Voices in the Media

Advances in Sociolinguistics Series

Series Editor: Tommaso M. Milani, University of the Witwatersrand, South Africa

Since the emergence of sociolinguistics as a new field of enquiry in the late 1960s, research into the relationship between language and society has advanced almost beyond recognition. In particular, the past decade has witnessed the considerable influence of theories drawn from outside of sociolinguistics itself. Thus rather than see language as a mere reflection of society, recent work has been increasingly inspired by ideas drawn from social, cultural, and political theory that have emphasized the constitutive role played by language/discourse in all areas of social life. The *Advances in Sociolinguistics* series seeks to provide a snapshot of the current diversity of the field of sociolinguistics and the blurring of the boundaries between sociolinguistics and other domains of study concerned with the role of language in society.

Discourses of Endangerment Ideology and Interest in the Defence of Languages
Edited by Alexandre Duchêne and Monica Heller

Globalization and Language in Contact Scale, Migration, and Communicative Practices
Edited by James Collins

Globalization of Language and Culture in Asia
Edited by Viniti Vaish

Language, Culture and Identity: An Ethnolinguistic Perspective
Philip Riley

Language Ideologies and Media Discourse Texts, Practices, Politics
Edited by Sally Johnson and Tommaso M. Milani

Language Ideologies and the Globalization of 'Standard' Spanish
Darren Paffey

Language in the Media Representations, Identities, Ideologies
Edited by Sally Johnson and Astrid Ensslin

Language and Power: An Introduction to Institutional Discourse
Andrea Mayr

Language Testing, Migration and Citizenship
Edited by Guus Extra, Massimiliano Spotti and Piet Van Avermaet

Linguistic Minorities and Modernity, 2nd Edition: A Sociolinguistic Ethnography
Monica Heller

Multilingual Encounters in Europe's Institutional Spaces
Edited by Johann Unger, Michał Krzyżanowski and Ruth Wodak

Multilingualism: A Critical Perspective
Adrian Blackledge and Angela Creese

Semiotic Landscapes Language, Image, Space
Adam Jaworski and Crispin Thurlow

The Languages of Global Hip-Hop
Edited by Marina Terkourafi

The Language of Newspapers: Socio-Historical Perspectives
Martin Conboy

The Languages of Urban Africa
Edited by Fiona Mc Laughlin

The Sociolinguistics of Identity
Edited by Tope Omoniyi

Voices in the Media

Performing French Linguistic Otherness

Gaëlle Planchenault

Bloomsbury Academic
An imprint of Bloomsbury Publishing Plc

BLOOMSBURY
LONDON · OXFORD · NEW YORK · NEW DELHI · SYDNEY

Bloomsbury Academic
An imprint of Bloomsbury Publishing Plc

50 Bedford Square	1385 Broadway
London	New York
WC1B 3DP	NY 10018
UK	USA

www.bloomsbury.com

BLOOMSBURY and the Diana logo are trademarks of Bloomsbury Publishing Plc

First published 2015
Paperback edition first published 2017

© Gaëlle Planchenault, 2015

Gaëlle Planchenault has asserted her right under the Copyright, Designs and Patents Act, 1988, to be identified as the Author of this work.

All rights reserved. No part of this publication may be reproduced or transmitted in any form or by any means, electronic or mechanical, including photocopying, recording, or any information storage or retrieval system, without prior permission in writing from the publishers.

No responsibility for loss caused to any individual or organization acting on or refraining from action as a result of the material in this publication can be accepted by Bloomsbury or the author.

British Library Cataloguing-in-Publication Data
A catalogue record for this book is available from the British Library.

ISBN: HB: 978-1-4725-8802-9
PB: 978-1-3500-3627-7
ePDF: 978-1-4725-8803-6
ePub: 978-1-4725-8804-3

Library of Congress Cataloging-in-Publication Data
Planchenault, Gaëlle, author.
Voices of the Media : performing linguistic otherness / Gaëlle Planchenault.
pages cm. — (Advances in sociolinguistics) Includes bibliographical references and index.
ISBN 978-1-4725-8802-9 (hardback) — ISBN 978-1-4725-8804-3 (epub) —
ISBN 978-1-4725-8803-6 (epdf) 1. Mass media and language—France.
2. French language—Style. 3. French language—Usage. 4. Sociolinguistics—France. 5. France—Social aspects. I. Title.
P96.L342F73 2015
306.442'41—dc23
2015014295

Series: Advances in Sociolinguistics

Typeset by RefineCatch Limited, Bungay, Suffolk

To my father, whose illness deprived him of his speech.

May your voice endure in your singing

Contents

Acknowledgements	xi
Introduction	1

1 The Sociolinguistic Study of Voices and Performances in the Media 15
   1.1 Studying language in the media: A brief review 16
   1.2 Genre, style and stylization in the media 24
   1.3 The performer, the performance and the audience 30

Part 1 Voices in French: Performances of Linguistic Differentiation in the French Media

2 Performances of Non-standard Voices in French Films 47
   2.1 Standard language ideology, accents and orders of indexicality 48
   2.2 Contexts of linguistic ideologies framing the films 50
   2.3 Cinematic realism and linguistic stylization 59
   2.4 Reception of the films and ideological shift 61
   2.5 Conclusion 65

3 Performances of Feminine Voices on the Internet 67
   3.1 Performance, appropriateness and gender in computer-mediated communication 68
   3.2 Sense of community on the transvestites' website 73
   3.3 Data 75
   3.4 Conclusion 83
   Post-script 84

4 Performances of Ethnic Voices in French Films 89
   4.1 *Coloured* voices: Prejudices and discrimination in the lip-synching industry 90
   4.2 Commodification of ethnic voices on a mainly white market 92
   4.3 Ethnic voices in French cinema: What voices in what films? 95
   4.4 Conclusion 99

Part 2 Voices in French-accented English

5 Performances of French-accented English in Hollywood Films — 107
  5.1 Characters speaking French-accented English in Hollywood films: Types and linguistic practices — 108
  5.2 The French-accented voice of Inspecteur Clouseau — 118
  5.3 Conclusion — 122

6 The Case of Poirot's Voice — 125
  6.1 Folk linguistics and stylized French English — 126
  6.2 French stylization in Hercule Poirot's *The Mystery of the Blue Train* — 129
  6.3 Conclusion — 137

7 Performances in French on Vancouver's Dining Scene: The Case of French Restaurants' Menus — 139
  7.1 Menus, French gastronomy and French language in English-speaking restaurants — 141
  7.2 French restaurants in Vancouver — 150
  7.3 French language and the French dining experience in Vancouver — 153
  7.4 Conclusion — 156

Conclusion — 157

Appendix: A Framework for the Study of Voices in the Media — 163
Notes — 167
References — 183
Filmography — 201
Index — 205

Acknowledgements

I am grateful to the editors of the following publications for permission to reproduce copyright material:

Planchenault, G. (2008), '"Who can tell, mon ami?": representations of bilingualism for a majority monolingual audience', in E. Ellis (ed.), special issue on 'Monolingualism', *Sociolinguistic Studies*, 2 (3): 425–440.

Planchenault, G. (2010), 'Virtual community and politeness: the use of female markers of identity and solidarity in a transvestites' website', in M. Locher (ed.), special issue on 'Politeness and impoliteness in computer-mediated communication', *Journal of Politeness Research: Language, Behaviour, Culture*, 6 (1): 83–103.

Planchenault, G. (2012), 'Accented French in films: performing and evaluating in-group stylizations', in J. Androutsopoulos (ed.), special issue on 'Language and society in cinematic discourse', *Multilingua*, 31 (2/3): 253–275.

I would also like to thank Michel Jacob, chef and owner of *Le Crocodile*, for allowing me to reproduce an excerpt from the restaurant's website.

Last but not least, I am grateful to my family for their constant support and their enduring love and patience.

Introduction

> *[The voice] is an absolutely available signifying substance.*
> Jacques Derrida, *Voice and Phenomenon* (1967) 2011: 68

For Derrida, the recording of voices was one of the twentieth century's major phenomenons. After being recorded, archived and/or broadcasted (by the means of radio or cinema), an infinity of voices are brought back to existence: '[the phenomenon] gives to the *living presence* the occasion to "be here" again, with no equivalent or precedent' (Derrida 2001 – my translation).[1] Recorded voices, such as the stylized voices performed by actors in films or stand-up comedians on TV or on the Internet, surround us in our daily life; this polyphony often feels as natural as the common voices. In this book, I intend to show that performed voices do not exist in a vacuum, that they are echoes of the voices that preceded them, but also that they permeate our very voice or influence the way we *envoice* others (i.e. envisage their ways of speaking). What I call a *performed voice* or a *performance of voice* refers to 'a mode of language use, a way of speaking' (Bauman 1975: 293) created during the artistic performance of an actor as well as, if more unconventionally, a performance of voice that takes place in the written media (the press and the Internet). What these artistic and discursive creations have in common is that in those instances, language is used in a way that creates a discrepancy between the stance taken by the performer and his/her *real* voice (i.e. identity). To be understood as performances, and as the following anecdote will show, they call for a specific *interpretative frame* (Bauman 1977, based on Goffman 1974).

French fictional voices, such as Clouseau's hyperbolized verbal Frenchness in the *Pink Panther* or Poirot's French-accented English in the TV series, are familiar to audiences around the world. Such ways of speaking have come to constitute varieties that now exist independently from the natural languages/vernaculars that they were originally parodying and can be no more evaluated by comparison to them (to be convinced of this, see Steve Martin's French-accented English stylization in the *Pink Panther* reboots). There is little doubt that most spectators would not be fooled into believing that this is the way the French speak (at least outside the realm of films), nor that it is the way people of French origin speak English. However, parodic ways of speaking exist in their own right and stylized voices entertain complex relationships with their objects of reference (i.e. the actual linguistic practices). At the end of 2012, the British media gloated over what journalists called the 'faux French accent' displayed by the *Olympique de Marseille* footballer, Joey Barton, during a French press conference. While some journalists, such as *The Guardian*'s commentator Jean Hannah Edelstein, saw in the Liverpudlian midfielder's vocal performance nothing more than 'an expat trying to fit in',[2] others sniggered at the exercise of *'Allo 'Allo!*'s cod-French accent, such as the *Daily Mail*, which entitled its cover of the event: 'Excusez-moi, Joey? Football bad boy Barton gives an interview in English . . . with a comedy French accent.'[3] Interestingly, more than Joey Barton's lack of fluency in the French language, the object of ridicule here is the fact that the footballer confuses a fictional accent with reality. In other words, the reproach made to him stems from his mix-up between a fictive rendering of a foreign accent and the real linguistic practices of the depicted community (even though the former is based on shared social representations of the latter), as well as the embarrassing infringement on the neighbourly etiquette that requires one not to present the mocked community with a stylized performance of their *funny* ways of speaking. This example shows that the distinctions between performances of voices in the media and real linguistic practices are not clear-cut and may become blurred in real-life interactions.

In this introduction, I wish to prove that performances of voices are complex social and discursive phenomena that need to be studied more systematically than they have been in past research. In fact, it seems that there has been a consistent trend in social sciences to treat them as rather passive – if not innocent – objects. One of the main reasons behind this is the fact that performances of voices are often considered as mere *representations*. As such, theatrical and literary performances of voices have been treated as windows to inaccessible (whether in time or space) linguistic varieties or, as is still the case in stylistics, an index to characters' social and cultural features. Moreover, since Plato's theory of *mimesis*, there has been a prevalent idea that artistic representations should be evaluated in terms of less when compared to reality: less *real*, less *authentic*, etc. One major argument for philosophers and theoreticians is that the copy has less existence than the model – that it is 'ontologically weaker than the original' (Hobson 2001: 140). Also, as performances, verbal art (Bauman 1975) has been studied as utterances in which 'meaning [is] somehow cancelled out or rendered inoperative by the nature of the utterance as verbal art' (p. 292), and evaluated as aesthetic forms in which language is 'used not seriously, but in ways *parasitic* upon its normal use' (Austin 1962: 21–22). Finally, with regards to ideologies, performed voices have been studied as simple vectors of popular ideas and stereotypes. However, an argument that I shall support in this book is that performed voices are also performative. Taking into account Austin's point that '*in* saying something we do something, and even *by* saying something we do something' (Austin 1962: 94), and considering that both 'performance' and 'performative' are derived from the old French verb *parformer* ('to accomplish/to form'), questions that arise are: what does language *accomplish* when voices are performed? What work do performed voices do? Any answer to these questions should take into account not only the role played by language in the creative act of verbal performance, but also the effects that the chosen words – and the way they are said – have on audiences (and eventually on societies). Performances of voices are sites of discourse where ideologies are realized and can therefore be highlighted by the analyst. In order to deconstruct the multiple levels of meaning encapsulated in verbal art, I shall argue that not only are language ideologies actualized in performances of voices, they are also realized in them as social representations, registers, performed voices and exchangeable commodities. Silverstein (1979: 193) defines linguistic ideologies as 'sets of beliefs about language articulated by users as a rationalization or justification of perceived language structure and use'. For Rumsey (1990), basing his definition on that of Silverstein (1979), linguistic ideologies are 'shared bodies of common sense notions about the nature of language in the world' (1990: 346). A hasty reading of these definitions would lead one to believe that language ideologies are no more than sets of views on languages, and that their use in societies is distinct from these societies (they are beliefs *about*), and, therefore, that they do not take part fully in the social life of languages or in the linguistic practices themselves. However, this understanding would ignore the facts that the goal of Rumsey's (1990) study was to demonstrate a Whorfian interrelationship between linguistic ideologies and social life, and that Silverstein demonstrated that language ideologies were not mere false consciousness, in the Marxist sense, but that they actually had an influence in the evolution of linguistic structures. As such, there is little doubt that language ideologies are a force behind the well-oiled machinery of daily interactions as well as the (most often) unquestioned consumption of media discourses.[4] To support this argument, I would like to present another example, taken this time from the French media.

After the release of the film *L'Esquive* (*Games of Love and Chance*, Kechiche 2003), Serge Kaganski, a well-known journalist of the weekly magazine *Les*

Inrockuptibles, entitled his review with the surprising and somewhat rude *Nique Rohmer!*[5] (Kaganski 2004). The title functions as a pun that mixes the notorious swearing *Nique ta mère* (defined by the French dictionary *Petit Robert* as 'an insult used by young males who live in the suburbs') with the name of the famous Nouvelle vague French filmmaker, Eric Rohmer, who directed intimate films in which characters were mostly from an all-white and privileged background (intellectuals and bourgeois). The irreverence of the title is made possible by the fact that the magazine's readers are familiar with its insolent and mildly subversive style.[6] Moreover, there is no doubt that, in such an instance, the analyst deals with a performance of voice or 'verbal art' (Bauman 1975):

> [P]erformance represents a transformation of the basic referential ('serious', 'normal'...) uses of language. In other words, in an artistic performance of this kind, there is something going on in the communicative interchange which says to the auditor, 'interpret what I say in some special sense; do not take it to mean what the words alone, taken literally, would convey.' This may lead to the further suggestion that performance sets up, or represents, an interpretive frame within which the messages being communicated are to be understood, and that this frame contrasts with at least one other frame, the literal.
>
> Bauman 1975: 292

Of course, the frame through which Kaganski's (2004) title is to be read is 'joking' ('in which the words spoken are to be interpreted as not seriously meaning what they might otherwise mean (cf. Austin 1962: 121)' – quoted in Bauman 1975: 292), as readers are expected to understand that neither the film reviewer nor the imaginary persona behind the performed voice (a youngster from the suburbs? The film director Abdellatif Kechiche? A symbolic embodiment of the film?) is wishing any ill on the French new wave director.

Verbal performances use phonological (performed accents) or lexical (slang, emblematic words, etc.) hints. In such cases, performers make use of salient features (in my example, the verb *niquer*) that are linked to stereotypical views on the linguistic community and whose symbolic meaning needs to be shared with the audience if the performance is to be understood fully. What is taking place here is a complex semantic construction that needs to be read at several levels. I shall now unpack the assumed shared knowledge on which Kaganski's (2004) verbal performance is based while developing the previously mentioned four realizations of language ideologies in performances of voices: (1) social representations; (2) registers; (3) performed voices; and (4) exchangeable commodities.

Social representations

Firstly, language ideologies are realized as social representations (Duveen and Lloyd 1990, Moscovici 1998a, Moscovici and Marková 1998). Through childhood socialization and, later on, through other forms of socialization and with the intervention of mediatization, socially shared knowledge about groups precedes and frames individuals' development and understanding of their own (as well as others') positions in society. Through emergent processes of identity-construction, social representations are constantly negotiated as they are re-interpreted and re-presented. As individuals' socio-cognitive activity integrates and (re)produces social representations, these become social reality, 'ways of world making' (Moscovici 1988: 231).[7]

Social representations on social classes and what is taken as their inherent ways of speaking are what makes Kaganski's (2004) title work. In France, there exist hegemonic social representations on ways of speaking that divide social classes by opposing legitimate (i.e. standardized) French to varieties (i.e. non-standard, popular, regional, suburban, rural, etc.). They often function as an *us-versus-them* distinction (Tajfel and Turner 1979), and therefore participate in the linguistic construction of otherness. In the studied example, the formula *Nique Rohmer* clearly polarizes what are seen as popular/young/suburban ways of speaking and the appropriate way of speaking that is expected in the written press. But what takes place in the semantic background of the magazine title does not occur solely at a linguistic level. According to Moscovici's theory of social psychology, social representations serve: '(a) to establish a social order that enables individuals to orientate themselves and master the material and social world they live in, and (b) to enable communication among members of a community through a shared code for social exchange and for naming and classifying various aspects of the social world including their individual and group history' (Sammut and Howarth 2013: 1799). Along with linguistic representations, one way to establish and maintain this social order is the organization of space, and the distribution of urban space is indisputably an expression of social hierarchy and power relations between social classes. In France, with regards to major French cities, social representations of urban spaces often function in a binary fashion that divides the privileged from the disadvantaged neighbourhoods (such as the suburbs), the centre from the periphery. Even though rich suburbs exist, the French term of *banlieue* is predominantly evocative of social misery and of social groups that have literally and symbolically been pushed to the margins (i.e. foreign, unemployed, criminal).

The French historian Alain Faure (2006) recounts the history of the word in an article evocatively entitled '*Un faubourg, des banlieues, ou la déclinaison du rejet*' ('A faubourg, a suburb, or the inflection of rejection'), and he describes the suburb as 'the degree zero of a city, a thousand miles from a real city. But that was nothing yet, as from 1985, the word was used to describe all at once the places, the ills and the fears[8] associated with the crisis of a French society, born at an age of unemployment and racism that today compromise the integration of an important part of the migrants' children' (p. 19).[9]

In France, the expression '*nique ta mère*' is notoriously used in suburban slang, arguably by the youth of Maghrebi origin whose parents are Algerian, Moroccan or Tunisian immigrants (*niquer* is a French verb that comes from the Arabic – more precisely from the French *forniquer* through North-African pidgin – and that was originally used as a familiar version of *to make love*). Though it seems that the created suburban voice is only playfully mocking the arty French cinema, Kaganski (2004) nonetheless conforms to common representations of suburban individuals, depicting them as failing to adhere to social order (i.e. the curse), a linguistic etiquette (i.e. the use of slang in the written media) and the nation's cultural heritage (i.e. Rohmer's cinema).[10]

Finally, I would like to extend the analysis to the other meanings of the word *representation* as it is worth noting that it carries an artistic connotation and may be used as a synonym of the words *performance* or *show*. According to Derrida (2011), the word includes the 're' of *repetition*[11] as well as the meaning of 'taking place of another' (p. 42), while *pre-sent* means 'being in-front' (p. 46). The persona that is performed by a performer (the voice's carrier) *in front of* an audience is also *present* in the interaction. Moreover, in order to perform voices, actors and authors access symbolic resources and, by doing so, produce and reproduce symbolic material.

Registers

If there is no doubt that language ideologies play a role in the evolution of languages (or non-evolution, as one would argue by focusing on the conservative process of standardization), they also contribute to the formation of registers as 'living social formations, susceptible to society-internal variation and change through the activities of persons attuned to alignments with figures performed in use' (Agha 2005: 45 – I shall later come back to Agha's concept of *enregistered* voices). The register displayed in *Les Inrockuptibles*' title – and more specifically by the use of the verb *niquer* – is categorized as *populaire* in the French dictionary

Larousse. In the written press, the use of taboo words in such prominent position is intended to hail (if not to shock) the reader. In this particular case, it also signals a specific register (popular, urban, suburban, young and of Maghrebi origin) and therefore stands for the voice of a community (young people of diverse ethnic origins who live in the suburbs of major French cities); it presumes what it (or the film) says to a conservative audience and cinema. The title of the film review should therefore be read as the promotion of a refreshing new stance in French Cinema (a stance to which the rather young readership of *Les Inrockuptibles* would adhere to). Even though the emblematic insult to the mother is common to different cultures, it is arguable that the urban '*nique ta mère*' has some commonalities with the African-American notorious swear words. As it is the case for the stigmatized urban North-American communities, non-standard varieties participate in constructing the voice of a counterculture.[12]

Performed voices

One cannot theorize about voices without mentioning the Russian literary critic Michael Bakhtin's well-known concepts of heteroglossy and polyphony. While Bakhtin (1981, 1986) worked predominantly on the novel, the concepts that he created are easily transferable to media texts. One can therefore argue that media discourses are often heteroglot, 'multiform in style and variform in speech and voice' (Bakhtin 1981: 261). These discourses most often embed, within *unmarked* journalistic speech, *marked* voices that stand for linguistic and social communities. By means of a textual performance, *Les Inrockuptibles*' journalist has created a voice that is linguistically marked in order to index a suburban and young identity.

Regarding performances, Bauman and Brigg (1990: 73) state that 'performance puts the act of speaking on display – objectifies it, lifts it to a degree from its interactional setting and opens it to scrutiny by an audience'. But more than simply actualizing acts of speaking, verbal performances also *put on display* social stereotypes (Bell and Gibson 2011: 555). Moreover, if performances of voices in the media are framed by hegemonic language ideologies in society (this is an argument central to this book, and on which I shall expand in several chapters), they are also embodied and contextualized. They are the results of performers' acts, and these acts take place at particular times and places. In other words, they are *anchored* in varied contexts of performances (Bauman and Briggs 1990: 73). During performances, performers tap into a vast linguistic and symbolic capital assumedly shared with their audiences[13] (including language ideologies that vary according to fluctuating dynamics between standard language ideologies and alternative language ideologies). In this sense, they activate varied semantic values, selected according to the contexts of discursive action and the performers' communicative intents. In the French media, the use of words and expressions coming from the *parler banlieue* has been very common since the 1990s, as it appears that journalists have been besotted with its novelty and hip associations. In the last twenty years, the articles published on what was covered by the media as a linguistic phenomenon, commonly comprised glossaries (lists of translated expressions) and interviews of language experts (linguists, lexicologists, writers, etc.).

However, it is important to note that the press coverage has also shown different trends: ten years ago, French linguists, such as Alain Bentolila, and politicians, including former minister Azouz Begag, defended the popular opinion that saw the suburban ways of speaking as impoverished forms of French. They argued that, rather than marvelling at the creativity of the linguistic community, one should worry at the '*fracture linguistique*' ('the linguistic divide' – in Potet 2005) that condemned young people to a 'linguistic ghetto' (Bentolila 2007) and prevented them from benefiting from the Republican ideal of social levelling through an education in standard French. From then on, polarized values (popular/standard French; street/legitimized culture; language's innovation/corruption; social conformity/sedition) have been embedded in any display of *parler banlieue* in the media. Judging by the wording as well as the entextualization (Bauman and Briggs 1990) of the suburban voice, there is no doubt that Kaganski's (2004) title builds on this polarization. Moreover, by reinforcing binary views on standard and non-standard ways of speaking, this performance of voice contributes to strengthen the polarity of language ideologies (the dominant vs. the alternative views). Even though Kaganski (2004) appears to take the side of the alternative culture (his review is full of praise for Kechiche's film), his linguistic position remains conservative. It is noticeable that most of his article is written in standard French, except for a short excerpt at the beginning where the journalist writes: 'Pour le dire dans la langue du film: «Putain, L'Esquive, sur la tête de ma mère, je kiffe sa race, Inch'Allah»' ('To say it in the language of the film: "Fuck, *L'Esquive*, on my mother's head, I bloody love it, God willing"' – Kaganski 2004). Building on the use of suburban slang and Arabic, this is not only an obvious exercise of pastiche; it is also what Bourdieu (1991: 68) calls a 'strategy of condescension' as a speaker who is undoubtedly able to use the legitimized variety purposely uses a lower-status way of speaking (while the audience recognizes the hierarchy). In doing so, the speaker not only profits from the 'distinctly symbolic negation of the hierarchy'

(1991: 68), he or she also draws on the positive associations (hip and urban, in the case of Kaganski's performance) that constitute the symbolic capital of the lower-ranked variety. According to Bourdieu (1991), far from threatening the established social order (even though they may pass as a 'subversion of objective hierarchies in the sphere of language', p. 69), these strategies reaffirm the higher ranking and strengthen the hierarchy: it is only because the speaker is confident of his or her position that he or she is free to subvert it. In other words, and as Hill (1998) puts it, it is a form of 'orderly disorder'. In our example, Serge Kaganski cannot be 'suspected of resorting to the stigmatized language *faute de mieux*' (Bourdieu 1991: 69). And if this was not obvious enough to the reader, the journalist highlights his performance by mentioning that he is borrowing 'the language of the film' (Kaganski 2004). Finally, note that, in this case, the strategy of condescension is addressed not to the linguistic community that it stylizes, but to a readership that is for the most part educated and economically privileged.

Before closing this section on performance, I would like to reflect further on the character that is embodied by the performed voice and question whether Kaganski's (2004) title presents an instance of reported speech. In the title, no graphic marks (i.e. inverted commas or italics) indicate that it is the case. In a study on radio presenter's stylized reported speech, Carroll (2013) argues that:

> In Goffmanian terms the speaker can be said to be emitting, or animating, talk but attributing those words to some other figure (Goffman 1981). It may be that the EMITTER/ANIMATOR (the physical speaker) is also the AUTHOR of the utterance and that s/he is attributing it to some (known or unknown, real or hypothetical) third party or that s/he is repeating something actually authored by the FIGURE to establish a PRINCIPAL, or stance.
>
> Carroll 2013: 262

As with the ethnic stylizations studied by Carrol (2013), there is no doubt in our case that the stylized sentence should be attributed to a third party (it is a form of *speaking as*). However, as the latter remains *unnamed* and *hypothetical*, it is unclear who this third party would be: the director, a suburban youth or the film's anthropomorphic figure?

Exchangeable commodities

Developing his famous concept of *linguistic market*, Bourdieu (1991) defined any linguistic exchange as 'an economic exchange which is established within a particular symbolic relation of power between a producer, endowed with certain linguistic capital, and a consumer (or a market)' (p. 66). Linguistic exchanges take place on a market, a linguistic market in which utterances have value and are *signs of wealth* (1991: 66). In the background of this concept, there is Bourdieu's fundamental viewpoint that uses and structures of language contribute to maintain power relations within social groups. In other words, social reality is achieved through everyday talk. As such, the linguistic market is a site of power relations 'whose variations determine the variations in the price that the same discourse may receive on different markets' (Bourdieu 1991: 69). On some markets (such as formal ones), certain speakers are legitimate (i.e. they possess the authority to speak), and, as such, they have more power to manipulate the market and to gain higher prices/profits for the discourses that they produce.

Going back to the studied example and as already mentioned, borrowings from *Banlieue* French were common occurrences in the French media, especially at the turn of this century. Stemming from the 1990s media interest in the French suburbs that followed societal events such as the birth of *cinéma de banlieue*[14] or the series of riots that affected the suburbs of major French cities throughout that decade, one witnessed a multiplication of stylized suburban voices ('spectacular fragments'[15] – Rampton 1995) in newspapers and on TV screens. When performing suburban vernaculars, legitimate speakers do not only benefit from their symbolic values; they also contribute to increase the performed voices' economic value. But who exactly benefits from such increased value on the media markets? Following Bourdieu, one needs to ask who the legitimate speakers are according to the diverse contexts of mediatization. In the case of the studied example, I argue that it is the journalist. Indeed, if higher prices are obtained by speakers who are 'more or less formally delegated to speak' (Bourdieu 1991: 69), it appears that film reviewers are delegated by the general public to inform them on the quality of the new film releases. Indeed, some of them may believe that they are the best placed to judge the *value* of a film. However, to develop the argument further, in the case of the review's title, one may question whether what is effectively sold is the voice of a journalist or the voice of the suburb. I shall raise a similar question in the section of the book dedicated to the stylized performances of accents in *L'Esquive* (chapter 2).

Furthermore, if one follows the economic argument that the value of a commodity varies according to the market, one may claim that the voices performed in *Banlieue* French will not bear the same value when performers and markets vary. Considering that, according to Bourdieu (1991: 69), 'certain agents are incapable of applying to the linguistic products offered, either by themselves or by others, the criteria that are most favourable to their own products', one may be tempted to believe that stigmatized speakers are not able to market their linguistic product and profit from the added value. Indeed, as the suburban vernacular is still very much stigmatized,[16] one can argue that community members would be unable to benefit from the use of their vernacular. However, this is not always the case, as there are notable exceptions in popular music (rap) and in the film industry with *films de banlieue* (which have sometimes been directed, if not produced, by members of the community). Moreover, I shall argue that since such performances of voices have gained market value, these voices have been reclaimed by stigmatized communities (see chapter 4). In some cases, varieties were consequently reassessed and legitimized. In a surprising example of such a phenomenon, one will find on the website of a French publisher of Arabic textbooks, and more specifically in a part of the website dedicated to Arabic language, a whole page on 'parler banlieue' where one reads: 'The emergence of the "beurs" [i.e. the second generation of North-African immigrants] in French society, particularly after 1981s political change, permitted the birth of a new language, coming from the disinherited suburbs and that shone as far as the *quartiers chics* of the capital, influencing the media and the intellectual circles.'[17] What is interesting in this statement is that it not only includes common views on the suburban language (i.e. the role played by the Arabic language in the creation of the sociolect), it also reformulates the positive appraisals that were made in the media to give the language its own agency (note that the writer chooses the word *langage* instead of the usual *parler* or *argot* 'slang'). Another example of speakers that were able to market their vernacular is to be found in recently published dictionaries of non-standard urban varieties that were created by community members' initiative (the *Lexik des Cités* – Permis de vivre la ville 2007[18] is one of these).

This very detailed study of a simple instance of performed voice shows that media performances of voices function thanks to a complex interplay between linguistic structure, socio-cultural knowledge and language ideologies. Analysing such performance of voice means 'teas[ing] out the social mechanism through which particular ideas or beliefs about linguistic practices are produced, circulated and/or challenged through meaning-making activities under particular conditions' (Johnson and Milani 2009: 4), a practice that requires close scrutiny of texts. In this book, I shall analyse many more occurrences of such media stylizations. Among the varied ways to analyse such performances, the approach that I adopt is situated in discourse analysis of media texts, but all my studies are also framed by a linguistic anthropological approach to language ideologies. I wish constantly to bear in mind a few paradoxes that will frame many of the analyses conducted in the book:

- Though diverse and varied, media performances of voice take place within a constraining framework that incites them to conform to dominant language ideologies.
- Performance contrasts are entextualized: an analysis of these performances should not ignore the interaction that exists between media genres (article, film, website, etc.) and the ideological contexts of media discourse.
- Understanding of language ideologies and salient features in media discourses is often taken for granted; one should always leave space for misinterpretation and resistance.
- Performances of voices are embodied as well as detached from their source.

The types of performed voices analysed in this book are varied (film dialogues, articles, new-media texts, etc.), and were selected foremost to address the following series of questions.

The first questions focus on the form adopted by performances of voice:

- What does language do when voices are performed?
- How different are the voices created in media *performances* (in Bauman's sense of the term) from the voices produced by everyday life performances (in a Goffmanian sense)?

Second, I research the performer's role and agency:

- What happens when one speaks like someone that one is not, someone that one knows that one is not, someone that the audience that one is addressing knows that one is not, i.e. when one speaks like an *Other*?

The third series of questions address the semantic interaction between performers and audiences:

- How do the stereotypic personae that performed voices contribute to build become familiar to national as well as transnational audiences? How are these shared frames of reference established?
- How is a performed voice's meaning negotiated between performers and audiences?

Finally, the book questions the role of performed voices in society:

- To what social work do performed voices contribute?

- How do stylizations of the *Other*'s language contribute to reinforce hegemonic systems and processes of differentiation? How do performed voices reproduce ideologies of standard and non-standard languages and perpetuate social discriminations?
- How are performed voices commodified into cultural products of otherness that may also be reclaimed by stigmatized communities?
- How do local processes of linguistic differentiation inform transnational studies?

In the first chapter, I start by taking a look at the diverse approaches that were chosen to study language in the media. I then follow by exploring the varied dimensions (in terms of style, performance and audience) that will be considered in the varied studies of voice performances presented throughout the book.

1

The Sociolinguistic Study of Voices and Performances in the Media

A couple of decades ago, the back cover of Scannell's (1991) book on *broadcast talk* stated that '[t]he fundamental significance of the media as communicative outlets in a modern society is widely understood, but the language in which this communication takes place is as yet little studied'. However, this is far from being the case today, as dozens of articles and books are published every year on language in the media, in fields as diverse as applied linguistics, sociolinguistics, anthropology, media studies, political science, etc. This occurs to such an extent that drawing a state-of-the-art review of such studies would amount to a Sisyphean task. It is nevertheless useful to go back in time and to look at the origin of linguists' interest in media texts.[1] It seems that, since the last decade of the twentieth century, the reasons to study language in the media have gone beyond Bell's (1991: 3) laconic formula: 'because it is there'. Although everyone seems to agree on media discourses' ubiquity, I distinguish throughout my readings between two ways of looking at language in the media. For some studies, the media is a social context where discourse practices are social practices in their own rights and in which – like in any other social contexts – context-bound ways of using language are worthy of study. For others, the media generate their own *languages*, or rather new varieties of the national languages (an approach seen frequently in the studies of the new media). For example, when Conboy (2010: 1) studies the written press, he insists on the importance of 'deal[ing] with the very stuff of newspapers: their language'. Furthermore, these two tendencies are seen in the format chosen in the monographs' titles, the latter often following common matrices such as Language and Media X (Crystal 2004, Durant and Lambrou 2009, Tannen and Trester 2013); Language in the Media/ Media X (Fowler 1991, Johnson and Ensslin 2007); Media X Language/ Discourse(s)/Linguistics (Fairclough 1995, Bell and Garrett 1998, Aitchison and Lewis 2003, Matheson 2005, Lorenzo-Dus 2008, Crystal 2011); or The Language of X Media (Reah 1998, Bednarek 2010, Conboy 2010, Seargeant and Tagg 2014).

In the introduction of this book, my aim was to demonstrate the interest of studying voices in the media. In this chapter, I intend to give a selective account of the genres and language features that were traditionally studied in the different types of media, as well as the approaches that were commonly favoured in these studies. After this review and in order to draw on the theoretical background of the book, this chapter will focus on the following questions:

- What does language do when voices are performed?
- What happens when one speaks like someone that one is not?
- How are the voices created in media *performances* different from the voices produced by everyday-life *performances*?

In answering these questions, this chapter also presents recent insights from research on genres, stylizations and performances.

1.1 Studying language in the media: A brief review

Nearly two decades ago, Bell and Garrett (1998: 3) acknowledged that the interest in media texts is not recent as 'the media have been a focus of attention among those working within the broader field of communication studies'. They cited four reasons: the availability of media texts to researchers and students; the media's influence on attitudes towards language; the fact that media texts can inform us on social meanings and stereotypes; and finally, because of the fact that they are formatted to fit the culture where they are circulated.[2] Media texts reflect the cultural, ethical and political dimensions of societies. However, it is in particular the last decade of the twentieth century that saw an unprecedented growth in linguistic studies of media texts. Wodak and Busch (2004) argue that the present trend in approaches to media texts was caused by a major shift taking place in the period, characterized by what Meinhof (1994) defined (developing Fiske's (1987: 249) argument that 'text-as-meaning is produced at the moment of reading, not at the moment of writing') as 'moving from purely text-internal readings, where readers are theorized as decoders of fixed meanings, to more dynamic models, where meanings are negotiated by actively participating readers' (p. 212). For Wodak and Busch (2004: 106), this shift resulted in an 'interactive model of communication, which is far more complex than the traditional models in mass communication. Media texts are perceived as dialogic, and the readings depend on the receivers and on the settings.' This has had the effect of encouraging researchers in media studies to pay more attention to the role played by audiences (see Bell 1984, 1991). With regards to relationships between media texts and audiences, another major source of influence to researchers in media studies and media discourse is the work of cultural theorist Stuart Hall. He describes how 'events are "made to mean" by the media' (1978: 54) as follows:

> An event only 'makes sense' if it can be located within a range of known social and cultural identifications. If newsmen did not have available – in however routine a way – such cultural 'maps' of the social world, they could not 'make sense' for their audiences of the unusual, unexpected and unpredicted events which form the basic content of what is 'newsworthy'. Things are newsworthy because they represent the changefulness, the unpredictability and the conflictful nature of the world. But such events cannot be allowed to remain in the limbo of the 'random' – they must be brought within the horizon of the meaningful. This bringing of events within the realm of meanings means, in essence, referring unusual and unexpected events to the 'maps of meaning' which already form the basis of our cultural knowledge, into which the social world is *already* 'mapped'. The social identification, classification and contextualisation of news events in terms of these background frames of reference is the fundamental process by which the media make the worlds they report on intelligible to readers and viewers.
>
> Hall 1978: 54

The 'social-cognitive model' later developed by Van Dijk (1988) is based on similar cultural 'maps of meaning' (called 'models of situation' and 'schemata') that guide the production as well as the reception of news texts.[3] At the origin of linguists' and scholars' interest with language in the media, the news, described by Bell (1991) as *dominating* media discourse, is a common object of analysis (Van Dijk 1988, Fowler 1991, Bell 1991, Fairclough 1995, Bell and Garrett 1998). Most of the studies of 'news language' (Bell 1991) were inspired by Halliday's systemic-functional theory of language, according to which texts should be analysed for their language users' choices in the *ideational*, *interpersonal* and *textual* functions of language (1978: 45–46). With regards to language in the news, the first and second functions correspond to the representations that journalists produce of societies and their portrayal of social identities and relations, both of which are central in Fairclough's study of media texts (1995). In these seminal references, discourse analysis and critical discourse analysis (CDA) approaches (Fairclough 1989) have been favoured to highlight power relations, ideologies and prejudices (most often racism) in the news (print, radio and TV). According to researchers, news cannot be value-free, because language itself is loaded with cultural and social values. These studies' goals are not only to point out 'double standards' and 'biases' in news coverage but also to present a *framework* for analysing media language (Fairclough 1995: 2). While Bell (1991), with his well-known theory of *audience design*, focuses on the study of 'styling' the news for audiences, Fairclough's book (1995) adopts a more holistic approach: media texts are discourse practices which are embedded in social practices. It is then necessary to consider the role of the media in ongoing processes of social reproduction and change, as well as contexts of 'marketization' where the viewer is also a consumer. This is why Fairclough (1995) insists that media discourses are simultaneously constituted by social practices and constitutive of such practices (bearing in mind that they also serve ideologically hegemonic forces). In a nutshell, two important approaches emerged during this period: a critical approach that is concerned with the study of the ideologies present in media discourse, and a structural approach that focuses on the analysis of media styles and genres. Both form a strong heritage and, to this day, these two axes constitute the backbone of most current studies on media discourse (see, for example, Johnson and Esslin 2007, Johnson and Milani 2010). Not forgetting authors who adopt a more applied approach, I would like to mention a series of books aimed at students in media studies, communication or linguistics (Reah 1998, Matheson 2005, Durant and Lambrou 2009), and structured around a variety of 'real texts' (Durant and Lambrou 2009), to showcase the varied approaches used to analyse media discourse.

The following review does not attempt to give an exhaustive inventory of the sociolinguistic studies of media discourse. It rather aims at providing a general idea of the frameworks that were used to analyse media texts, as well as at situating studies of films and the new media within a history of studies of language in the media.

1.1.1 Print media

Since Fairclough's (1995) and Van Dijk's (1988) seminal works, many studies of the written press, such as the news, have adopted a CDA approach (Kress and van Leeuwen 1998, Reah 1998, Teo 2000, Richardson 2007). According to Matheson (2005: 12), '[t]hese approaches, certainly in the analysis of media texts, often come under the heading of critical discourse analysis, because it is the work of scholars who seek not just to understand how language works in society, but in whose interests and with what effects on the world that is constructed in language.' In most cases, the researchers' goal was to bring to light the characteristics of the written press grammar (Kress and van Leeuwen 1998).

Traditionally, linguistic studies of newspaper articles have focused on the linguistic expressions of ideologies and prejudices, such as racism (Teo 2000, Van Dijk 2000, Cottle 2000) or sexism (Jaworska and Larrivée 2011), with the goal to show that news language contributes to reproduce inequality. As an example, Teo's (2000) study of two Australian newspapers' depictions of Vietnamese gangs uses Van Dijk's (1988) framework of micro/macrostructures analysis to highlight the newspapers' lexical choices and syntactical structures, and to demonstrate that generalizations, quotation patterns and over-lexicalization are evidences of 'systematic "othering" and stereotyping of the ethnic community by the "white" majority' (2000: 7). Other examples of the studies of media biases are to be found in the post-9/11 analyses of newspapers' discourse on Islam and Muslims (Burger 2006, Blackledge 2009, Baker et al. 2013). Among these, some recent studies choose to combine different approaches to produce an 'objective picture of media attitudes'. For example, Baker et al.'s (2013) recent book uses a detailed analysis of newspaper articles on Muslims and Islam in the British press (over 140 million words of media texts) and, combining corpus linguistics (such as the study of collocates) to discourse analysis methods, attempts to demonstrate that corpus linguistics provides more robust and valid sets of findings and therefore improves the objectivity of critical discourse analysis. Not surprisingly, their study shows that most often newspapers tend to link Muslims to concepts of extreme belief or fundamentalism. They also highlight differences across newspapers, as '*The Guardian* described Muslims as extreme only about one in thirty-five times, while this figure was one in eight for *The People*' (Baker et al. 2013: 259).

Finally, taking after Kress and van Leeuwen's work on a *grammar of visual design* (1996, 1998, 2001), a recent multimodal trend in discourse analysis has developed. However, as most studies of media texts are almost entirely devoted to the linguistic component, multimodal analyses are still rare and typically found in studies of the audiovisual media, such as TV or the Internet.

1.1.2 Broadcast media

After Goffman's (1981) seminal work on radio talk, studies of broadcast-media language have traditionally focused on macro-structural analysis of broadcast talk (Scannell 1991) or conversation analysis of interviews (Heritage 1985, Hutchby 1991). Two areas of analysis, as yet not studied in the written press, are given renewed attention in the audio(visual) media: sociolinguistic diversity (Jaffe 2011), and the presence/representations of minority languages on the airwaves and on TV (De Fina 2013). Among the latter, studies of accents' stylizations have focused on dialect stylization (Coupland 2001) and ethnic stylization (Carroll 2013). Coupland (2001) analyses data from English-language national radio broadcasts in Wales to demonstrate that Welshness is self-consciously evoked, partly through dialect performance. The phonological variables used by performers are a rich semiotic resource ('stylization is the knowing deployment of culturally familiar styles and identities that are marked as deviating from those predictably associated with the current speaking context' – Coupland 2001: 345), but are also linked to non-dialectal means of evoking Welsh cultural stances and practices (such as performances of archetypal personas). Kelly-Holmes and Atkinson (2007) study attitudes to Irish language in a radio satire and focus on parodied instances of code-switching accented Irish-English slang performed by the Irish radio presenter Hector Ó hEochagáin. They argue that '[a]s would be expected with radio satire, language and accent are key factors in the construction of characters' (2007: 179). In her study, Carroll (2013) uses interactional discourse analysis and acoustic analysis to compare a disc jockey's ethnical stylizations with unmarked uses of reported speech. Interestingly, her analyses demonstrate the difficulty to identify what counts as stylizations and that the selection of salient features is often therefore 'left to the researcher's intuition' (2013: 261).

Minority language practices on radio and television reflect societies' perceptions of language standards, authority and authenticity (Androutopoulos 2010). Jaffe (2007) examines the use of Corsican (such as lexical choices and instances of code-switching) on a regional Corsican radio in order to explore the constitutive role of media practices and representations with regard to the community's languages and the audiences indexed by those languages. According to her, these issues are 'related to fundamental questions about how the minority language speech community is collectively imagined, and what kinds of speech and speakers are considered authoritative and/or authentic' (Jaffe 2007: 149). With regards to linguistic studies of TV programmes, next to the traditional studies of TV news and political interviews (e.g. BBC's *Question Time* in Lorenzo-Dus 2008), innovative studies focus on new formats. As an example, Lazar (2009) studies the strategic use of Singlish on Singapore's national television during the 2003 government's campaign to tackle the SARS pandemic that was affecting the country. The national endorsement in public media discourse of the otherwise discriminated colloquial variety of Singapore English was significant in demonstrating the complexity of positioning towards language ideologies and language planning.

1.1.3 Fiction (TV and cinema)

The study of language in fiction (TV series and feature-films) does not differ widely from more traditional analyses of media language (in the written press or the broadcast media), at least in terms of the methodological approaches chosen in the analysis of dialogues: discourse analysis (Rossi 2011); critical discourse analysis and language ideology research (Planchenault 2012); phonological analyses of accents (Gibson and Bell 2010); analysis of styling (Higgins and Furukawa 2012) and stylizations (Coupland 2004, Tsiplakou and Ioannidou 2012); studies of multilingualism and sociolinguistic diversity (Petrucci 2008; Bleichenbacher 2008, 2012; Androutsopoulos 2012b); etc. Other studies combine such approaches with other methodologies that are more specific to the study of fictional language, such as stylistics (Richardson 2010; Bednarek 2010, 2012).

Why study language in fiction and in dialogues? If it were often the case that films were used as a readily accessible data for the study of *real* languages (Rossi 2011), recent studies have highlighted the problematic relationship between the fictional depictions of languages and authenticity (Alvarez-Pereyre 2011). Going beyond mere 'fidelity checks' (i.e. studying the authenticity of cinematic language in comparison with a language that would be considered as the 'original' – Androutsopoulos 2012a), these studies attempt to link fictional languages to systems of indexicalities and to show that such media texts contribute to maintain current ideologies of standard languages and minority languages, as well as representations of the communities who speak them (Johnson and Milani 2011).

Since Lippi-Green's (1997) seminal study of accents in Walt Disney's films, scholars have studied film dialogues at phonological, lexical or discursive levels, in order to highlight the salient features that are used to index specific characters and speech communities. Below are a few examples of these studies:

- **Phonological level:** At this level, most articles focus on the study of performed accents (Gibson and Bell 2010; Planchenault 2008a, 2012). Bell and Gibson (2011: 570) argue that '[a]ccent is perhaps the most obvious linguistic means by which performances index identity'. In their study of the sociophonetic processes used in performed stylization of Pasifika English in a New Zealand TV programme (Gibson and Bell 2010), they hypothesize that compared to the 'natural' variety, such performances may overshoot quantitatively (by increasing the frequency of a feature's occurrence) and qualitatively (through lengthening or exaggerated phonetic positioning), selectively produce some features of the variety, but omit others (perhaps on grounds of salience or lack of it), and mis-realize other dialect features in an unlimited number of ways. My own study of *accented* French in films (Planchenault 2012) is included in chapter 2 of this book.

- **Discursive level:** Such articles study instances of bilingualism such as code-switching or absence of code-switching taken as tokens of linguicism (Bleichenbacher 2008, 2012); mock languages (Hill 1993, 1995; Higgins and Furukawa 2012), and ethnic stylizations designed for monolingual audiences (Meek 2006, Androutsopoulos 2007, Planchenault 2008a, Chung 2013).
- **Repertoire analysis (Androutsopoulos 2012b) and character-based analysis (Bednarek 2012):** These studies look at what code(s) is/are assigned to which characters and analyse the ideological implications of these associations.
- **Film language in translation:** In the dedicated field of Audiovisual Translation (Orero 2004, Díaz-Cintas 2009). Other studies focus on dubbing and synchronization (Planchenault 2008b; Guillot 2010, 2012a).

Most studies combine several levels of analysis. For example, the study of stylizations often combines the studies of phonological features and genres (Coupland 2004, Tsiplakou and Ioannidou 2012); and Petrucci (2012) and Guillot (2012b) analyse the losses that occur in the translation of stylization.

1.1.4 New media

Studies of the new media have focused on different genres (blogs, institutional websites, social media or Web 2.0 such as YouTube, Twitter or Facebook) and most of them have made the previously mentioned binary approach to the study of language in the media a central focus of their reflection. If statements such as 'The internet has revolutionised the way we live our lives in untold ways, but the most far-reaching is the impact it is having on the way we communicate' (Seargeant and Tagg 2013) sound very similar to arguments that were held during the heyday of print media or, centuries later, that of broadcast media, it is true to say that the linguistic study of computer-mediated communication has fuelled new debates on whether the new media creates new ways of speaking and writing (see Crystal 2011) – prompting the emergence of a new domain of linguistic study: Internet Linguistics. Technology (e.g. typed text in synchronized online communication) and new media contexts do not only shape the forms of communication that take place online (Tannen and Trester 2013). According to scholars, the broad influence of the new media goes beyond shaping the way we speak/write on the Internet; it also profoundly affects the way we live and the way we are. For Seargeant and Tagg (2013), 'how we communicate online has a profound and lasting impact on language and society ... on how we relate to each other, the communities we live in, and the way we manage and present a sense of self in twenty-first century society.'

However, the study of language on the Internet has not only focused on the changes in language patterns of social interaction and communicative practices that were caused by the physical constraints of technology (Seargeant and Tagg 2013, Tannen and Trester 2013) or on the impact the new media have on individuals' sense of identity. Other studies have turned to domains such as folk linguistics, and looked at the ways languages are discussed in terms of standard and the presence of minority languages (see Johnson et al.'s (2010) study of the BBC Voices' website), or considered the impact that shifting social-economic priorities (such as globalization) have on the prevalence of diversity and the status of various languages on the Internet (for example, in the new field of study 'Minority Language Media studies' – see Gruffydd Jones and Uribe-Jongbloed 2013).

Finally, and to wrap up this review of literature, I would like to highlight the fact that one important characteristic of mediated texts pertains to the presence of *contrasting voices* (which were also central to the novel, see Bakhtin's studies of polyphony and heteroglossia). This is even more evident when looking at the studies of language in the media, as linguistic analyses of media texts often focus on instances where the language is considered as marked, or as deviating from standard forms of speaking (the use of bold, italics or underlined features in the analysed media excerpts makes this quite clear). As a process of differentiation, voice contrasts permit us to distinguish between a norm (*our* way of speaking) and other linguistic forms (*their* ways of speaking): 'Speakers can simply alter their voices, writers their style, to suggest voices *from outside*' (Johnstone 2007: 61 [my emphasis]).

In the case of fictional language, the 'double plane of communication' – that is, what is said between the characters in the story vs. what information is intended to be given to the film audiences (Piazza et al. 2011: 1, also called the 'double articulation' of films – Lorenzo-Dus 2008) – complicates the matter further. In fiction, voice contrasts occur as a consequence of the physicality of the performance (i.e. different actors talking to one another), but also as a result of an artificial construct (intended by authors, with the use of accents or other stylistic devices, and for narrative as well as ideological purposes).

As the premise of the studies of voices presented in the following chapters, there is the fundamental notion that the performed media voices are to be analysed as framed and entextualized discourses. To grasp better the consequences of this premise, I now present the theoretical background of this book: it combines important concepts taken from the research on genre, stylization and performance (all of which are socially shared constructs that shape the use of language(s) in contexts). I start with the concept of *genre*, bearing in mind that for Bell and Gibson, 'genre is a key concept in studying performance, but both variegated and slippery in its definition' (2011: 565).

1.2 Genre, style and stylization in the media

Most media genres are unmistakably attached to media types (TV, radio, the written press, the Internet, etc.). News articles, evening news programmes, TV advertisements, films, blogs, chats and tweets ... each one of these media genres follows specific sets of rules that dictate their forms, contents as well as the way they make use of language. Media discourses are so intricately embedded in our daily life that most people after being presented with a media text are instantly able to recognize the genre to which it belongs. In this section, I argue that other speech genres are embedded within these familiar media genres. Bauman (2001) offers a definition of genre as

> ...one order of speech style, a constellation of systematically related, co-occurrent formal features and structures that serves as a conventionalized orienting framework for the production and reception of discourse. More specifically, a genre is a speech style oriented to the production and reception of a particular kind of text. When an utterance is assimilated as a given genre, the process by which it is produced and interpreted is mediated through its intertextual relationship with prior texts.
>
> Bauman 2001: 79

For Halliday (1988: 162), genre is 'a cluster of associated features having a greater-than-random ... tendency to co-occur'. And for Bell and Gibson (2011: 565), it is defined by 'patterns of language [that] yield typical collocations'. It is, however, important to note that for Biber and Conrad (2009), genre, register and style do not fundamentally differ from one another but all three are 'different approaches or perspectives for analysing text varieties, not different kinds of texts or different varieties'. They are categories that have been used in the systemic-functional study of diatypic variation ('The dialect is what a person speaks, determined by who he is; the register is what a person is speaking, determined by what he is doing at the time' – Halliday 1978: 110). Turning one's attention to definitions of register and style (such as: 'register is used as a cover term for any language variety defined in terms of a particular constellation of situational characteristics' – Biber and Conrad 2001: 3), one finds the same fundamental characteristics that could be summarized under the terms of *clustering* (i.e. the association of salient features), *co-occurrence* (i.e. the appearance of these features in the same stretches of language and in particular contexts or situations), and *distinctiveness*:[4] stretches of language are marked with comparison to other ways of speaking taken as the norm ('styles achieve their meaning through contrast and difference' – Coupland 2007: 21), and produced in such ways in order to be perceived as holding specific social meanings.

Categories of stylistic variations are therefore described in terms of typical linguistic characteristics (lexical, grammatical and discursive) in relation to situational contexts, as well as with regards to the indexical relationship between mediated stylistic features on the one hand, and situated social meanings and discursively constructed personas on the other hand. How does the notion of genres informs the study of performed voices in the media? Next to obvious macro-genres (films, stand-up comedians, TV advertisements, etc.), there also exist micro-genres that are embedded in the former, *stratified* in what Bakhtin (1981, 1986) calls sub-genres or speech genres ('relatively stable types' – 1986: 60; 'more complex and comparatively highly developed and organised cultural communication' – 1986: 62), that hold specific relations with macro-genres and are used to index specific personae or groups. In performances, sub-genres (such as impersonations and other familiar narrated styles) are used as frames for interpretation, and are recognized by enculturated audiences thanks to the cluster of stylistic features that they present (phonological features such as accents, lexical features such as emblematic words, discursive features such as code-switching), which are then taken as marked to index specific characters. For example, the French-accented English displayed by Clouseau, Hercule Poirot or Depardieu's characters in Hollywood productions makes use of salient phonological features (i.e. thrilled /r/, alveolar /th/ or absent /h/) and stylistic features (i.e. token code-switching in French) that bear social and narrative connotations (see part 2, chapters 5 and 6). How do people become familiar with these genres? In other words, how has the performance of selected features come to embody specific voices? According to Conboy (2010: 7), 'genre is also a form of social contract between writer and reader. A reader knows what to expect from a particular genre or combination of genres.' It is through 'processes whereby distinct forms of speech come to be socially recognized (or enregistered) as indexical of speaker attributes by a population of language users' (Agha 2005) that performers and audiences alike become competent to the point that they can read into the linguistic features which are produced, reproduced and circulated in varied media genres and draw from the associated social meanings. In other words, according to Agha's concept, 'enregisterment is the process by which a style becomes engraved in the public mind as indexing certain social personas or characterological figures' (Bell and Gibson 2011: 561). When applying the concept to performed voices in the media, one faces two paradoxes that will subsequently need to be dealt with: how should one address the complex relationships between, on the one hand, genre and diversity (how can enregisterment survive the huge diversity of voices audible in the global media?) and, on the other hand, enregisterment and authenticity (how do enregistered media styles relate to the ways of speaking that exist in the *real world*?). The indexical link between language use and social meaning is not direct, but is instead mediated or derived through ideologically connected indexical orders (Silverstein 2003). Moreover, considering that 'the success of a performance does not necessarily require accuracy' (Bell and Gibson 2011: 568), one has to acknowledge that quite often, imitation goes beyond simplification.

The relationship between media macro-genres and the sub-genres found across varied media is based on complex dynamics. For Bell and Gibson (2011: 558), audiences have a 'heightened awareness of the existing repertoire of cultural texts, and value is placed upon their skilful recontextualization'. In the same journal, Bauman (2011) gives a linguistic-anthropologic definition of the concept of genre as a 'metapragmatic orienting schema for entextualization … that is, the production, reception, and circulation understanding of particular orders of texts and for the production of intertextuality' (p. 711). Performances of voices loosen media texts by embedding a genre within another genre. For example, French-accented English may be found in films as well as in TV advertisements (I shall later mention a French TV commercial that paradoxically makes use of such an accent) or in spectacular fragments of language that appear in the written press (in articles or commercials). If encultured audiences know about genres, spectators are also able to recognize recontextualization of familiar orders of texts and to evaluate the relevance of the transfer from one macro-genre to another (for example, from street speech to political speech in the case of *verlan* – see note 16 in the Introduction). With regards to the new media, one may question whether the Internet has created new genres or if existing ones have been embedded in new genres (websites, blogs, tweets, etc.). For example, the menus posted on restaurants' websites do not differ widely from paper-based versions commonly handed out in restaurants. For Bakhtin (1986), genres are not fixed forms, but transform constantly. Or is it rather that they are constantly remade to fit better the transformations of macro-genres (as according to Bolter and Grusin's (1999) concept of remediation, prior media forms are refashioned into new media technologies)? For Wodak and Busch (2004: 106), 'Media texts also depend on intertextual relations with many other genres, diachronically or synchronically. Texts relate to other texts, represented by the media, through quotes or indirect references, thus already adding particular meanings or decontextualizing and recontextualizing meanings. Media thus produce and reproduce social meanings.'

1.2.1 Styling

One traditionally thinks that, contrary to genre where features serve important communicative functions, style features are preferred for aesthetical reasons (see Irvine's (2001) introduction on the common understanding of style as distinction). However, comparing style to genre, Eckert (2008: 455) states that 'style has a similar function in everyday language, picking out locations in the social landscape'. Just as with genre, style can foremost be understood as a bundle of linguistic features with specific social meanings. In his seminal studies, Labov (1984) considered style from a variationist perspective: 'By "style shifting" we mean to include any consistent change in linguistic forms used by a speaker, qualitative or quantitative, that can be associated with a change in topics, participants, channel, or the broader social context' (p. 29). Here, style shifting refers to a single speaker changing style in response to context. If Labovian studies of style have focused on the attention paid to speech ('*styles can be ranged along a single dimension, measured by the amount of attention paid to speech*' – Labov 1972: 208) or shifts from vernacular to more formal ways of speaking, more recent studies have been interested in seeing style-shifting as acts of identities that permit speakers to express personal stances: '[F]ocus [of study] has turned from the reactive to the creative' (Schilling 2013: 328). Recent studies consider the way people use stylistic resources in unfolding linguistic interactions, and according to Eckert's three waves of stylistic variation study (2005), in the third wave, individuals make social meaning as 'speakers place themselves in the social landscape through stylistic practice'. However, for some, speakers' agency is also limited. For Irvine (2001), an ideological framework is necessary to interpret styles and Eckert (2008: 456) argues that 'ideology is at the center of stylistic practice: one way or another, every stylistic move is the result of an interpretation of the social world and of the meanings of elements within it, as well as a positioning of the stylizer with respect to that world ... stylistic moves are ideological'. She proposes the notion of 'indexical field' (Eckert 2008) as an 'embodiment of ideology in linguistic form' (2008: 464) and to account for the cluster of social meanings embodied by a style and available to interlocutors in the meaning-making of unfolding interactions.

The notion of 'styling' opens a dynamic perspective on style, and highlights the action that takes place during the act of performing (reminding us that for Halliday the diatypic variation should be considered according to what the speaker is *doing 'at the time'*) as well as the liminal space that separates performance from normal talk. In a 1999 special issue of the *Journal of Sociolinguistics*, edited by Rampton and entitled *Styling the other*, Bell argues that '[t]he notion of "styling the other" presupposes that a variety has a distinguishable and rather stable core of linguistic features in order for it to be modelled at all' (p. 525).

If styling can be perceived by audiences as 'talking strange' (Bell 1991: 17–18), it is not generally perceived as incongruous with the context of interaction or the intentions of the speaker. The next section will show that stylizations often present themselves as obvious performances and are usually understood as deviations from the style that one would normally expect in given situations.

1.2.2 Stylizing

Coupland (2001: 346) distinguishes stylization from styling as stylization deals with performance in a theatrical way: 'it brings into play stereotyped semiotic and ideological values associated with other groups.' Later, in an article written in 2004, he gives the example of a waiter's style in a high-end restaurant, and compares it with an instance where he would pretend to perform the waiter's style at his own dinner table, arguing that the latter case is an instance of stylization. According to his own definition (Coupland 2004: 249): 'Stylised utterances [are] bounded moments when others' voices are, in somewhat more literal sense, displayed and framed for local, creative, sociolinguistic effect.' In a few words, and going back to the scholar to whom we owe the concept of stylization, for Bakhtin (1981: 362) stylization is the 'artistic representation of another's linguistic style'.[5] What differentiates the social performance of self in everyday life in the Goffmanian sense from the theatrical performances of actors? Are all theatrical performances of voice stylizations? For Bell and Gibson (2011: 558): 'we expect staged performance to often be linguistically *stylized* – that is, rehearsed, self-aware, stagey, and at times hyperbolic', and with regard to films, Androutsopoulos (2012a: 151) argues that:

[s]tyling is the concept with the broader extension, understood as the design of character in terms of language style, leaving stylisation to focus on more specific discourse processes. Thus stylisation can focus on a particular mode of character styling, which draws on overtly stereotyped and obviously exaggerated realisations of dialect or language/dialect mixing (Tsiplakou and Ioannidou). Stylisation can also focus on the tension between an actor's ordinary voice and their put-on voice in a film (Planchenault). Alternatively, and closer to the term's conventional usage, stylisation captures the cinematic moments when characters step out of their ordinary voice and into adopting a different voice.

Androutsopoulos 2012a: 151

Stylization is often a caricature; it sometimes verges on the grotesque. In the case of films, spectators' suspension of disbelief is always threatened as they are constantly being reminded of the performance. However, for Coupland (2001: 345), 'Although stylization is a form of strategic deauthentication, its ultimate relationship with authenticity is complex. As a facet of cultural performance, stylization can be part of a process of cultural reproduction.' In studies of language in the media, Carroll (2013) argues that it is difficult to scientifically identify what counts as stylizations and that it is therefore often 'left to the researcher's intuition' (2013: 261).

In his theory of *crossing*, Ben Rampton depicts situations 'in which the conventional persona normatively associated with one situation is transposed to another setting where it initially seems anomalous but subsequently makes sense as some kind of artful effect' (Rampton, ms., as quoted in Coupland and Jaworski 2004: 35). It is language style 'out of place' (Coupland and Jaworski 2004). Even though the concept has some commonalities with stylization (as it refers to the use of a language which is perceived as not 'belonging' to the speaker), language crossing involves a sense of movement across quite sharply felt social or ethnic boundaries, and raises issues of affiliation and legitimacy that participants need to reckon with in the course of their encounter (Rampton 1998: 291). While instances of crossing are generally stylizations, none of the performances of voice studied in this book is an act of crossing.

1.2.3 The politics of style, stylization and mock languages

One should not forget the strategies behind the act of styling/stylizing language (Coupland and Jaworski 2004: 33). The intentions behind, as well as labels used to define, these manipulations of language vary. Carroll explains this clearly: 'While Rampton and others (eg. Jaspers 2006, T. Rahman 2009, Mason Carris

2011) have argued that stylizing is a means for members of politically disadvantaged groups to resist the social order, there is also literature on the topic that uses the term "mock" rather than "stylized" to highlight the pejorative motives of this type of language use' (Carroll 2013: 260). However, Hill (2009), who created the label, has herself put into question its use by ethnographers for analytical purposes and encouraged them to think about its implications. In this book, I use different labels ('accented French'; 'ethnic voices'; 'French-accented English'; 'French-stylized English'), all of which carry important ideological and political connotations.

But for now, and more importantly perhaps than agreeing on which terms should be used to define such instances of language, one has to acknowledge the fact that, in such studies of language use and representations, sociolinguists 'step away from taken-for-granted, relatively transparent, apolitical sense of social meaning to [adopt] a perspective that seeks out agencies in meaning-making' (Coupland and Jaworski 2004: 38). In Coupland and Jaworski's words, it is the 'end of innocence' (2004: 38).

The last section of the chapter focuses on the specificity of performed voices in their artistic sense as well as in their theatrical contexts.

1.3 The performer, the performance and the audience

With regards to the artistic sense of the term, the word 'performance' has two meanings: it is an action in progress (the performing act) as well as the result of this action (the performed text), or, according to the Merriam-Webster dictionary, 'the execution of an action' and 'something accomplished (deed, feat)'. In past studies of performances, the cultural text often took the forefront of the analysis, while the context was relegated to the background, sometimes at the expense of the performance's ecology. As early as 1975, in a seminal article that was, according to its author's own words (Bauman 2011), under the strong influence of Dell Hymes' and Goffman's works on performance, Bauman defined the concept thus:

> Performance involves on the part of the performer an assumption of accountability to an audience for the way in which communication is carried out, above and beyond its referential content. From the point of view of the audience, the act of expression on the part of the performer is thus marked as subject to evaluation for the way it is done, for the relative skill and effectiveness of the performer's display of competence. Additionally, it is marked as available

for the enhancement of experience, through the present enjoyment of the intrinsic qualities of the act of expression itself. Performance thus calls forth special attention to and heightened awareness of the act of expression and gives license to the audience to regard the act of expression and the performer with special intensity.

Bauman 1975: 293

From the first sentence, what this quote tells us is that, although the focus of studies is most often on performances as decontextualized cultural objects, analysts should adopt a holistic approach and never lose sight of the ecology of *verbal art* (Bauman 1975). In other words, they should not ignore any side of the triad Performer-Performance-Audience. Before considering separately each angle of this performance's triangle, I would like to say a few more words on the two specificities under which I circumscribe my study of language in performances: mediation and stage.

What distinguishes ordinary and everyday performances of self from the performances that Bauman talks about? If Goffman's (1959) work has brought to the forefront the necessity to study attentively the management of face-to-face interactions and, in particular, to pay careful attention to what people do when they are co-present to each other, it is important to consider that quite often, in the context of performances that are technologically mediated, people are not necessarily co-present to each other. Moreover, in the case of performances that are not live, or with regards to films and the new media, spectators/readers take part in the *interaction* in an asynchronous manner (for example, spectators can view/listen to a recorded performance long after it has been produced, even long after the performer's death: a characteristic that contributes to the magic of mediated voices,[6] see Derrida 2001). This is one of the reasons why Bell and Gibson (2011) prefer to speak not of media performances, but of *mediated performances*. The chosen term calls for a mention of Peirce's difference between *immediate* and *mediate* perception that defines two sorts of objects: the ones that the conscience perceives immediately and the ones that the conscience perceives in a mediated way. However, since for the semiotician, all perception is mediated, it is more fruitful to turn to another concept.

A key word that could help to differentiate the two sorts of performances is the notion of *staged* language (Bell and Gibson 2011). In this regard, I argue that, even though they do not involve the presence of a stage in the conventional sense of the term, the performances of voices studied in this book (i.e. performances that take place in films, the written press or the social media) are all instances of *staged* language. I take the meaning of stage in a figurative fashion: it is a place that can be virtual and where an object, a person or a linguistic act, is put on display. In this regard, it is not unlike Goffman's concept of *platform*. In his studies of what he calls *platform events* (e.g. lectures, plays, concerts), Goffman (1981, 1983) defines orders of interaction 'in which an activity is set before an audience' (1983: 7). Such *platforms/stages* that I study in this book are films and websites. They are more than a simple medium but, like a theatre stage, they too offer performances to the ears and gazes of more than a mere interlocutor and to audiences for reception and evaluation. This fact involves three consequences as follows, which will be developed below:

- For the performer, this is most often a **deliberate**, **knowing** and **reflexive** act that involves individual positioning as well as competence (the part left to improvisation is usually minimal).
- For the performance, being *staged* has several implications: it is **constructed**, therefore it is **artificial** and **prepared** (i.e. drafted and/or rehearsed).
- For the audience, there is a tacit agreement that taking part in the reception of a performance of voice is to adopt the spectator's role. More than a simple gaze or special attention (Bauman 1975), it requires **intellectual participation** that may take the form of an aesthetical evaluation, but most of all it calls for the **cognitive processing** of a discursively coded information.

1.3.1 The performer

Since his seminal article (1975), Bauman never ceased to refine his view on performance and revisited several times what he considered to be the key features of the cultural act of performing. In a recent article written for the special issue of the *Journal of Sociolinguistics* on performance, he says that, just as Goffman's work is, his approach is 'rooted in the Durkheimian tradition which looks to cultural performances as highly reflexive display events – *cultural forms about culture* – in which *the deepest meanings and values of a culture are embodied*, enacted, and placed on display before an audience' (Bauman 2011: 715, my emphasis). As a consequence, the performer has a responsibility and a commitment with regards to the form of his/her production or what Bauman describes as an act of *stance-taking* (which Jaffe defines as 'the taking up [of] a position with respect to the form and the content of one's uttering' – 2009: 5). To develop further this definition of stance-taking as related to performances, I would like now to raise the following questions: what position do performers take with regard to the characters that they perform? And to go back to Goffman's well-known functions (1981), are performers mere *animators* (and sometimes authors) of the lines that they utter, or are they also *principal*? In other words, do they speak in the name of 'we'? Bell and Gibson (2011: 562) argue that '[t]his does not mean that when a performer does a particular accent they are necessarily trying to identify with the people who speak with that accent in any simple sense. They are referring to the accent, and such referencing may embody a variegated range of linkages and intentions.' Dealing with more complex implications still, one should question where performers stand with regards to the ideologies that are commonly circulated on the voices that they perform, especially when their performances seemingly make use of hegemonic ideologies as a common ground between them and their audiences (I shall return to this last point in chapters 2 and 4 of this book).

More than performers' stance as well as confidence in their position as being legitimate (as speaker and as performer), performances often require *virtuosity* (Bauman 2011). As Coupland (2004) says about the act of stylizing, 'some speakers will be more adept than others' (p. 253). Not only do performers need sufficient knowledge in the specific genre (or, in Chomskyan terms, to be *competent*), they need to perform (in Dell Hymes' sense and in the double sense of the term: to play and to excel). Good performers may also need to be inventive as each performance is a re-enactment of already circulated voices (see chapter 5). As an example, the creative pun written by Kaganski (2004) can be evaluated with comments such as 'well put!' or 'well said!' In some cases, performers are so talented that they seem to summon personae who come to exist by themselves – 'cancelling the assumption that we are even hearing "the same" speaker' (Coupland and Jaworski 2004: 35). This is undoubtedly the case of Poirot's voice, which will be studied in the second part of this book. In the case of very talented performers, these summonings are awe-inspiring and performers may appear *possessed* by the character(s) that they play (see, for example, Margaret Cho's impersonation of her own mother[7] or Philippe Caubère's marathon one-man shows,[8] in which he embodies up to 115 different characters).

1.3.1.1 *The Performer's Voice*

Studying media text as a voice implies studying language that is embodied. Film scholars such as Chion (1999), in his seminal book on the voice in films, have come to the conclusion that:

> The voice is ceasing to be identified with a specific face. It appears much less stable, identified, hence fetishizable. This general realization that the voice is

radically other than the body that adopts it (or that it adopts) for the duration of a film seems to me to be one of the most significant phenomena in the recent development of the cinema, television, and audiovisual media in general.

Chion 1999: 174

Sociolinguists such as Heller (2009: 279) argue that '[t]he media are not disembodied (although they have resources for making the bodies which produce and consume disappear, a move which serves to naturalize media discourse in powerful ways); they are not timeless or free-floating'. Faced with such contradictions, it is necessary to address the deceptively simple question: What is *a voice*? In its singularity the word refers principally to the articulated sounds produced by the larynx and the vocal human organs but is also seen as the property and the specificity of an individual person (to the point that the word is used as a synecdoche to stand for the presence of an individual or a group of individuals' stance as in the expression 'voices against …'). In linguistics (and particularly phonetics), the voice is usually studied with a functional approach (it is generally reduced to its physical aspect: the vibration of the vocal cords) that chooses to ignore its individuality or the role played by culture and society in shaping its form. However, in order to deal with all its richness, one has to face a couple of paradoxes. A voice is embodied (i.e. unique) yet socialized (i.e. collective and generic), making it impossible to distinguish between the 'uniqueness of an individual's voice and the social and cultural determination that shape its performance' (Neumark et al. 2010: ix). In films, a voice is made in the very fabric of a human vocal production, yet as a costume, it varies widely according to the characters being performed (this vocal versatility is the trademark of voice talents). A performer's voice is bound to its bodily origin yet partly disembodied when it is performed (i.e. it does not fully 'belong' to the speaker).

1.3.2 The performance

The production and reception of performances of voice are determined by four key characteristics: the facts that, in performances, language is (i) staged, (ii) mediated, (iii) entextualized and (iv) commodified.

1.3.2.1 *Staged*

As already mentioned, saying that something (e.g. an event) is *staged* implies that it has been deliberately and carefully constructed. Regarding instances of language that are produced and recognized as staged, one seems to recognize implicitly that one is not dealing with *natural* everyday communication but with language that is produced in specific and out-of-the-ordinary circumstances. For Bell and Gibson (2011: 558), 'The focus here shifts to the non-everyday and the non-vernacular – or to the vernacular which is intentionally reproduced.' However, performances are not disconnected from the real, and in fact they seem to occupy an in-between position from which they entertain complex relations with authenticity and artifice. This defines the very particular nature of the performance as a form of speaking *as if* and one that is also undoubtedly fake: spectators are aware, most of the time,[9] that they are watching someone who is pretending to be/to speak like another person. Developing further the theatrical metaphor of the stage, the performance appears to be framed (the way the performance that is taking place on a stage is framed by the set). Once again, this has the effect of always keeping the performance at a distance from its audience as well as to objectify it – thereby reinforcing the audience's consciousness of the artifice. This frame is also 'a window on the world of the creative and the self-conscious, the kind of language excluded from sociolinguistic work which targets "natural, unselfconscious speech"' (Bell and Gibson 2011: 558). Moreover, as enacted cultural forms, performances are well placed to become an ideal object of study. This is true to such an extent that, for Bauman (2011: 715), 'cultural performances, in this line of inquiry, afford the anthropologist, theologian, sociologist, or historian a privileged vantage point on culture, an illuminating point of entry into how participants see themselves as they are and as they might be'.

1.3.2.2 *Mediated*

Mediation has a few effects on the way one relates to performances' linguistic content. First, as already mentioned, individuals taking part in performed events (i.e. performers and audiences) are not necessarily co-present (with the exception of what Coupland (2007) calls 'high performances' – viz. concerts, theatre plays, stand-up comedians' performances, etc. – which are space-bound and time-bound). When a performance is mediated, the moment of reception is most often deferred through representation (i.e. the performer is not directly present and does not share the same timeframe with spectators). A representation can therefore be repeated (one can replay the same DVD or reread the same article as many times as one wants), giving ample time and opportunity for audiences to scrutinize the displayed ways of speaking. Second, by dressing a barrier between performances and audiences, mediation acts as the fourth wall of the theatre stage (i.e. the fictive wall that separates actors from the audience and creates a narrative space), and reinforces the performance's hybrid nature of being fictive, albeit situated and embodied. Finally, reminding ourselves of the oft-cited McLuhan's 'the medium is the message', it appears that the medium frames the content of the performance and, therefore, its interpretation (to such an extent that one would not fully comprehend a media text if ignoring the fact that it is mediated). Mediation has come to shape frames of reference to language. To paraphrase Stuart Hall (1980), if the dog that is represented in the media can bark, it does not bite. In other words, if what is presented in the media performances of voices looks like *natural* language, it is not natural language *per se*; it is closer to people's assumptions about natural language. In fact, I shall repeatedly argue in this book that studying such performances amounts to studying metalanguage (Coupland and Jaworski 2004, Coupland 2004) or, because they hold the key to commonly shared beliefs on language, to study what Preston calls metalanguage 3 (Preston 2004).

1.3.2.3 Entextualized

As a reminder of the origins of the concept of entextualization, I quote Silverstein and Urban (1996):

> To turn something into a text is to seem to give it a decontextualized structure and meaning, that is, a form and meaning that are imaginable apart from the spatiotemporal and other frames, in which they can be said to occur. Such an autonomously meaningful object, indeed, becomes a trope for culture, understood in the sense of an ensemble of shared symbols and meanings.
>
> Silverstein and Urban 1996: 1

For Bauman and Briggs (1990: 73), despite anchoring counterforces that make them dependent on a context, performances are 'decenterable': i.e. the discourse that it presents is extractable and can be 'lifted out of its interactional setting' (1990: 73). As a result, this discourse does not depend on the context of the performance any more and may stand autonomously: 'A text, then, from this vantage point, is a verbal utterance rendered decontextualisable' (Bauman and Briggs, 1990: 73). Before being reshaped for Kaganski's (2004) journalistic intents, the '*Nique ta mère*' that was studied in the introductory chapter had been entextualized as a swearword, a joke, and abbreviated to become a band's name. For Coupland (2007: 155), a performance 'packages up stylistic and sociosemantic complexes and makes them transportable'. Expressions that originated from the suburbs have travelled to other mediated forms (films, raps songs, etc.)

and have been read and heard in the most improbable of places: the title of a film review or the political scene. When 'decentered', voices may become the site of tensions and negotiations. Because they are open to audiences' scrutiny, they also present a space for resistance, as it was the case when the ex-secretary of state was blamed for using suburban slang (see note 16 in the Introduction). As Bauman (2011: 715) argues, 'Thus materialized and placed on view, these enactments allow not only for the contemplation of received and authoritative truths, but for experimentation, critique, even subversion.' As well as being appropriated, such enactments can also be reclaimed by the stigmatized groups that the performances represent. I shall, however, discuss the meanings associated with acts such as appropriation and reclaiming.

1.3.2.4 Commodified

Paraphrasing Bourdieu (1991), I argue that performed voices are commodities that are negotiated between a producer (in the case of a movie, this person can be the actor or the person in charge of the commercialization of the film) and a consumer (to follow with my example, the latter may in-turn be the filmmaker, film producer or spectator) and exchanged on media markets in multiple ways.

The most obvious way is linked to the nature of artistic performances. As the product of a professional competence, performances can be traded and sold, in exchange for a salary and via the revenues generated by the end product. Moreover, it is usually believed that the value of the commodity depends on the talent of the performer. However, this value also depends on the existing demand for the performed voices (and for the genre to which they belong).

Second, verbal performances are the demonstration of a linguistic competence, which as an added value (Heller 2010, Duchêne and Heller 2012) can also be traded. By displaying linguistic ability and legitimacy (even in the case of stigmatized languages' stylizations as successful performers often occupy a privileged position), performers benefit from professional recognition, work opportunities and high status.

Third, as framed by language ideologies, performed voices gain value according to the current state of the market. For example, performed voices have been sold at turns as ideologies of linguistic otherness (one could argue that, in the history of theatre, such language ideologies have occupied a major place – see, for example, the stump speech of the nineteenth-century black minstrels), as alternative ideologies that opposed conservative views on languages (first performed by legitimized speakers[10]), or as a mix of the two (see, for example, bell hooks 1992, 1997 for a critique of the commodification of rap culture). Therefore, what takes place through the transaction of performed voices as commodities is also a circulation of language ideologies. However, on media markets, it is not always clear what language ideologies are exchanged (legitimized or alternatives – see chapter 2), nor what speakers are legitimized to obtain the higher profits from the commodified voices. For Duchêne and Heller (2012), there are 'complex ways in which older nationalist ideologies which invest language with value as a source of pride get bound up with newer neoliberal ideologies which invest language with value as a source of profit'. As argued above, if it is clear that when the street language is appropriated by the media, the source of pride becomes a source of profit, one may also argue that it may also be regained as a source of pride (and profit) when reclaimed by the stigmatized community (this was, for example, the case with the suburb's *parler caillera* – literally the speak of the *racaille*, 'the scum').

1.3.3 The audience

For Bell and Gibson (2009: 563), 'Audience is crucial to performance. Audiences have their roles as do performers.' Audiences' engagement may start with demonstrations of interest (such as buying a theatre ticket, renting or downloading a DVD, connecting to a particular website) that are usually accompanied by the willingness to dedicate sufficient time and attention to the performances. But apart from this first commitment, what can be said of the intellectual engagement that defines the nature of spectatorship? How different is the reception of a mediated performance from the performance that takes place in a face-to-face interaction? Fifty years ago, one would have answered these questions in terms of activity (individuals taking part in a social interaction) and passivity (spectators being spoon-fed the content of, for example, a TV programme). However, after decades of media studies dedicated to audiences, it is now obvious that spectators are not mere receptacles of the media message, and that if they sometimes align with the dominant ideologies that are conveyed by media performances, they may also be indifferent to them or even resist them (Hall 1980: 59–61). Wodak and Busch (2004: 106) urge researchers to consider the way that readers and listeners interact with the media 'not only by writing letters to the editor but also by interpreting and understanding them in specific subjective ways'. This being said, and following Hall (2000), the studies of media voices conducted in this book will more specifically address the assumptions that these performances entail with regard to audiences:

One such background assumption is the *consensual* nature of society: the process of *signification* – giving social meanings to events – *both assumes and helps to construct society as a 'consensus'*. We exist as members of one society *because* – it is assumed – we share a common stock of cultural knowledge with our fellow men: we have access to the same 'maps of meanings'. Not only are we all able to manipulate these 'maps of meaning' to understand events, but we have fundamental interests, values and concerns in common, which these maps embody or reflect.

Hall 2000: 425

If Bauman and Brigg (1990: 73) have argued that 'performance heightens awareness of the act of speaking and licenses the audience to evaluate the skill and effectiveness of the performers' accomplishment', I would like to argue that performance's evaluation is secondary in the audience's participation. Indeed, to enjoy fully a performance of voice, readers and spectators must first decipher the diverse meanings and linguistic associations that are encoded in the performance. To recognize instances of staged language and genres requires enculturated audiences (Coupland 2004), whose familiarity with varied registers (in and out of the realm of the media), developed through socialization and cultural experience (such as repeated contacts with films, the written press, or a particular magazine), enables them, for example, 'to read the semiotic value of a projected persona' (Coupland 2004: 253). During a performance of voice, a performer relies on this assumedly shared cultural capital from his/her audience. Bourdieu defines cultural capital as 'knowledge, skills and other cultural acquisitions, as exemplified by educational or technical qualifications' (Thompson 1991: 14). In its embodied form (the individual's capital), it is partly inherited, partly acquired over time, and includes linguistic capital, which in turn is converted into a linguistic habitus. The habitus as defined by Bourdieu is a set of structured and ingrained *dispositions* which 'generates practices and perceptions . . . and provides individuals with a sense of how to act and respond' (Thompson 1991: 13). These dispositions are inculcated, durable, generative and transposable (Thompson 1991: 12). As for the linguistic habitus, dispositions and attitudes are 'regular', predictable without being consciously co-ordinated. In the case of the example given in the introductory chapter, thanks to their linguistic habitus, *Les Inrockuptibles*' readers are equipped to perceive the words chosen in a predictable way. They also unconsciously react to the title's entextualization: by recognizing the utterance as non-standard, incongruous in the written press, and as a sample of coarse language. What is particularly remarkable in the case of Kaganski's title is that, in order to understand it fully, its readers not only have to be familiar with the salient linguistic features that have often been used in the media stylizations of the suburban French; they also need sufficient knowledge in the history of French cinema to understand the created duality between the two sorts of cinema. It is the combination of such competences that defines a particular readership[11] (and creates pleasure for the readers who are acknowledged in their *distinction*). Far from being inclusive, the process also reinforces division and reinstates the politics of otherness. Indeed, by being able to understand the performed stylization and read/hear a voice as different, readers also validate the markedness of a voice. The process of differentiation is complete.

In this section, I have attempted to show that studying voices and performances in the media implies having in mind the very specific nature of mediated instances of language that are under scrutiny. Performances of voice are not only mediated, they are also staged, entextualized and commodified, as well as embodied.

Consequently, the questions that I shall examine in the forthcoming studies of voices are as follows:

- In what way should one study the form that is specific to a performance of voice?
- What features/linguistic props/rhetorical devices are used during such performances?
- Why are certain genres favoured? Are the reasons for this preference to be found outside of the media? How do traits become salient within a genre?
- What part is played by actual performers in the choice of features and creation of a voice that is unique, albeit recognizable, by diverse audiences?

Appendix 1 provides additional questions and proposes a framework for the study of performed voices in the media.

Part One

Voices in French: Performances of Linguistic Differentiation in the French Media

The texture of a voice says a lot about who the speaker is: his or her identity (social, sexual, etc.) and origins (national and regional), as well as feelings, health, mood, the way he or she relates to his or her interlocutor(s) and to the context of the exchange (Revis 2013). When an actor performs a voice, what this voice says to an audience about the character that he or she plays goes beyond mere techniques of characterization (i.e. social and regional origins, sexual orientation, personality and emotions, or other traits important to the narration at play). Culpeper (2001: 206) argues that 'dramatists can capitalise upon the attitudes stereotypically associated with particular accents and dialects'. For Kozloff (2000: 26–27), 'dialect, mispronunciation, and inarticulateness have been used [in film dialogues] to ridicule and stigmatise characters.' For these reasons, the study of a performed voice also informs the analyst about the society in which the media discourse takes place, in terms of its relations to legitimate and non-standard ways of speaking, as well as with regard to groups that are discriminated against.

Accented voices in the French media: Stigma, prejudice and discrimination

As in many modern societies, and despite (or owing to) what Silverman (1999: 6) calls 'the archetypal Enlightenment model of the Republic' (comprising of emblematic values such as *laïcité* or *Liberté Égalité Fraternité* – the well-known French national motto), France has its own objects/subjects of stigmatization. As a result, stigmatized groups and individuals are stylized or ridiculed in the

French media. In this first part of the book, the following chapters will study three types of stigmatized groups: social and regional (suburban youth and rural communities in chapter 2), sexual (transvestites in chapter 3), and ethnic (North African and black communities in chapters 2 and 4). Among other stigmas, accents occupy a prominent position. This is not a recent or French phenomenon, as Chambers (2013) shows by quoting Cicero's (55 BC) encouragement to his readers to avoid 'not only the asperity of rustic pronunciation but the strangeness of outlandish pronunciation' (in Chambers 2013: 4). Giles and Coupland (1991) report that since the 1960s, research has repeatedly demonstrated that speakers of non-standard varieties are evaluated – mainly on the basis of their accent (see the 'Speaker Evaluation Paradigm' and matched-guise technique, for example) – as being less intelligent, competent, confident and/or ambitious. For Goffman (1963), perceptions of such features play an important role in the way people are categorized into social groups and in the process whereby the virtual social identity comes to prevail on the real one:

> Society establishes the means of categorizing persons and the complement of attributes felt to be ordinary and natural for members of each of these categories ... When a stranger comes into our presence, then, first appearances are likely to enable us to anticipate his category and attributes, his 'social identity' ... We lean on these anticipations that we have, transforming them into normative expectations, into righteously presented demands ... the demands we make might better be called demands we make 'in effect' and the character we impute to the individual might better be seen as imputation in potential retrospect – a characterization 'in effect', a *virtual social identity*.
>
> Goffman 1963: 2

The media is an important place where such traditions of language discrimination are maintained, in particular in the way marked voices contrast with standardized voices: accent-free, 'uniformed and cloned voices' (Le Breton 2011),[1] performed by mainly white speakers. As Hodson (2014: 60) puts it in this strong statement, 'completely true-to-life accents are never captured on films', and performed accents remain, for the most part, imitations of natural vernaculars.

In this part of the book, I use the words 'accented voice' and 'accented French', terms that bear significant pejorative connotations. In the cases that I study, the performed voices most often appear to the general audience (spectators or readers) as being marked and, in their most caricatured forms (i.e. stylizations or impersonations), these marks are based on linguistic stigmas (accents, emblematic lexicon, code-switching, etc.). According to Goffman (1963), a stigma is an attribute that is deeply discredited by a given society and because of which the individual who bears it may be rejected: the reaction of others to the stigma *spoils* the individual's social identity. Suburban varieties of French (see also Derville 1997, Truong 2010) bear such social stigma. If stigmas are usually understood as physical or psychological marks borne by individuals that as a result have them categorized as different, Goffman defined a third category that he called 'tribal stigmas' (1963: 4). With these terms, he referred to the phenomenon whereby traits are given to ethnic, national or religious groups that are seen as a deviation from a prevailing normative ethnicity, nationality or religion (which is clearly the case with *parler banlieue*). Since Goffman (1963), social sciences have preferred to use the concept of *prejudice* to refer to the preconceived judgment (positive as well as negative) of individuals or groups, usually because of their ethnicity, religion or race. Prejudices may be the result of individual experiences, but are most often shared within a given society. There is little doubt that films make use of such preconceived judgments, in particular in relation to language; for Lippi-Green (1997: 81), 'film uses language variation and accent to draw character quickly, building on established preconceived notions associated with specific regional loyalties, ethnic, racial or economic alliances'. Films do not only use such preconceived judgments, they participate in their perpetuation and, even though there are other means by which social and ethnic representations may be disseminated (daily interactions, institutional discourses, etc.), they also contribute to the construction of prejudices by disseminating opinions and propagating stereotypical attitudes.

If this phenomenon of differentiation may be perceived as essential to the nation-building process ('It is through the Other that the nation forms its boundaries' – Haque 2012: 21), one should bear in mind that xenophobic discourses share similar tools of exclusion. In this vein, Goffman (1963) explains how the *normals* construct a stigma-theory to explain the *stigmatized*'s inferiority and account for the danger that they represent (1963: 5). Such processes of stigmatization appear in varied genres; but comic genres (films, stand-up performances, jokes, etc.) are favoured sites for stylizations built on such prejudices (and often resulting from stigmas). According to Eitzen (1999: 95):

> [M]ost humor involves some breach of social norms or accepted behavior ... humor can be explained as a relatively non-violent and therefore socially acceptable form of aggression towards others or correction of social deviancy. The pleasure of humor, in [superiority] theory, stems from ego affirmation: humor makes us feel part of a privileged in-group or otherwise superior to those at whom our laughter is directed.

If one likes to believe that laughter frees us from accumulated tensions, that it helps release stress and diffuses aggression, anthropological studies have shown that laughter is also a sign of submission or a tool to exclude or humiliate. Comic discourses may conceal acts of stigmatization. Humour is often ambiguous. Otherwise progressive and open-minded people are sometimes found telling racist or sexist jokes, counting on the fact that their words will not be taken seriously because their interlocutors will know that they are not fundamentally sexist or racist. And it is fairly common for French people to believe that being able to laugh about anything or anyone is the sign of a healthy freedom of expression (the argument was, for example, put forward during the 2006 Muhammad cartoons controversy and, more recently, after the attack of the satirical newspaper *Charlie Hebdo*) and the refusal of a global PC trend led by English-speaking cultures. In this vein, the makers of the film *The Intouchables* (Toledano and Nakache 2011) defended themselves against the charge of racism by showing that the film's humour recycled overused stereotypical jokes that not only targeted blacks, but also indiscriminately made fun of the bourgeois, those with disabilities, women, South-East Asians, migrants, etc.

The media rely heavily on stereotypical assumptions about ethnicity, sex, class and language to construct intended effects on audiences (for humour and/or narrative purposes). Studying cinematic displays of 'interlanguage German' in a German ethnic comedy about second-generation Turkish immigrants, Androutsopoulos (2012b) asks whether recent films (i.e. Turkish-German cinema) are 'playfully exposing rather than endorsing the stereotypical language-ideological assumptions it operates with' (p. 323). He also argues that while language ideologies in fiction are not only shaped by predominant language ideologies, they also have the potential, by exposing (if not challenging) stereotypes, to shape audiences' ideologies (Androutsopoulos 2012b). Building on his argument, I would like to add that media have the potential to subvert dominant stereotypes. In the following chapter, and in particular in my study of the stylizations of a northern French vernacular in the film *Bienvenue chez les Ch'tis* (2008), I show that laughter is a powerful tool of subversion, as the oppressed may laugh about the self and about stereotypes concerning the self. They may also laugh against the oppressor (Bayle and Fix 2013). Filmmakers' stylistic choices interact with dominant language-ideological discourses, endorsing, opposing or in some way negotiating them.

By framing discourses, genres remove them from everyday talk, and by making them somewhat special, they allow performers to adopt a different stance. In performances of voice, when *one* speaks as if it is not he or she who is speaking, *one* is masked. Because their words should not be taken *seriously* (Austin 1962), performers are able to push the limits of acceptability or appropriateness (such as starting an article with a curse). In her study of griots and Xaxaar insult poetry, Irvine (1993) shows that using stylistic devices permits performers to evade responsibility, because the words that they utter are obviously not theirs and because of the fact that they are being paid to perform (i.e. it is a job/temporary occupation). Audiences may also evade responsibility (when jokingly repeating film lines, for example), because the words are not theirs either. Performed voices therefore have a subversive potential. In a carnivalesque spirit (Bakhtin 1984), performed voices contest what society establishes as the norm. During carnivals, everyday social hierarchies are profaned and overturned by normally suppressed voices. In the media, performed voices have the potentiality to overturn social categories. And if there is no doubt that carnivalesque grotesque and excess (Bakhtin 1984) may be found in comic performances (Sacha Baron Cohen or the French stand-up comedian Coluche are good examples among many others of this grotesque style), one may rightly question whether such performances offer a carnivalesque vision of the world – that is, a vision of a *world upside down*. By taking individuals away briefly from their ordinary lives, carnival allows self-transgression through processes of masking, for example ('a bodily participation in the potentiality of another world' – Bakhtin 1984: 48). This is a central argument of my study of transvestites' voices on the Internet (chapter 3) – where voices are 'jarringly reassigned to "inappropriate" bodies via language crossing and stylization' (Bucholtz 2011: 256). Such practices have been described as 'the quintessential linguistic reflex of late modernity' (Bucholtz 2011: 256), and as Derrida (1984: 79) argues, technology has certainly played a large role in allowing voices to detach themselves from sexualized bodies:

> Nowadays, some technical devices offer us the occasion to witness this demonstration: the telephone, the radio, the record, etc. . . . A voice may detach itself from the body, from the very first instant it may cease to belong to it. By which it traces, it is a trace, a spacing, a writing, but neither a simple presence nor a dispersion of meaning. It is part of the body but because it traverses the body, because it disposes of it, it retains almost nothing of it, it comes from elsewhere and goes elsewhere, and in passing it may give to this body a locus but does not depend upon it, that is, for example, it does not depend on it insofar as 'its own place' is sexually determined. 'Sexually determined' is to be understood here according to dominant criteria. Voice can betray the body to which it is lent, it can make it ventriloquize as if the body were no longer anything more than the

actor or the double of another voice, of the voice of the other, even of an innumerable, incalculable polyphony. A voice may give birth – there you are, voilà – to another body.

Derrida 1984: 79

Whereas there is no doubt that transvestites' performances of another self/another voice may be constructed as being in discordance with their physical origin, my study will also question whether such voices escape pre-established binary representations of masculinity and femininity, as for Bucholtz (2011: 256), 'despite the linguistic remapping of gender, race, and other social categories via crossing and stylization, these practices may reinscribe rather than subvert essentialized mappings of body and voice'.

Chapter 4 raises similar questions with regards to the representation of ethnicities and ethnic voices in films. Looking at it from the other side, it questions how one may be disserviced by one's body and have a *fetishized* preformatted *voice* imposed on oneself. In this chapter, I also show how markedness and prejudice on voices result in stigmatization and discrimination. Unlike prejudices, which remain at the stage of judgments, discrimination manifests itself in unequal treatment of an individual who bears a characteristic seen as a negative property in the society where the discrimination is taking place. As a result, individuals or groups may be excluded from full participation in a society. The media commodification of voices has led to such forms of discrimination.

By studying performed voices as commodified, the first part of the book demonstrates that accented voices in the French media, and particularly the social, sexual and ethnic voices studied in the three following chapters, are commodities on a discursive market of differentiation. When Bourdieu (1991) mainly focused his theory of linguistic market on national markets, where the key issue is the high value of standard languages relative to vernacular dialects, I argue that when vernacular dialects gain value, they are also subjected to the control of legitimate speakers. The second part of the book will later be concerned with transnational and global linguistic markets, in which what is considered locally as non-standard languages may be considered elsewhere as national languages.

2

Performances of Non-standard Voices in French Films[1]

In the 2000s, the French audience saw, within the space of a few years, the release of two movies that made heavy use of accented French: *L'Esquive* ('Games of love and chance', 2004) and *Bienvenue chez les Ch'tis* ('Welcome to the sticks', 2008). Both were to become major successes: a critical success in the case of the first one (four Césars won in 2005), a phenomenally popular hit for the second one (with 20.2 million viewers, it is the most successful film in France since the Second World War). Both films are very verbal and place language in a prominent position: not merely as a dramatic device but at the core of a reflection on the place and legitimacy of French non-standard varieties. The two movies were taken to be accurate linguistic depictions, as in both cases the directors, as well as the actors, are members of the communities they portray. But both films propose an ambivalent linguistic display as dialogues are used at one moment to alienate the audience (the characters are unintelligible) and at another to endear characters to the spectators, or at least to provoke one's sympathy for what is shown as the expression of a community's identity. But apart from those similarities, there is a major difference between the two films: one is a comedy, the other one a realistic drama. The question that this difference of genre entails concerns stylization. Stylized language is produced by means of performances in which 'presenters make it clear to their audience that the images they manufacture ... are "put on", "for now", and "for show"' (Coupland 2001: 347). It entails a display of others' voices in the production of '"as if" utterance[s]' (Coupland and Jaworski 2004: 35). Exercises of stylization are obvious in the case of comedies, which often border on caricature and where the very act of putting on a voice is comical. However, can the term be used to define the performance of non-professional actors who present themselves as equal to the characters they play? Should one rather be talking in this case of a *realistic performance* that aims at having the audience forget that it is a mere copy of the original? It is true to say that, from the audience's point of view, a major difference in the perception of the two films lies in the degree of veracity that is ascribed to the dialogues. For example, *L'Esquive* was often used as a primary source of *banlieue* slang: in the absence of authentic documents, scholars rely on such fiction films to display *realistic* linguistic behaviours and analyse speech characteristics. However, *playing* oneself is certainly different from *being* oneself, and one should consider to what extent non-professional actors reproduce expected performances of themselves as the Others.

This chapter is organized as follows: I first provide a brief theoretical overview of ideologies related to standard language, French non-standard varieties and accents. I then present a contextualization of the linguistic discourses framing the films studied. By comparing the supposedly *true-to-life* display of French urban vernacular in *L'Esquive* with dialectal stylizations (also called *hyperpicard*) in *Bienvenue chez les Ch'tis*, I discuss whether the actors' performances in the former film are cases of stylization. However, this study is neither an exhaustive analysis of the cinematic texts nor a comparison of the dialogues with what the vernaculars are like *in the real world*, but it rather examines the directors' linguistic choices. Thirdly, I discuss the theoretical implications of the concept of realism in films and argue that, notwithstanding the genre, a film can only display linguistic stylization. Finally, I discuss the ways in which the viewers' commentaries on the two films, *L'Esquive* (Kechiche 2004) and *Bienvenue chez les Ch'tis* (Boon 2008), bear evidence of a significant shift from second-order indexicality to first-order indexicality.

2.1 Standard language ideology, accents and orders of indexicality

'Standard Language Ideology' (coined by Milroy and Milroy 1985) is the backdrop for this chapter. It was defined by Lippi-Green (1994: 166–167) as 'a bias toward an abstracted, idealized, homogeneous spoken language which is imposed from above'. In France, the media have played an important part in its legitimization. In films, the choice of spoken varieties and the way they are performed entail complex implications that guide audiences' perceptions of the characters. Regarding the common perception of the French standard, Lodge (1993) argues that the French have a strong tradition of linguistic prescriptivism. He says that '[the average layperson in France] is sensitive to the most subtle distinctions among the particular "accents" and styles he or she encounters ... It is quite usual for French-speaking laypersons to regard slang or regional forms as not being French at all: "Ce n'est pas du français ça, c'est de l'argot"' (1993: 4). I acknowledge that to refer to cinematic displays of non-standard varieties as '*accented* French', as I do in this chapter, is ideologically loaded: it alludes to the fact that the stylized performances are embedded in a sociolinguistic context. Comparing *Bienvenue chez les Ch'tis* and *L'Esquive*, I found that both films bring into focus non-standard varieties whose status as French language has been commonly put into question: the first because it is seen as extremely low culture, the second because of its hybrid form. Regarding popular perception of accents, Lippi-Green (1994: 165) explains that 'for most people, accent is a dustbin category: it includes all the technical meanings, and a more general and subjective one: accent is how the other speaks'. For Yaguello (1988: 32), 'the word *accent* is usually understood as a deviation from a norm, which is an *absence* ([hence the expression] "to speak without an accent")'. And finally, Fagyal, in her monograph on '*accents de banlieue*' ('suburban accents'), argues that 'every perceived accent is a social construction of the Other, and often an identity that is imposed on the Other' (2010: 15, my translation). For film audiences, accented forms are marked. Depending on the speaker, addressee and spectator, accented French indexes a macro-context (a community to which the speaker belongs or of which he originates, this community being geographical or social) or a micro-context (in the case of stylistic variation as speakers may tend to accommodate or even drop their accent in formal situations). Furthermore, in France, stereotypical views have long linked strong accents to lower classes or rural origins (Boughton 2006), which the media have played a large part in sustaining. On the back cover of her aforementioned book, Fagyal (2010) notes that the *banlieue* accent is a real stereotype of contemporary French: 'it is recognised, imitated and makes the headlines'.

Androutsopoulos (2010: 182) calls such social practice 'ideologizing', a term that he defines as follows: 'Ideologizing refers to the process by which ways of using language become socially recognized, classified, evaluated, debated – in short invested with language ideologies' (Androutsopoulos 2010: 182). The gerund emphasizes the activity of ongoing processes in which language ideologies are 'constantly produced, reproduced, circulated in a variety of discursive arenas, including (but not restricted to) mediated public discourses' (Androutsopoulos 2010: 184). These processes are co-constructed by media and audiences and the meanings that are given to the 'ways of using language' are negotiated according to interfaces (media to media in the case of film reviews, or media to audience when the film is received by heterogeneous audiences) or to the circularity of these processes (audience to media to audience in the case of spectators interviewed for a newspaper article, or media to audience to media for spectators' comments posted on blogs).

In order to contextualize the linguistic representations proposed in films, it is necessary to analyse the way directors' language ideologies interact with dominant discourses – in other words, whether they endorse them or oppose them. Moreover, a study of the perception of the end result is needed: Are spectators aware of the directors' intentions to reframe language attitudes? Do preconceived linguistic beliefs influence their interpretation of the film? In the latter case, I argue that most often, a flattening of indexical orders is taking place. With regard to Silverstein's concept of *orders of indexicality*, Woolard (2008: 437) points out the following:

> Language users everywhere tend to associate particular linguistic forms with specific kinds of speaker or contexts of speaking... In Silverstein's system, which builds on Peirce's work, *first-order indexicality* is the pre-ideological but still semiotic work of forming these associations.... If first-order indexicality involves a semiotic act of noticing, *second-order indexicality* brings ideology to bear on the relationship noticed.
>
> Woolard 2008: 437

Taking *L'Esquive* as an example, choices of words and accents are not intended solely to index a social background, but they also index a specific ideological framework. Furthermore, by having the same actors switch between youthspeak and Marivaux's eighteenth-century French, Kechiche's goal is to show that speaking in a voice is a performance. Second-order indexicality is to be found in the filmic discourse that frames the dialogues, and I shall show that in both films the directors are well aware of the current ideologies regarding non-standard varieties and aim at changing common stereotypical views by reframing them. However, is this second-order indexicality perceived as such by film viewers?

Before going any further into the analysis of the films' discursive flows, a presentation of the language ideologies displayed by *L'Esquive* and *Bienvenue chez les Ch'tis* is necessary, as their linguistic standpoints are complex. Assuming the aims of both films were to reframe discourses on non-standard varieties, they appear to exploit, nonetheless, standard language ideology and the underlying assumptions on which it is built, especially those that separate deviations from the norm.

2.2 Contexts of linguistic ideologies framing the films

Abdellatif Kechiche shot *L'Esquive* ('Games of love and chance', 2004) on location in one of the Courneuve council estates, a notorious Parisian suburb situated in

Seine-Saint-Denis, one of the poorest French departments, crippled by social inequalities. *L'Esquive* tells the story of a group of ethnically diverse, economically disadvantaged high school students and friends, and the difficulties they encounter in their project to stage Marivaux's eighteenth-century classical play, *Le jeu de l'amour et du hasard* ('The game of love and chance'). The characters are constantly engaged in verbal encounters, making a highly talkative film that alternates between scenes of interaction among the young people who, like any teenagers, joke, court and argue – 'continually jockeying for position in a youth culture clearly dominated by *their very striking sociolect*' (Strand 2009: 262 [my emphasis]), and scenes where they rehearse for the play. In doing so, the film juxtaposes two varieties which are usually situated at the two extremes of the French varieties continuum: 'Marivaux's hyper-legitimized French [and] a suburban back-slang spoken by the adolescents' (Swamy 2007: 60). The French audience is well acquainted with these two varieties of French as, in the French *linguistic imaginary* (Houdebine-Gravaud 2002), they embody diametrically opposite stances on language. Regarding the first, the common use of the periphrasis 'la langue de Molière' or 'la langue de Racine' to refer to the French language shows that it is described with pride as the creation (or possession) of the most celebrated French writers. As for *verlan, français des cités* or *parler banlieue*, as the youth speak is usually named, it has been highly mediatized, with three different sorts of coverage: at times it is depicted as inventive, buzzing and excitingly counter-cultural; at other times, it is denounced as a symbol of linguistic and social impoverishment, not to say the cause of a 'linguistic ghettoisation' (see Bentolila's controversy);[2] and finally, more recently, it has been described as a multiethnic (mainly influenced by the *beur* population's Arabic language) youth speak (Boyer 2001).

By using a 'fiery mélange of back-slang and high classical French' (Swamy 2007: 60) and having the two coexist with equal dramatic importance, Kechiche aims at giving some legitimacy to the youth language that he sees as beautiful and enriched by its diverse origins (in Fajardo 2004); creative, intelligent and harmonious (in Melinard 2004); in short, as cultured as Marivaux's language. Moreover, by having the characters switch with ease from one to the other, Kechiche undermines the determinist position that directly links ways of speaking to one's identity or social condition (the latter associated with the view that the teenagers are victims of a linguistic *confinement*), and implies, in Goffman's style, that speaking a language – any language – is a performance. Moreover, one should not neglect to note that Marivaux's text also proposes an exercise of stylization as the characters of the play swap positions and do an impression of their companion.[3] For the actors who play the parts, it means performing a performance. And there is much irony in the fact that Krimo, the young hero from the Parisian suburb, is asked to play the role of a valet who pretends to be an aristocrat.

The two *extremes* of the dialectal continuum are not the only forms of French spoken in the film. The varieties and the characters who speak them can be categorized as follows:

- *Parler banlieue*: the teenagers.
- Marivaux's written-literary text (spoken during rehearsals and in the final performance of the play): the high school students and their teacher.
- Standard French: the parents, the teacher of French, the police.

The only characters that code-switch between the three are the Courneuve teenagers. Interestingly enough, in the film, suburban slang and Marivaux's eighteenth-century French coexist peacefully. It is with Standard French that the youth vernacular comes into conflict. On this point, I would like to highlight the fact that, in the film, most speakers of the dominant variety are different embodiments of authority: parental, academic and coercive. Of course, the choice of Marivaux's play has political implications. *Le jeu de l'amour et du hasard* is a story of social determinism, as emphasized, in Kechiche's film, by the teacher's interpretation of the play:

> We are completely prisoners of our social condition. When one is rich for 20 years or poor for 20 years, one can always dress up in rags if one is rich, in designer clothes if one is poor, but we cannot get rid of a certain language, a certain type of conversation, a particular form of expression, the way we behave, all of which indicate where we come from. And moreover, it [the play] is called *Games of Love and Chance*, but it shows us that there is no chance involved.
>
> trans. by Swamy 2007: 62

The teacher's comment refers to a linguistic stigma. It implies that one may try to speak like someone one is not (usually above one's condition); one will never fool one's interlocutor into believing one is from a different social background. In other words, according to this view, one cannot change language or perform another variety. If this is very much in line with Bourdieu and Passeron's (1990) view of schools as the institutionalized rationalization of social inequalities, it seems to be in complete contradiction with the republican Education Nationale's mission, as expressed in another scene of the film when, irritated by Krimo's silence and incapacity to play the scene, the teacher loses her temper and bursts out: *Sors de toi! Amuse-toi! Libère-toi!* ('Come out of yourself! Enjoy yourself! Free yourself!'). In this scene, what is implied is that in order to free oneself of a social stigma and to fit into French society, these teenagers will have to adopt the dominant variety: standard French. In what appears to be a scene of symbolic violence, Krimo is being told to take pleasure in being someone else, in a schizophrenic use of the Other's language. To go back to Bourdieu's words:

> What circulates on the linguistic market is not 'language' as such, but rather discourses that are stylistically marked, both in their production, insofar as each speaker fashions an idiolect from the common language, and in their reception, insofar as each recipient helps to *produce* the message which he perceives and appreciates by bringing to it everything that makes up his singular and collective experience.
>
> Bourdieu 1992: 39

With respect to cinema, the recipient's participation is surely the case of any film spectator who brings into the theatre personal views of the world as well as his/her own interpretative strategies. However, I would like to argue that linguistic production and perception take place within a restricted set of possibilities. For example, interpretative schemata have been formed by one's social experience of movie-going, an experience that takes place within a specific society that shares a limited set of values and linguistic ideologies. Moreover, this experience is inscribed in a discursive framework.

If Kechiche's film had to be categorized in a genre, it would be 'film de banlieue'. According to Carrie Tarr (2005: 2), '*Banlieue* filmmaking refers to the work of directors aiming to represent life in the deprived housing estates on the outskirts of big French cities. *Cinéma de banlieue* emerged within French film criticism in the mid-1990s as a way of categorising a series of independently released films set in the rundown multi-ethnic working-class estates' (Tarr 2005: 2). Another of Carrie Tarr's arguments is that a common denominator of these *banlieue* films is their desire to 'reframe difference' by reframing the symbolic spaces of French culture, addressing issues of ethnicity and difference in order to question what it means to be French and to speak French. In this vein, Kechiche said, in reference to the suburban vernacular, that he 'wanted to demystify the verbal aggressiveness and to make it appear in its true dimension of communication code; a pretence aggressiveness that hides a sort of shyness, even fragility, rather than a strictly-speaking violence'.[4] Moreover, the fact that Abdellatif Kechiche is a *beur* filmmaker, i.e. a second-generation North-African immigrant (his parents moved from Tunisia to France when he was six: he then grew up in Les Moulins, a council-estate of the French southern city of Nice), places his cinema in what has been labelled 'accented cinema', defined by the *Migrant and Diasporic Cinema in Contemporary Europe*'s website as a cinema that 'comprises different types of cinema made by exilic, diasporic, and postcolonial ethnic and identity filmmakers who live and work in countries other than their country of origin.... Accented films are often bi- or multilingual.' In accented cinema, multilingualism encompasses the use of different languages as well as varieties of the same language, alongside code-switching practices. The choice of the word 'accented' is interesting because it does not refer to a phonetic property of the languages displayed in the films, but Naficy (2001) uses the linguistic concept of accent 'as a trope to highlight that the kind of cinema he identifies is "different" from the standard, neutral and value-free dominant cinema produced by the society's reigning mode of production'.[5]

L'Esquive is a small budget film. Six weeks of shooting and digital camera filming were economic choices (Melinard 2004). However, they became stylistic choices. As Tarr argues, referring to French-born directors of North-African origin: '[t]hey draw on *realist modes of filmmaking* to demonstrate the basic humanity of the *beurs*, placing them at the center of the diegesis, privileging points of view which make them subjects rather than the objects of the gaze, and constructing them as complex individuals whose feelings and emotions are likely to elicit sympathy' (Tarr 2005: 210–211, my emphasis).

Bienvenue chez les Ch'tis ('Welcome to the sticks', 2008), the second film studied in this chapter, does not obviously draw on realistic modes of narration. Its humour relies on the culture shock experienced by a high-ranking post office administrator from the South of France who is transferred to the North of the country; a region he sees as a cold, foreign land inhabited by Barbarians who speak an 'obscure language' called *ch'timi*. However, thanks to his employees, especially the postman played by the film director Dany Boon, he soon discovers that behind the accent that he initially found grotesque lies a very endearing vernacular and a warm-hearted community. Dany Boon was born in the North of France: his father was of Berber origin, and his mother is a *ch'ti*. On his official website, Dany Boon explains that he made the film for her and to turn the tables on people who hold prejudiced views against the North of France. In his own words, *Bienvenue chez les Ch'tis* is an 'ethnological comedy'. In the film, every member of the northern community speaks the stylized variety, with no difference between sexes, ages, social classes, and most importantly no stylistic variation (whereas, interestingly, the southern character speaks 'non-accented' French). The accent is an essential comic motive as this first encounter (1) between the two main characters shows (after the manager's car nearly runs over his future employee, Mr Bailleul):

(1) Excerpt 1 [0:21]: *Bienvenue chez les Ch'tis* (Boon, 2008)

1. *Oh* Vindieu, *ça va, vous n'êtes pas mort?*
   – The manager: 'Oh *God*, you're not dead?'
2. *Bienvenue monsieur le directeur*
   – Mr Bailleul: 'Welcome sir'
3. *Monsieur Bailleul?*
   – The manager: 'Mister Bailleul?'
4. *Ouais* **sh**'*est* **mi**. *Ouille,* Vindiou!
   – Mr Bailleul: 'Yes, it's *me*. Ouch, *God*!'
5. *Bougez pas, bougez pas, vaut mieux appeler les secours.*
   – The manager: 'Don't move, don't move, we should call for help'
6. *Non non* **sh**a va
   – Mr Bailleul: 'No, no, I'm fine'
7. *Oh la la, j'aurais pu vous tuer!*
   – The manager: 'Oh dear, I could have killed you!'
8. *Non mais c'est pas grave,* **sh**a va, *j'vous ai reconnu à vot' plaque qu'est 13, ici c'est 59. J'vous ai fait signe d'arrêter vot' carrette, mais vous . . . Mais* **sh**a va, *j'ai* **rin**, *j'ai* **rin** . . .
   – Mr Bailleul: 'No, it's nothing, I'm fine, I recognized your number plate that shows 13, here it's 59. I made a sign for you to stop, but you . . . But that's ok, I don't have anything'
9. *Vot' mâchoire, vous êtes blessé là?*
   – The manager: 'Your jaw, you're hurt?'
10. **Hein?**
    – Mr Bailleul: 'He?'
11. *Vous avez mal quand vous parlez là, non?*
    – The manager: 'It hurts when you speak, no?'
12. **Quô?**
    – Mr Bailleul: 'Wha'?'
13. *Vot' mâchoire, ça va là?*
    – The manager: 'Is your jaw ok?'
14. *Non, non, non, j'ai mal à ma* **tchu**, *j'suis tombé sur ma* **t'chu**, *quoi*
    – Mr Bailleul: 'No, no, I fell on my arse . . . I fell on my arse'
15. *Le* **t'chu**? *Oh la la, c'est pas terrible quand vous parlez. Vous voulez pas qu'on aille montrer vot' mâchoire à un médecin?*
    – The manager: 'Your arse? Oh dear, it does not sound too good when you speak. You don't want to see a doctor?'

16. *Non, j'ai **rin** Vindiou!*
    – Mr Bailleul: 'No, I don't have anything for Pete's sake!'
17. *Oh j'vous assure, vous vous exprimez d'une façon très particulière!*
    – The manager: 'Believe me, you express yourself in a very peculiar way'
18. *C'est parce que j'parle ch'ti **sh'est sha**?*
    – Mr Bailleul: 'It's because I speak ch'ti, isn't it?'
19. *Pardon?*
    – The manager: 'Excuse-me?'
20. *Be', j'parle ch'timi **quô**!*
    – Mr Bailleul: 'I speak ch'timi!'
21. *Oh putain, c'est ça le fameux cheutimi!?*
    – The manager: 'Jesus, is this the famous cheutimi?!'[6]

The communication difficulties encountered by the two characters illustrate nicely Lodge's (1993: 3) description of French prescriptivism as 'the belief that the ideal state of the language is one of uniformity and that linguistic heterogeneity is detrimental to effective communication is firmly entrenched'. In excerpt (1), I emphasize a few lexical variants used to stylize South and North varieties (note the humoristic variation between *Vindieu* and *Vindiou*, lines 1 and 4, that seems to indicate that the two characters have more in common than they believe). The salient phonological features used by Dany Boon to stylize the Picard variety are in bold letters. Pooley's (1996) work on Picard stereotypical features points out the use of /ʃ/ for standard /s/ (such as 'sha' for *ça* and 'sh'est' for *c'est* in the excerpt – lines 4, 6, 8 and 18). He notes as well that some Picard morphological forms, such as the pronoun *mi,* are obsolescent. Yet it is used in the dialogue (line 4) by the youngish character played by Dany Boon, surely because the form, being part of the word *ch'timi* that means 'it's me', is emblematic. With the transcription of excerpt (1), I do not aim to propose a detailed analysis of the *Ch'timi* lexical or phonetic features present in the film, but rather to show that the accent itself is an object of ridicule. The native speaker is shown as an unintelligible creature (who in this scene looks very much like the famous hunchback of Notre-Dame) and the cause for his peculiar accent is mistakenly thought to be a displaced jaw. As Lodge pointed out regarding folk perceptions of French, the spectator is meant to believe that 'non-standard varieties are merely failed attempts to express oneself properly' (Lodge 1993: 6). However, one important difference between *L'Esquive* and *Bienvenue chez les Ch'tis* is that the Northern variety is not as familiar to every French person as the suburban sociolect is. As for Coupland (2004: 253) stylization 'requires an enculturated audience able to read the semiotic value of a projected persona', the film ought to provide a short introduction to *ch'timi* pronunciation. It is given to the main character, as early as ten minutes after the beginning of the film, with the very short formula: 'They [the Northerners] say /o/ instead of /a/, /k/ instead of /ch/ and /ch/ instead of /s/'. The fact that, in the film, the *snapshot* is comical is due to its reliance on French standard ideology. Furthermore, the performed accent makes use of features that, in the French linguistic imaginary, are interpreted as 'patois' or rural. In this vein, it is interesting to note that, in both films, the characters who use accented varieties of French are from a lower-class background.[7]

I shall now focus on the first scene of *L'Esquive* in order to demonstrate that the film uses similar linguistic strategies. The opening sequence of the film shows a group of male friends speaking vehemently about the attack that targeted a few of their peers:

(2) Excerpt 2 [0:01]: *L'Esquive* (Kechiche 2004)

1. *J'vais y aller, j'vais y **niquer** leur mère!*
 – Voice 1 (off-screen): 'I'm gonna go, I'm gonna fuck their mother!'
2. *De toute façon, leur quartier, c'est pas l'Bronx ou quoi, j'vais y aller et j'vais tous leur **niquer** leur mère!*
 – Voice 2 (off-screen): 'Anyway, their estate is not the Bronx, I'm gonna go and I will fuck their mother to them lot!'
3. *Allez, on y va maintenant.*
 – Voice 3 (off-screen): 'Come on, let's go now'
4. *Y en a un ... j'vais l'serrer, j'vais l'séquestrer sa mère, ce fils de pute.*
 – Voice 1 (off-screen): 'There's one ... I'm gonna get him, I'm gonna do him, this motherfucker'
5. *Le premier qu'on voit là, la vie d'ma mère qu'on lui baise sa mère. Y a qu'ça à faire, y a pas ...*
 – Makou: 'The first we see there, on my mother's life, we'll fuck his mother. There's nothing else to do, there's no ...'
6. *D'vant tout l'monde, les gens y faisaient rien, tu crois c'est normal ou quoi? Ils passent à côté de toi, y m'regardaient.*
 – Slam: 'In front of everyone, nobody did anything, you think it's normal or what? They were walking by, looking at me ...'
7. *C'est tous une bande de fils de pute!*
 – Fathi: 'They're all motherfuckers!'

L'Esquive, L'avant-scène Cinéma 542, 2005

I am aware that the transcription and translation of excerpt (2) may give a wrong impression of the scene and that the repetitive use of f* words in a written form may appear grotesque. In the original scene, the characters are often unintelligible and the swearwords are not so salient. The non-standard lexical features (among which only a few are characteristic of the youth vernacular – see my emphasis in the excerpt) are combined with phonological traits (for more detail see Armstrong and Jamin 2002; Fagyal 2003, 2010; Trimaille and Billiez 2007) to give a general impression. As in *Bienvenue chez les Ch'tis*, spectators are alienated and the non-standard variety is first experienced as a foreign language. The performances of both films are meant to be excessive. In *L'Esquive*, it is an exercise of *tchatche* – i.e. a virtuoso display of suburban slang – in which the teenagers seem to compete for the most abusive language. This first scene puts the spectator in the middle of a group of young men who seem to be discussing a plan to get retaliation over the theft of a bag by a rival gang. It is a tongue-in-cheek depiction of the suburbs, as Kechiche seems to say to the audience: 'Isn't this what you expected from the suburbs, i.e. violent language and a violent theme?'

All the actors, apart from Sara Forestier, are amateurs from the Parisian suburbs. Kechiche worked with them for over six months before shooting the film (Swamy 2007: 64) in order to have them *appropriate* the text (in Gignoux 2004). The spectators are meant to believe that, using Goffman's terminology (Goffman 1981), the actors are not mere *animators* of the lines they utter, but they are *authors*, too.[8] Paradoxically, Kechiche explained that they had to rehearse a lot to find *sincerity*: 'I like to give the illusion that everything is true. I want my film to give the impression that what I show is there for real, alive' (in Piazzo 2004). However, it seems that Kechiche had to go against young actors' tendency to overdo it. In an interview given for *Libération*, Kechiche (in Aubenas 2004) recalled his amazement, during the exercise of free improvisation that they used to cast actors, at seeing the teenagers' inability to do other than reproduce the clichés they hear about the estates. One of the actresses justified this tendency with the fact that the audience expects them to present something impressive. Moreover, regarding the way the script was conceived, Kechiche insisted on the fact that the 'dialogues were written. Stylisation consisted in striking a balance ... not going too far in the use of *banlieue* slang, limiting *verlan* so that the film would not be incomprehensible' (in Lalanne 2004).

At this point in the chapter, it appears clearly that *L'Esquive* stages linguistic stylizations, even though the film generally adopts a realistic mode of filmmaking. I would now like to discuss to what extent a film may claim to present authentic (linguistic) behaviours per se.

2.3 Cinematic realism and linguistic stylization

The depiction of the real in films has always been a hot topic of cinema studies. Many renowned theorists expressed their views on the matter as early as the turn of the twentieth century. Later, the famous French film theorist André Bazin remarked, in his seminal article 'An aesthetic of reality', that 'realism in art can only be achieved in one way – through artifice' (1967: 26). In the same vein, the philosopher Gilles Deleuze (1989: 146) argued that the artist is a 'creator of truth, because truth is not to be achieved, formed, or reproduced; it has to be created'. With this artificial or created sense of reality, what is implied is that the real is not to be accessed freely. As soon as there is human intervention (i.e. someone holding the camera), there is a bias. And, for technical reasons, this subjectivity will get in the way of any pretence to display the world as it is. For Bazin (1967: 26), filmmakers have to make a selection in the real world of 'what is worth preserving and what should be discarded'. What is deemed good enough to be preserved in the film is charged with high semiotic value, and what is judged as being redundant, meaningless or incoherent with the ensemble, is discarded (these two processes being very similar to *iconization* and *erasure* as described by Gal and Irvine 1995).

What does this *manufactured* real entail? It tells us that the real is subverted by ways of representation that 'operate more or less corrosively and thus do not permit the original to subsist in its entirety' (Bazin 1967: 27). For Edgar Morin (1980), '[i]t is under the cover of "cinema of the real" that we have been shown, proposed, and imposed, the most incredible illusions.' In return, illusions 'induce a loss of awareness of the reality itself, which becomes identified in the mind of the spectator with its cinematographic representation' (Bazin 1967: 27). Similarly, Roux (2008: 60) argues that, in *Bienvenue chez les Ch'tis*, 'the real only exists by the idea that is formed about it, so as to erase any tension or asperity to the benefit of a deauthentifying fantasy'. However, as mentioned before, Dany Boon does not think of his film as a fantasy but rather, in his own words, as an 'ethnological comedy'. As for *L'Esquive*'s director, his film, as realistic as it may be, remains a fiction nonetheless. In an interview with *Cineaste*, he told a journalist who was questioning him about the *L'Esquive*'s documentary-like style: 'It kind of bothers me that you use the word documentary. The film has a script, the actors and actresses did not know each other beforehand, and they came from different schools' (in Porton 2005: 47). The cinematic depiction of the French suburbs interacts with a general ideological framework about French *banlieues* (by subscribing to it or opposing it). Furthermore, the varieties displayed in the film and the ambient linguistic ideologies coexist in a dialogical rapport. I have said elsewhere (Planchenault 2008a) that, to the extent that a character's lines respond implicitly to dominant discourses and reflect shared assumptions regarding non-standard varieties, filmic dialogues can be analysed as a source of folk linguistics (Preston 2004). And, to go back to the notion of stylization, Coupland (2001: 350) argues that 'it brings into play stereotyped semiotic and ideological values associated with other groups', hence highlighting them for the analyst.

Generally speaking, one assumes that actors benefit from a verbal agility that allows them to switch easily from one voice to another. Coupland (2001, 2004) says that stylization implies that actors obviously speak in *altera persona*, that is, they put on a voice. Dany Boon is a famous stand-up comedian, well-known for his farcical impersonations, and his Ch'timi persona. In *Bienvenue chez les Ch'tis*, the performance that he accomplishes is a definite exercise of pastiche, a genre that the linguist Fernand Carton calls *hyperpicard* (in Haydée 2008). In the behind-the-scene documentary that accompanies the DVD, Dany Boon is shown on set, expressing himself in Standard French, but switching to his accented *voice* as soon as he is hailed by fans. In the same manner, all the other actors of the film, when interviewed for the making-of, express themselves in *non-accented* French. In the case of non-professionals, one decisive criterion directing the choice to cast an individual has to do with the linguistic flexibility necessary to perform the required role. For *L'Esquive*, according to Strand (2009), a proof of stylization is to be found in the fact that the actor playing the sullen and introvert Krimo (Osman Elkharraz) is in fact a 'self-assured boy from the projects who memorized stylized script written to imitate a contemporary sociolect' (2009: 265). The dichotomy between stylized performances and reality is not straightforward, as for Coupland (2001: 345): 'Although stylization is a form of strategic deauthentication, its ultimate relationship with authenticity is complex.' Even though Dany Boon appears to give a caricature of the Northern dialect, he says that his first goal is to introduce the French audience to the language and culture of his origins. Not only the animator and the author of the dialogues that he voices (he is the scriptwriter and the main performer of *Bienvenue chez les Ch'tis*), Dany Boon is also a principal, which for Goffman (1981: 145) means that 'the individual speaks, explicitly or implicitly in the name of "we"' – i.e. in the representation of a group. In this vein and according to one of the actresses in the film, Dany Boon is seen by his linguistic community as an 'ambassador' of the Ch'timi culture. In the case of *L'Esquive*, even though, as mentioned earlier, actors are not fully the authors of their lines, they, too, can be considered as 'principals' (Goffman 1981) because they 'believe personally in what is being said and take the position that is implied in the remarks' (1981: 167), or because they believe in *the way* it is being said.

In the same way that Kechiche battled against prejudices toward youthspeak,[9] Dany Boon, when preparing *Bienvenue chez les Ch'tis*, was well aware of the pejorative image associated with strong regional accents. In the making-of, he explained how crucial the choice of the right actress was, as, in his own words, she has to be able to *be sexy* while speaking with a *ch'timi* accent. He then added that it is her accent that makes her moving when she declares her love to the main character. Following the phenomenal success of the film, Dany Boon played a part in restoring the image of the northern vernacular. The success of the film was a godsend for the economy of Nord Pas-de-Calais as it increased the popularity of the region. Quotes from the film were reproduced on T-shirts and souvenirs to be sold to the tourists. Appropriation of film quotes by all sorts of spectators is a common phenomenon (see Kozloff 2000: 27). However, it is quite perplexing to see the film's stylizations reappropriated by the linguistic community itself. One example of this is to be seen in the use of '*biloute!*', which, from the release of *Bienvenue chez les Ch'tis*, became a rallying call among film fans (the word itself was commented on by a more purist speaker of *picard*, interviewed in *L'Express* magazine and deemed to be not appropriate to the situation).[10]

In the last section, I have demonstrated that studies of stylization cannot be limited to excessive cases of pastiche. Taking spectators' beliefs into account and, in the case of cod-French accents (such as Poirot's or Inspector Clouseau's accents), I found, in past research, that it is often possible for the audience to comment on the quality of an impersonation or on the appropriateness of a voice (Planchenault 2008a). However, in the case of the two films studied in this chapter, because of the fact that the directors and actors are members of the communities that they stylize, this sort of evaluation is rarely given, and stylizations are not always recognized as such: their performances are then judged not for their quality but rather on the basis of their faithfulness to reality, i.e. their authenticity. In the last section of this chapter, I shall argue that, in this case, second-order indexicality is often misinterpreted as first-order indexicality.

2.4 Reception of the films and ideological shift

Any research that studies audience perceptions faces the problem of the heterogeneity of its object of analysis as well as the difficulty in accessing diverse types of data. For example, Richardson (2010: 86) mentions that there is an unavoidable bias towards what she calls an 'articulate audience', which she defines as 'viewers with the desire and ability to verbalize their reactions and opinions'. I shall first comment on a couple of scientific articles, before including the articles that were written during the film release and spectators' comments. Considering the current trend depicting French varieties of youthspeak as multi-ethnic slang, one would think little at reading the descriptions of *L'Esquive*'s staged vernacular made by Strand (2009: 263): 'an aggressive discourse that mixes *verlan*, a French version of back-slang, with borrowings from languages other than French (Arabic, Wolof, English), a generous sprinkling of profanity, and staged brinkmanship'; or Swamy (2007: 58–59): an 'Arabic-inflected street slang of the Parisian *banlieue*'. By first quoting two academic sources, my aim is to show how widespread the iconization of specific linguistic features is. In most French reviews written on the film for its release,[11] three linguistic features were brought to the forefront: verbal aggressiveness; Arabic influence; and lexical features (*verlan* – 'back slang').[12] Excerpt (3) presents a few instances from the French reviews referring to the violence of *L'Esquive*'s language:

(3) a. 'Everyone speaks wildly ... resonant outburst, frenzy of words ...'
Les Cahiers du Cinéma, in Tessé 2004

b. 'Words erupt at the speed of a submachine gun'
Le Monde, in Piazzo 2004

c. '... in a salvo of indignation in *verlan* that stays incomprehensible for most people'
Les Echos 2004

d. 'This language strikes the audience straightaway in the stomach'
La Croix, in Gignoux 2004

With regard to the second linguistic feature used by the media to iconize the suburban youthspeak, newspapers mention the vernacular borrowings from Arabic (*La Croix*, *Les Inrockuptibles*). For example, Kaganski (2004), in an article entitled *Nique Rohmer!* ('Fuck Rohmer!' – playing with the sonorities of the stereotyped formula *Nique ta mère*), starts his review with a pastiche: *Pour le dire dans la langue du film: «Putain, L'Esquive, sur la tête de ma mère, je kiffe sa race, **Inch'Allah**»* ("To say it with the language of the film: "Fuck, *L'Esquive*, on my mother's head, I bloody love it, **God willing**"' – my emphasis). In the film, there are actually a handful of Arabic words: *mabrouk* ('congratulations'), *hchouma* ('shame'), *ouallah* ('I swear'), *tayib* ('ok'), *Inch'Allah* ('God willing'), *zarma* ('that is'), *wesh* ('what's up?'), *kahba* ('whore').

As for *verlan*, despite Kechiche's conscious choice to avoid overusing stereotyped lexical features, a few newspapers still mention it. However, it is interesting to note that, in the 117-minute film, hardly twenty words are verlanized[13] and that occurrences of more than one *verlan* word per sentence are rare. Moreover, *verlan* words that are familiar to a general audience (e.g. *ouf, meuf, keum*) are favoured throughout the film. Finally, it is the secondary characters (especially males) that use them most.

Throughout *L'Esquive*, standard French lexicon is dominant. Nevertheless, reviews focused primarily on non-standard features. In these instances, Arabic words and *verlan* forms are perceived as *hypersalient* features or 'spectacular fragments of language' (Rampton 1999). For reviewers, the staged suburban vernaculars index an ethnic origin, this perception relying on the French *imaginaire linguistique* (Houdebine-Gravaud 2003). However, one can argue that they relay Kechiche's desire that the audience should perceive the vernacular's hybrid origins. Moreover, the newspapers' focus on non-standard features is not surprising since they are often seen as the heralds of the French norm (and regularly come under attack for not using *correct* French). This position is made clear by excerpt (4), where the journalist ironically adopts Marivaux's literary French to translate an exoticized sample of youth vernacular:

> (4) «*Je la kiffe à mort, c'te bouffonne*» *s'enflamme Krimo soudain épris de la coquette*
> '"I bloody fancy her, the bitch" cries out Krimo, suddenly enamoured with the coquette'
>
> Gignoux 2004

This example shows that exercises of stylization are not restricted to films, but that they may be demonstrated in film reviews as well. If it is necessary for the audience to be *enculturated* to understand exercises of stylization (Coupland 2004: 253), it is noticeable that this ability to actively stylize a persona may be shared with the audience.

However, in the same article, the journalist comments on the spontaneity and realism of the dialogues. The ideological stance is erased in favour of a pre-ideological or semiotic level: what the accent supposedly tells about the social or ethnic origin of the characters. This, alongside the aforementioned comments, seems to indicate that, in the way the cinematic image flattens a three-dimensional plan into two dimensions, the viewing of the film operates a flattening of indexical orders, from second to first.

Two weeks after the national release of *L'Esquive*, the Catholic newspaper *La Croix* interviewed a group of young spectators (was it a coincidence that most of them were of African and North African origin?), as they were leaving the Seine-Saint-Denis theatre after seeing the film, to ask their impressions of the language. Excerpt (5) presents some of their comments:

(5)

a. Kama
Franchement, ils disaient trop de gros mots. Les filles emploient des termes hypervulgaires, c'est exagéré, même si c'est vrai que ça existe dans certaines cités.
'Sincerely, they swore too much. The girls used really vulgar words, that's exaggerated, even if it's true that's like that in some estates'

b. Rachid
Elle parle comme une racaille, cette meuf.
'She speaks like a scum, this chick'

c. Nawel
C'est très cliché et amplifié.
'It's very cliché and amplified'

in Bouillon 2004

It is worth noticing that, by the very fact that they mention processes of 'amplification' and 'stereotypification', Kama and Nawel concur with Kechiche's argument on seeing the film as fiction. Were these spectators able to read the exercise of stylization because of the fact that they were more *enculturated*? Kama and Rachid's comments insist on the inappropriateness of the female characters' speech. In his review of literature on youth vernaculars, Pooley (2008) notes that informants attributed the use of *banlieue* vernacular to boys and evaluated its use by girls negatively: 'Such girls challenge the perceived masculine hegemony in terms of control of sub-cultural capital' (2009: 336). I argue that it is this idea that Kechiche favours: a counter-attitude that he chooses at the price of realism.[14] Interestingly, it seems that, considering the young spectators' insistence on the vulgarity and violence of the dialogues, Kechiche did not manage to reach his goal, i.e. to oppose the usual negative cliché and propose an alternative depiction of youthspeak. However, one should note that the young people who were asked to judge the authenticity of the staged vernacular are considered as experts, notwithstanding the fact that their discourse may conform to mainstream prescriptive views (for example, Fagyal 2004 remarks on her young informants' belief that they spoke bad French). Ironically, Kama's comment ('in some estates') seems to imply that the inappropriate words are used by inhabitants from neighbourhoods other than hers, and reinforces a common tendency to associate the disapproved language with the Other.

Finally, if *L'Esquive*'s linguistic performances did not seem to be validated by the speech community that it depicted, it appears that the contrary happened at the release of *Bienvenue chez les Ch'tis* as Dany Boon was greeted with wild applause by thousands of fans who congregated to welcome their fellow countryman during the film tour in Lille.

2.5 Conclusion

In this chapter, I have argued that two very different cases of filmic stylization entertain complex relations with *reality*, both in their claim to authenticity/realism and with regard to whether the performances are validated or not by the linguistic community they represent. It appears that the linguistic community depicted may choose to recognize itself in the caricature offered by the films (as was the case with *Bienvenue chez les Ch'tis*), to the extent of taking pride in it, and of re-appropriating linguistic *spectacular fragments*. One may argue that the genre of the films played a role in the extent to which members of the community were willing to validate the dialectal/sociolectal stylizations. Is it the lack of a formal stance on language, in the case of the comedy, that was felt as less threatening?

The position of authority that is given or not to the authors of the films reflects notions related to an emic or insider's point of view – the latter associated with the popular belief that the community member *knows best*. This reminds me of Terry Eagleton's (1991: 9) statement that 'ideology is less a matter of the inherent linguistic properties of a pronouncement than a question of who is saying what to whom for what purposes'. I would add that ideology depends on the context in which the discourse appears, on which the right interpretation of the author's intentions depends. Moreover, as an anonymous reviewer stressed to me, it is noticeable that stigmatized varieties have gained a high value in the linguistic market of cinematic discourses. There has been, since the early days of the cinema industry, a commodification of stylized accents. However, one could argue that what was highly marketable as a skill (i.e. an actor's competence in impersonating others) has gained, since then and more specifically since voices have been reclaimed by the stigmatized communities, a symbolic value.

To conclude, I would like to highlight a point that I find disturbing: the fact that, despite 'good' intentions, both directors' *response* to standard language ideology brought them willingly to portray non-standard varieties as unintelligible. I have argued elsewhere (Planchenault 2010) that there is an ideological link between 'unintelligible' and 'non-intelligent' and what could be regarded as 'unarticulated' is often interpreted as indexing 'non-articulated' individuals.

3

Performances of Feminine Voices on the Internet[1]

It seems obvious to say that when one wants to join a group for the first time, one should keep a low profile and test the water before drawing too much attention to oneself. Displaying a positive face – that is, demonstrating that one's face wants to be desirable to fellow interlocutors (Brown and Levinson 1987) – plays a part in the creation of a sense of community. In this chapter, I propose to establish a link between joining a virtual community and using positive politeness strategies – that is, showing that one has the same wants as the virtual audience of the message (Brown and Levinson 1987: 328). A new member will necessarily have to comply with the appropriate behaviour (a set of specific rules and codes adopted by the community of practice that he is joining) if he wants to be included and not rejected. And acceptance is particularly important for a marginal population such as transvestites. The data for this study is drawn from 'texts of introduction' written by members of a virtual community of transvestites for a French-speaking website. It was first created by French-Canadian members but then developed with members from France, Belgium, Switzerland and other French-speaking countries. Today it counts more than 1.3 million visitors. For this chapter, I shall study a section of the website called *Le coin des copines* – literally 'girlfriends' corner'. On these pages, members post presentations of self with an optional picture in order to introduce themselves to other members. Their goal is often to initiate correspondence or future meetings. More than 250 members posted their text of introduction on these pages. The data will be analysed using a pragmatic as well as a discourse analytic methodology.

Analysing this sort of stylistic exercise (i.e. the presentation of self to a community), which is written and involves minimal interaction, allows researchers to study the writer's expectations of a group's face wants or of fellow members' rights and duties. This is the first point of contact for members of the website and a crucial moment in time, especially when one takes into account the fact that for such websites danger often comes from outsiders, who might not comply with the rules, and webmasters are wary of this. Moreover, with these texts, I shall be able to work on linguistic ideology and representations, especially regarding gender. Expectations about *feminine* talk and politeness, such as cooperation and avoidance of rude language (Holmes 1995), stand in the forefront here. In this chapter, I wish to propose that transvestites use gender-coded politeness in order to construct a feminine identity. In the computer-mediated texts analysed here, I argue that this feminine identity is essentially constructed through linguistic means.

In order to support this argument, I shall first define relations between performance, appropriateness and gender in computer-mediated communication (Section 3.1). In Section 3.2, I shall show how through this writing exercise and expressions of solidarity, transvestites participate in building a *sense of community*, defined by McMillan and Chavis (1986: 9) as 'a feeling that members have of belonging, a feeling that members matter to one another and to the group, and a shared faith that members' needs will be met through their commitment to be together'. In Section 3.3, in the data analysis, I shall focus on pragmatic markers, specifically forms of address (feminine forms such as *amie, copine, consoeur* – 'friend', 'girlfriend', 'fellow sister', use of inclusive pronoun *nous* – 'we'), as well as on linguistic means used by transvestites to express sameness, membership and mutual assistance. Finally, I shall analyse the choice of vocabulary used to respect a *netiquette* (overuse of formulaic politeness) and to avoid rude messages.

3.1 Performance, appropriateness and gender in computer-mediated communication

Two seminal concepts from the work of the American sociologist Erving Goffman (1959) are those of *face* and *performance*. My chapter will bring together a couple of research fields where these two notions have been prominent in recent decades: Politeness Studies and Gender Studies. In *Presentation of Self in Every Day Life* (1959), Goffman shows that the presentation of self is a performance in which every individual adjusts his or her behaviour according to a social setting and in order to guide the impressions that others have of him/her. The ways a person presents himself/herself (i.e. one's appearance, mannerisms or body language) as well as the setting of the interaction give the audience a lot of information about the speaker and serve to construct an image of him/her. Goffman (1967: 5) defines *face* as 'the positive social value a person effectively claims for himself [sic.]'.

In Gender Studies, Butler's (1990) seminal work introduced the notion that gender should be seen as performative, meaning that, rather than being the expression of a prior reality, it is constructed in interaction and is formed according to the context and through the enactments of appropriate behaviour, which are assumed by the interactants to be relevant to a particular context or Community of Practice. These assumptions are linked to cultural representations of gender roles and can be read clearly in transvestites' interactions. For Butler (1990: 187), '[i]*n imitating gender, drag implicitly reveals the imitative structure of gender itself – as well as its contingency*' (emphasis in original). Feminine behaviour is something that speakers achieve through the use of different cues, such as stylistic devices or behaviours which are coded as polite.

Regarding computer-mediated communication, Herring (2007: 8) underlines the fact that '[d]igital writing often takes on characteristics of artful, playful, stylized performance.' And for Danet (1998), in her article entitled 'Text as mask', interactants can play with gender identities in a carnivalesque way. This reminds us of Goffman's (1967) argument, for whom '[f]ace is a mask that changes depending on the audience and the social interaction'. But Goffman (1959) also claims that speakers give information about their gender unconsciously. And for Herring (2000), it is almost impossible to dissimulate one's gender for very long in a computer-mediated interaction because there are always signs which betray the user. Moreover, it seems that internet users have a tendency to rely on stereotypes about online gender styles in their interaction (Herring 2000), in their own performance as well as in their interpretation of others' behaviours.

In this chapter, I shall study what the implications of performing one's identity are for politeness and gender on a particular transvestites' internet platform. I shall focus on notions of appropriateness. In particular I shall analyse what behaviours are appropriate (gender and politeness-wise) for transvestites joining this web-based community. I shall show the link between joining a virtual community (when new members have to comply with the appropriate behaviour set by this community), female-coded politeness and displays of positive politeness, bearing in mind that feelings involved in positive politeness should be seen as specific to a certain community of practice: in the case of this particular community of transvestites this involves respect, empathy and mutual assistance.

3.1.1 Politeness and appropriateness

Brown and Levinson's model of politeness (1987) has been very influential in the field of politeness studies. It has been applied without modification by numerous researchers, but has been re-evaluated many times by others (Culpeper 1996, Mills 2003, Watts 2003, Locher and Watts 2005). One main source of critique concerns the fact that the model aims at being universal and restricts politeness to being nice or considerate, mainly a matter of avoiding what Brown and Levinson coined face-threatening acts (FTAs). Moreover, the bipolar model has been reproached because in daily interactions positive and negative politeness strategies are often used conjointly and cannot be kept apart. For some critics, it is necessary that politeness finds its place in a larger frame that has to do with relations and interactions. Arundale (2006), Locher and Watts (2005), and Locher and Bousfield (2008) have underlined the fact that politeness is only a part of facework or relational work, i.e. the negotiation of relationships with others. Going further than the classical dual notion of face (positive/negative), such as presented by Brown and Levinson (1987), and going back to Goffman's view of the concept, Watts (2003) and Locher and Watts (2005) propose that research should focus on the discursive struggle in which interlocutors engage. Cross-cultural studies on politeness have shown how elusive and culture-bound the term itself can be, thus highlighting the need for new terminology. Watts (2003: 257) chooses to talk about *politic behaviour*: 'Politic behaviour is that behaviour, linguistic and non-linguistic, which the participants construct as being appropriate to the ongoing social interaction'. The central place of the term *appropriate* is noticeable here. Locher and Watts (2005) propose that *appropriateness* be used for polite behaviours as well as politic behaviours that will not be conventionally judged as polite, and *inappropriateness* for impolite or overpolite behaviours. Watts (2003: 258) had previously argued that '[i]ndividuals have acquired fairly similar forms of habitus [permitting] a high degree of consensus in agreeing on what is and what is not politic behaviour'. This shows that there are representations – which are common to communities of practice – about what politeness or positive politeness is. The latter concept was defined by Brown and Levinson (1987: 70) as 'approach-based; it "anoints" the face of the addressee by indicating that in some respects, S wants H's wants (e. g., by treating him as a member of an in-group, a friend, a person whose wants and personality traits are known and liked)'. Or, according to Eckert and McConnell-Ginet (2003: 135), performing positive politeness is 'showing that you like or empathize with someone, that you include them in your "we", your "in-group"'. These are the two definitions of positive politeness that I shall use in this chapter, particularly when analysing expressions of sameness, empathy and inclusion in an *in-group*.

Finally, if face is relational and interactional, it might not seem so obvious to consider these two dimensions when working with asynchronous types of communication.² (This format does not make use of the usual rules involved in the appropriate pursuit of a conversation, such as turns, interruptions, overlapping, floor management, etc. – interestingly, elements that have often been studied as gender-coded). However, with regard to Brown and Levinson's model and the community of transvestites' writings analysed for the purposes of this chapter, it seems that the use of positive politeness is less for the hearer to feel good or respected, and more for the speaker to *look good*. With this idea in mind, I argue that a gender-coded politeness display takes place in the form of a performance of feminine identity and plays a role in the construction of a new persona for transvestites.

3.1.2 Gender and politeness

During the last two decades, scholars have started to speak about gender in terms of something that one *does* (West and Zimmerman 1987) or *performs* (Butler 1990), a 'routine accomplishment embedded in everyday interactions' (West and Zimmerman 1987: 125), and co-constructed through interactional work: '[G]ender is not part of one's essence, what one is, but an achievement, what one does. Gender is a set of practices through which people construct and claim identities, not simply a system for categorizing people. And gender practices are not only about establishing identities but also about managing social relations' (Eckert and McConnell-Ginet 2003: 305). Going beyond this notion of performance, I would like to link the performance that one achieves in interactions to notions of appropriateness and representations on gendered politeness. Gender identities are constructed according to assumptions of what is or is not appropriate for men and women in different communities of practice or cultures, seen in more or less monolithic fashions (i.e. French, American, Occidental cultures, etc.). These beliefs on suitable gendered roles are reinforced during interactions, but can sometimes be questioned. For Mills (2005: 277), 'The notion of appropriateness is not ideologically neutral ... But this process is informed by wider societal norms of what behaviour is considered to be gender-appropriate. Thus when individuals hypothesize what the Community of Practice would consider appropriate behaviour for them, they necessarily also invoke these social norms, whether to contest or affirm them.' One would argue that common beliefs about social norms verge on stereotypes. For example, stereotypical representations of appropriate feminine identity and communication in Western cultures involve notions of being nice, supportive and cooperative (Eckert and McConnell-Ginet 2003, Mills 2005), while male speech is often described by researchers as being more competitive and aggressive. According to Holmes (1995), women use more positive politeness, apologize and compliment more often than men. Her study has often been criticized for dealing with a stereotypical vision of feminine behaviour. But Eckert and McConnell-Ginet (2003) claim that stereotypes should not be perceived as fake representations of people's behaviours: '[they] constitute norms ... that we do not obey but that we orient to. They serve as a kind of organizing device in society, an ideological map, setting out the range of possibility within which we place ourselves and assess others' (McConnell-Ginet 2003: 87). In the following section, I try to see how these norms and orientations are displayed in computer-mediated communication (CMC) and gendered speech.

3.1.3 Computer-mediated communication, politeness and gender

Politeness in CMC has to do with how users construct norms of what they judge as being polite interactions within their own Community of Practice, creating therein a specific set of expectations (i.e. a *netiquette*), to the extent that deviations from these norms could result in what are perceived as rude or aggressive messages to members. Regarding gender, authors agree on the fact that there are differences between female and male CMC patterns or communicative styles on the internet (Herring 1999, 2000; de Oliveira 2007; Panayametheekul and Herring 2007). Herring (1999: 241) goes as far as to claim that '[w]omen and men appeal to different, partially incompatible systems of values with respect to their own behaviour on-line'. As for differences between genders in matters of politeness and appropriateness, what is appropriate or *acceptable* conduct on the internet seems to vary between men and women (Herring 1999). In her review of literature, Herring (2000) concludes that research has shown that '[m]ales are more likely to ... use crude language (including insults and profanity) and in general manifest an adversarial orientation towards their interlocutors'. Reminding us of Holmes' (1995) findings, Herring (2000) adds: 'In contrast, females ... are more likely to ... apologize, express support of others, and in general, manifest an "aligned" orientation towards their interlocutors'. Furthermore, women appear to seek polite exchanges (de Oliveira 2007) and react aversively to aggression in online interaction (Herring 2000).

As for CMC and gender dissimulation, Danet (1998: 129) notes a general tendency on the internet for 'textual cross-dressing' (most of the time male members pretending to be women for the fun of it), stating that 'the typed text provides the mask'. However, I argue that this is not the case in my study since it is clear for every user that members are male-to-female cross-dressers. Despite the fact that on the website studied for this chapter, it is not necessary for transvestites to *pass* (i.e. have other people believe that one is a woman, as the virtual audience will automatically assume that one is male), I shall, however, keep the concept of *textual cross-dressing* in mind, and show that it is even more evident in French due to the use of grammatical gender to index a female identity.

In the next section, I shall argue that, on the website, transvestites perform female-indexed behaviours. One such behaviour is a shared representation of what feminine politeness is and this representation is displayed through empathy, support and solidarity.

3.2 Sense of community on the transvestites' website

As mentioned before, I argue that a sense of community is established on the website through a feminine display of positive politeness and solidarity. Gusfield (1975) distinguishes between two major uses of the term *community*. The first is the territorial or geographical notion of the word (i.e. a neighbourhood or a city). The second is relational. Some communities have no geographical demarcation, as is obviously the case with internet communities. It is important to note that physical proximity or shared territory can be absent among members of a community, but that the relational dimension is indispensable. As for Sense of Community (referred to as SoC from now on), the psychologists McMillan and Chavis' (1986) descriptive framework has been widely accepted. In its definition it includes the crucial concept of *membership* in that community: 'Membership is a feeling that one has invested part of oneself to become a member and therefore has a right to belong . . . It is a feeling of belonging, of being a part' (McMillan and Chavis 1986: 9). Furthermore, reviewing the literature on dimensions of membership, the authors identify five attributes: 'boundaries', 'emotional safety', 'a sense of belonging and identification', 'personal investment' and 'a common symbol system' (1986: 9–10). I shall briefly develop the dimensions of *boundaries* and the *common symbol system*, as they will be of importance in this chapter. *Boundaries* are marked by factors such as language and dress codes, indicating who belongs to a community and who does not, and, as for *a common symbol system*, communities use symbols such as rituals, ceremonies, forms of speech (and forms of politeness) to indicate boundaries between who is and who is not a member. It reminds us of the Labovian notion of *speech community* which involves participation in a *set of shared norms* (Labov 1972).

According to McMillan and Chavis (1986), another side of membership is involved in the development of SoC: 'Fulfilment of needs, exchange of support among members'. Bringing this aspect together with the definition of positive politeness quoted previously ('showing that you like or empathize with someone, that you include them in your "we", your "in-group"' – Eckert and McConnell-Ginet 2003: 135), it now seems obvious that the two can be linked. The third element that comes into play is solidarity. In this chapter, I shall be analysing what I call *markers of solidarity*. I argue that the expression of solidarity plays a part in the construction of a SoC. The word *solidarity* has two definitions in the *Concise Oxford Dictionary*: the first definition highlights concepts such as unity and similarity between individuals 'united around a common goal or against a common enemy' (1999: 1366). The second definition puts a stress on the interactive side of the notion with the fact that individuals demonstrate 'a willingness to give psychological and/or material support' (1999: 1366). To summarize, solidarity encompasses a feeling of commonality; a sense of being part of a group and a desire to exchange support. One will note the similarity between the above definitions and SoC's descriptive framework, especially when concepts such as membership, boundaries and fulfilment of needs are taken into account. It is now generally acknowledged that solidarity is not a given, but has to be jointly constructed in the interaction through the use of specific markers.

For Baym (1995, 1998), computer-mediated communities are created under the influence of factors such as external context (e.g. pre-existing speech communities, in which members interact), as well as system infrastructures or group purposes; the medium creating new forms of speech and new ways to express identity and relationships. But how is a Sense of *virtual* Community (cf. Blanchard and Markus 2004) built and how does it apply to the group of transvestites that I am studying for the purposes of this chapter? Regarding membership and boundaries, it seems obvious that the feeling of belonging to a group is critical for transvestites, who often feel lonely in their surroundings since quite often people around them are not aware of this other aspect of their personality. A lot of these men have not come out of the closet and, if they have, they have a feeling of being judged as strange or deviant. Therefore they are looking for people who are similar, share the same views and make them feel that they are definitely not abnormal. They have a need to be part of a stable and dependable structure (McKenna and Bargh 1998). As for the common symbol system, I shall show in the analysis that the shared norms are expressed through the use of feminine forms of address, adjectives and participles.

3.3 Data

3.3.1 Presentation of data[3]

This current chapter is part of a larger research endeavour on the discourse of a virtual community of transvestites in a French-speaking website whose goal is clearly to establish an international community. It was first created by Quebecois members but then developed when members from France, Belgium, Switzerland, and other French-speaking transvestites from around the world joined the virtual community. Today it counts more than 1.3 million visitors. It is unquestionably a very successful website. For this chapter, I focus on a section of the website called *Le coin des copines* (literally 'girlfriends' corner'). On these pages, members are able to post a short text with an optional picture in order to introduce themselves to other members. Through this presentation of self they want to initiate correspondence or future meetings. More than 250 French-speaking members from France, Québec, Switzerland, and Belgium as well as Germany, Australia, the United States, etc. have posted their letter of introduction on these pages. For the analysis I focus on two groups of members: the *copines* from France (144 members) and the *copines* from Quebec (74 members). In these two groups, I noted a wide range of social backgrounds and ages (from 18 to 60). In the collected data, it is important to emphasize that the members' texts of introduction are not isolated pieces of work. Some members published their presentation of self on the website and were soon followed by other members. A few members commented that they found the courage to post their own text after reading presentations from other *copines*. Solidarity involves expressions of similarity and membership in the community and implies a desire to help, consideration (i.e. the display of positive politeness strategies) and a strong stand to avoid flaming or aggressive messages. The norms for appropriate behaviour on the website are enunciated by the webmistress in a page written for newcomers and entitled '*Quelques précisions de M.*' ['A few clarifications from M.']. In the following extract and hereafter, a superscript 'f' will be used to signal the use of the feminine form of the adjective or participle in French:

(1) Page to Newcomers

    a. *Chères amies qui venez chez nous pour la première fois, un peu surprises, sans doute, d'avoir trouvé asile ici, un peu déroutées peut-être devant sa richesse inattendue et inespérée, et très certainement séduites par son ambiance feutrée,* douce et amicale, c'est à vous que j'ai pensé en écrivant ce court texte de présentation, moi qui ai eu la chance de le découvrir dès sa naissance, voilà un peu plus de deux ans.

'Dear friends[f] who come here for the first time, a bit surprised[f] no doubt, to have found a sanctuary here, a bit confused[f] maybe to find this unexpected wealth, but surely seduced[f] by its refined, soft and amiable atmosphere, I thought of you when I wrote this short message of presentation, me who had the chance to discover it from its birth, that is two years ago now.'

b. *Et si vous êtes un homme... quelques conseils indispensables: Je pense qu'il est inutile de vous recommander de marcher sur des œufs, et notamment d'abandonner cette 'mâle assurance' qui se confond souvent avec la muflerie.*

'If you are a man ... some vital advice: I think that it is not necessary to remind you to be extremely careful, and most of all to leave this "male confidence" behind because it is too often mixed with boorishness.'

In these excerpts, one can note the use of feminine forms of adjectives, the term of address (*chères amies* –'dear friends[f]'), the amicable mood and the firm stand against rudeness or aggressive messages. Another welcome page defines the website as a support group created with the aim to help a community.

3.3.2 Data analysis

In the transvestites' texts of introduction, a few elements will be analysed. I want to show how these elements relate to a stereotypical idea of feminine speech and identity and build a display of positive politeness through a demonstration of solidarity and a sense of community. The following will be analysed:

- markers of feminine identity: words used to talk about self and to address others;
- markers of solidarity: utterances expressing similarity, membership in the community and mutual assistance; and
- formulaic politeness and utterances expressing the desire to avoid rudeness and aggressive messages.

3.3.2.1 *Markers of feminine identity: Presentation of self and forms of address*

Although most transvestites present themselves as such (*Je suis un travesti(e) / Je suis trav / Je suis tv*), some do not hesitate to call themselves *femme* (woman) or *fille* (girl). Similarly, the near majority uses feminine forms of adjectives or participles (here are a few examples among hundreds: *Je suis blonde* 'I am a blond^f'; *Je suis française* 'I am French^f'; *Je suis sexie*⁴ 'I am sexy^f'). In her article on transsexuals, Livia (1997) has shown that the French grammatical gender permits gender-bending possibilities and that speakers can play with gender to present themselves sometimes as male, sometimes as female (or both as in these two examples collected from our data: *Je suis une jolie travesti blonde* – 'I am a pretty^f blond^f transvestite^m'; *Je suis maintenant un homme très heureuse* – 'I am now a very happy^f man'). With reference to Brazilian transsexuals, Borba and Osterman (2007: 143–144) show that the use of both grammatical genders when referring to oneself allows for 'ambiguity perpetuated socially and linguistically' as well as for expression of 'specific places in [one's] identity market'. For the latter case, some transsexuals use masculine gender to refer to a more or less distant past before the transformation (i.e. the operation) took place. In this way, linguistic devices allow for the creation of 'complex multilayered identities' (Borba and Osterman 2008: 135). Livia (1997) also finds this use of both grammatical genders in her analysis of the autobiography of the French transsexual Georgine Noël. However, when the transsexual switches to the feminine grammatical gender, it is not to adopt a female identity: '[i]t is important to note that this linguistic strategy is not intended to reflect a feminine persona so much as to dissociate the speaker from the heterosexual alliance ... Speakers thereby underline their own alliance with the sissy, the nelly, the drag queen, and in fact create this alliance by their use of the feminine gender' (Livia 1997: 359). However, I argue that this is not the case with transvestites who, for the most part, feel that they are expressing a feminine alter ego when cross-dressing. On the website, because of the fact that photographic constituents are limited, linguistic cues are essential. Livia (1997: 363) further adds that '[s]peakers are not passive with regard to language and the possibilities its system of distinctions and similarities sets up.' This linguistic exercise contributes to the performance of a feminine identity: the sort of *textual cross-dressing* (Danet 1998) mentioned earlier.

The performance of feminine identity is not only to be found in the presentation of self but also in the chosen forms of address used on the website. Gay men use feminine terms to address fellows in the community (Livia 1997). In the data, I found forms such as *copines* (girlfriends); *amies* (friends^f); *filles* (girls); *consoeurs* (colleagues); *soeurs* (sisters); *cousines* (cousins^f) emphasizing a feminine friendship and sisterhood. I noted a similarity in the forms of address used by the transvestites in France and in Québec. The word *copines* (a favoured word in the gay community – cf. Livia 1997) was an obvious choice since the section is called *Le coin des copines*.

3.3.2.2 Markers of solidarity: Similarity, membership in community and mutual assistance

I would like to repeat Eckert and McConnell-Ginet's (2003: 135) definition of positive politeness as 'showing that you like or empathize with someone, that you include them in your "we", your "in-group"' as, for this part of the analysis, I focus on these two sides of positive politeness: empathy (one can keep in mind the etymology of the word: 'to suffer with') and the use of the pronoun 'we' in the French texts. Excerpts (2) and (3) present two examples from the data.

(2) A3 Québec

Je suis un travesti de 51 ans. Je te remercie bien fort de m'accueillir dans notre consœurie . . . En joignant les rangs, je sais que, dorénavant, je ne serai plus jamais seule.
'I am a 51 year old transvestite. I thank you very much for welcoming me in our sisterhood . . . Joining your ranks, I know that from now on, I will never be alone[f] anymore.'

(3) A10 France

Je suis heureuse d'avoir trouvé votre site, je me sens moins seule. Comme beaucoup d'entre vous, . . . je cherche à parler avec des amies, amis qui sauraient me comprendre.
'I'm happy[f] that I found your website, I feel less alone[f]. As many of you . . . I would like to talk to friends[f], friends[m] [masculine form] who will be able to understand me.'

As shown in excerpts (2) and (3), similarity and membership in the community are expressed through the expression of a feeling of not being alone and not feeling different anymore, as well as a feeling of sharing similarities and like-mindedness. In the data, I noted varied ways of expressing feelings of not being alone and of claiming similarity, in the French group as well as in the Quebecois group:

The French group:

Je croyais être seule 'I thought I was alone'; *Je suis loin d'être seule* 'I am far from being alone'; *en découvrant que je n'étais pas seule* 'discovering that I was not alone'; *Mon histoire est classique* 'My story is classic'; *être parmi vous* 'being among you'; *entre filles* 'between girls'; *Quel bonheur de se retrouver entre nous qui ne sommes pas tout à fait comme les autres* 'What a joy to be among us who are not really like others' – *comme moi; comme beaucoup; comme beaucoup d'entre nous; d'entre vous; comme toutes les filles; comme beaucoup de femmes;*

comme vous toutes 'like me; like a lot; like a lot of us, of you; like all the girls; like a lot of women; like all of you'.

The Quebecois group:

Je ne serai plus jamais seule 'I will never be alone anymore'; *On se sent moins seule* 'we feel less lonely'; *J'ai longtemps pensé que j'étais une espèce rare* 'I felt for a long time I was from a rare species'; *Plusieurs vivaient la même chose que moi* 'Several lived the same way that I did'; *qui ont les mêmes affinités que moi* 'who have the same affinities as me'; *les mêmes désirs que les miens* 'the same desires as mine'; *les mêmes craintes et les mêmes rêves* 'the same fears and the same dreams'; *Mon histoire est semblable à* 'my story is similar to'; *avoir une place avec vous* 'to have a place among you'; *faire partie du groupe* 'to belong to the group'; *me joindre au groupe* 'to join the group' – *comme moi; comme nous; comme plusieurs d'entre nous* 'like me; like us; like several among us'.

It is interesting to note that the same sentences are used – nearly word for word – by members of the two different groups. The expression of similarity clearly serves to give a feeling of belonging to a group and to sustain a sense of community. As for the 'we/in-group' category (Eckert and McConnell-Ginet 2003), I analysed the transvestites' use of the inclusive *nous* (i.e. the use of the pronoun 'we' as including the speaker as well as the addressee). When reading the letters of introduction for the first time, I noticed the important presence of the inclusive *nous* and its correlated possessive forms used by the members. In extract (4), instances are presented that contain the form:

(4)

a. *Il faut vivre pleinement ce que **nous** sommes.*
   'It's essential to live fully what **we** are.'
b. *J'espère qu'un jour **nous** pourrons toutes vivre au grand jour sans que **nous** soyons qualifiées des pires choses, comme c'est encore le cas.*
   'I hope that one day **we** will all[f] be able to live in the open without being called[f] awful names, as it's still the case today.'
c. *La France n'est pas un pays où **nous** avons le droit de cité. **Nous** sommes trop souvent obligés de vivre **nos** rêves dans une semi-clandestinité.*
   'France is not a country where **we** can live. **We** are too often forced to live **our** dreams in semi clandestineness.'
d. *Il faut être fière d'être ce que **nous** sommes car **nous** sommes toutes des personnes ouvertes et il faut d'abord apprendre à se respecter si **on** veut que le société **nous** respecte.*

'It is essential to be proud' of what **we** are because all of **us** are open people and it is necessary firstly to learn to respect oneself if **we** want the society to respect **us**.'

In excerpt (4), the inclusive 'we' appears as another linguistic device used by members in order to reinforce the 'boundaries' of the community ('we' as opposed to 'they') and to give a 'sense of belonging and identification' (McMillan and Chavis 1986) through the ongoing participation in *Le coin des copines*' pages.

Another way of expressing empathy and solidarity is to display a willingness to help. In the French and Quebecois groups, I noted expressions promoting support among members:

French group:

J'encourage 'I give encouragement'; *Je souhaiterais en faire profiter /donner quelques conseils / venir en aide / pouvoir partager mon expérience avec d'autres* 'I would like people to benefit from my experience / give some advice / come to your assistance / share my experience with others'; *Je suis disposée à aider* 'I'm willing' to help'; *Je serais heureuse de donner un petit bout de bonheur à l'une d'entre nous* 'I will be happy to give some happiness to one of you'.

Quebecois group:

j'ai senti le besoin de me rapprocher de la communauté car je vois qu'il y a beaucoup de copines qui ont besoin d'aide à différents niveaux 'I felt the need to get closer to the community as I see that a lot of girlfriends need help at different levels'; *Il me fera plaisir de vous initier* 'It will please me to initiate you ...'; *J'ai mon avis à donner sur l'utilisation des hormones* 'I have my opinion to give on the use of hormones'.

This linguistic practice reminds us of Herring's (2000) finding that, in CMC, women tend to 'express support of others, and in general, manifest an "aligned" orientation towards their interlocutors'.

As mentioned previously, the Quebecois part of the website predates the French one. This is noticeable in the greater number of thanks for help, as exemplified by the following collection:

grâce à ton site 'thanks to your website'; *grâce à ton site, je peux me définir comme réellement travesti* 'thanks to your website, I can really define myself as a transvestite'; *Quel plaisir de se savoir moins seule et c'est grâce à toi, Isabelle* 'It is a pleasure to feel less lonely' and it's thanks to you Isabelle'; *J'ai appris à maturer et* à devenir une adulte plus accomplie et tout ça en revient grâce à ton site qui m'a donné un point de référence 'I learnt to mature and to become a more accomplished ͑ adult and it is all thanks to your website which gave me a base point'; *Heureusement que vous êtes là!* 'Fortunately you're here!'

Finally, it is important to note that in the 250 texts of presentation of self, published on this part of the website, not one text of aggression or exclusion was found. I shall propose an explanation for this absence in the following section.

3.3.2.3 Formulaic politeness and avoiding rudeness

Formulaic politeness encompasses 'prefabricated linguistic expressions' (Coulmas 1981: 1) and verbal routines such as ritualized greetings and thanks. It is true to say that, since Fraser and Nolan (1981), it has been argued that no utterance is inherently polite and formulaic politeness is not necessarily used to demonstrate polite behaviour (note, for example, the ironic use of expressions such as 'thank you very much'). However, I argue that in the case of the data analysed here formulaic politeness is used as a means of displaying polite behaviour, since it allows individuals to express respect to interlocutors and 'anoints the face of the addressee' (Brown and Levinson 1987: 70).

On the website and in pages where formulaic politeness is not an essential part of the written exercise (such as *Le coin des copines,* where the goal is mainly to introduce oneself and not to interact with other members or with the webmistress), I noticed a significant number of instances of such forms. Two-thirds of the French members (92 *copines*) used formulaic politeness, mainly for greetings (*bonjour* 'hello'; *heureuse de vous rejoindre* 'happy to join you'; *à bientôt* 'see you soon'); thanks and congratulations (*merci; bravo; félicitations; bon courage*); closure and demonstration of affection (*tendresse; amicalement; amitiés; je vous aime; bons baisers; bises; bisous; je vous embrasse; kiss*). Three-quarters of the Quebecois (55 *copines*) used them for greetings (*bonjour; salut; allo; je daigne me présenter* 'I deign to introduce myself'; *permettez-moi de me présenter* 'let me introduce myself'; à *bientôt; bye; à plus; je vous laisse; salutation; au plaisir; à vous lire prochainement*); thanks and congratulations (*merci; bravo; félicitations; chapeau*); closure and demonstration of affection (*bises; bisous; kisses; xxx; tendresse*). Interestingly, there were more formulaic politeness markers in the Quebecois texts of introduction (used by three-quarters of the members) than in the French ones (used by two-thirds of the members), especially regarding greetings. On the other hand, I noticed more expressions of feelings on the French side and more written kisses (one may question whether this is due to a cultural habitus linked to the writing of letters, or to a stronger necessity for the transvestites from France to display positive politeness in order to see themselves as included in a community that was originally created by Quebecois). Excerpt (5) presents an example of formulaic politeness:

(5) M83 France

Bonjour à vous toutes, je suis très émue à la pensée de me trouver parmi vous et d'être la copine de la semaine je ne l'aurais jamais imaginé ... Merci de vos témoignages à toutes qui me donnent aussi la force d'être et un merci tout particulier à Isabelle pour son site.
'Hello to all^f of you^f, I am very moved^f to be among you and to be the girlfriend of the week. I would never have expected it. ... Thanks to all^f of you for your life stories; they give me the strength to be myself and a special thank you to Isabelle for her website.'

Regarding rudeness and aggressive messages, one can imagine why a transvestites' website would be so concerned with the need to avoid flaming or abuse from members or intruders since they are particularly vulnerable to such attacks.⁵ For the French group, I noted expressions showing the will to avoid adversarial or rude attacks: *Merci de m'avoir lue courtoisement* 'Thanks for reading me with courtesy'; *Merci d'accepter ces gens différents que nous sommes* 'Thanks to accept these other kind of people that we are'; *Ce que je n'aime pas: les machos, les gens bêtes, l'intolérance, les extrémistes, l'ignorance, la vulgarité, la stupidité, le sectarisme, la grossièreté* 'What I don't like: machos, idiots, intolerance, extremists, ignorance, vulgarity, stupidity, sectarianism and rudeness'; *Envoyez une petite lettre émaillée de jolis mots* 'Send me a nice letter peppered with pretty words'. And for the Quebecois: *Dans une atmosphère de respect* 'In an atmosphere of respect'; *Ce qui m'horripile: les esprits obtus* 'I find closed-minded people exasperating'; *Ce qui me deplaît: l'intolérance* 'I dislike intolerance'; *Je n'apprécie pas la vulgarité* 'I don't appreciate vulgarity'; *Je demande aux hommes de s'abstenir et encore plus de faire des propositions* 'I ask men to abstain, even more so to make propositions'.

To bring this section to a close, I should add that I did not come across blatantly face-attacking messages or occurrences of flaming in any part of the website. However, it is worth noting that there is no active chat room (the place where flaming would most probably occur). Furthermore, even in a section dedicated to letters to the webmistress, no adverse or challenging comments were found, but it could be the case that the webmistress moderated them and/or did not publish inflammatory messages.

3.4 Conclusion

In this chapter, I have argued that on the internet, when presenting oneself to a group and in order to gain membership or kinship, it is necessary to adopt what is considered by other members of the website to be appropriate behaviour. The set of behaviours generally used on the web are gender-coded but also based on a stereotypical vision of what a gender-based behaviour should be, as traits are often exaggerated because of the medium (Herring 1999, 2000, 2001). Moreover, the specific system infrastructure and form of the texts analysed (i.e. the presentation of self in asynchronous communication) certainly affect the content and the ways that writers choose to display politeness (Herring 2007); since they do not see their interlocutor(s), they are likely to adopt a positive face in order to avoid any misunderstanding or misinterpretation of their words. In my study, it seems therefore that the medium reinforces the use of formulaic politeness and the effort to prevent rude messages. Regarding CMC and feminine politeness, stereotypes involve notions of nice, supportive and co-operative behaviour (Mills 2005), in contrast to aggressive and face-threatening masculine forms of behaviour. In this chapter, I have tried to demonstrate that for transvestites, displaying a feminine politeness stance contributes to a broader performance and to the construction of a new identity as a woman. Female-coded politeness, essentially positive politeness, is one among many props used to perform a feminine identity. Markers of identity, solidarity and formulaic politeness are stylistic practices used in the construction of a female persona and a sense of community. In exercises of discourse analysis, classical bipolarities (male/female – positive/negative politeness – politeness/impoliteness) have to be examined critically. As Eckert and McConnell-Ginet (2003) advocate: 'If gender stereotypes are part of our sociolinguistic life, they need to be examined – not simply as possible facts about language use, but as components of gender ideology. Our linguistic behaviour is intertwined with ideology, our stereotypes are not simply "lies" about language, but exaggerations with a purpose. And that purpose is what makes a language tick' (Eckert and McConnell-Ginet 2003: 85).

Finally, I believe it is important to work on gender ideologies in computer-mediated texts in order to highlight the constructions of male/female/

transgendered performances and to study the common-sense representations of gendered discourses, appropriate behaviours and politeness.

Post-script

The research on which this chapter is based dates back more than ten years, more precisely to the time when I first came across the transvestites' website on which my study of the performances of feminine voices on the Internet is based. Ten years later, and considering the wealth of studies that have been published since then on gender and language (for French see Duchêne and Moïse 2011, Chetchuti and Greco 2012, Greco 2012 to name but a few), I feel the need to bring some clarification to the arguments that I held in this article. In recent publications, researchers claim not only that their goals are to rethink the difference between sexes, which is often taken as a rigid framework to understand societal values and attitudes (Chetchuti and Greco 2012), and to deconstruct the category 'female' that cannot exist outside discourse (Duchêne and Moïse 2011). They also highlight the necessity to consider the dynamics of resistance to the heteronormative man/woman binarity (Greco 2012). One case that illustrates such resistance is gender-bender Conchita Wurst who remembers the suffering he went through as a small boy being brought up in a conservative Austrian village and confided in a TV interview: 'I wanted to be part of the game and then I realised well *I* create the game'[6] (2014). This perspective on gendered performance as an individual creation says a lot on the current view about gendered identities. But how creative can individuals be in the face of gendered roles that are rigid social constructs (described by some as a psychological girdle)? For Greco (2012: 568), '[r]aising the issue of an individual's leeway in a normative context helps us account for the role played by gender norms in the construction of identity-related devices'. I would like nonetheless to argue that what is *created* is created with the help of available sociocultural and symbolic resources. Performances of gendered voices generally make use of coded vocal (height, melody, pitch, pace, etc.) and linguistic features, and reuse hegemonic gendered discourses. For Hall and Bucholtz (2013: 125): 'Because pragmatic meanings readily become bound to larger ideological distinctions such as "female" and "male" through sociohistorical processes of discursive sedimentation, utterances may also "pragmatically presuppose genders of speakers, addressees, overhearers, and referents"' (Ochs 1992: 339).

During my research, I viewed and read documents from transvestites and transsexuals who gave a wealth of advice on how to change one's voice. The objectives that were set were unambiguous. Quite often, the goal claimed by transvestites and transsexuals was to *'speak as a woman'*, to *'develop a female voice'* or to *'feminize one's voice'*. The question that arose for me was: if being a woman means to perform womanhood (West and Zimmermann 1987, Butler 1990), what does it mean to perform womanhood for someone who, using Fran Leibowitz' words (in Rasin 2010) 'has not been a girl' (i.e. someone who has not been socialized since the earliest age as belonging to this specific gender group)? The resulting performance requires constant attention to the minute details of any daily ritual (Garfinkel 1967) that is accomplished *naturally* by women. And there is no doubt that the performance goes beyond a simple act of mimicry. As Andy Warhol's' well-known transsexual actress Candy Darling, states: 'I am not a genuine woman but I am not interested in genuineness. I am interested in the product of being a woman and of how qualified I am.' It is quite often this discrepancy between essence (i.e. inner sense of identity) and nature (the biological sex) as well as the relationship between performance and the entitlement to express a gendered identity of one's choice that frames transvestites' testimonies.

For many of the individuals in the corpus that I studied, this second identity as a woman is expressed in terms such as 'when I am a woman', 'when I live *as a woman'*, 'I go out *as a woman'*; 'I love to *be a woman*' [my emphases]. The individuals who expressed themselves on the website have different motivations to cross-dress or to express another gendered identity (as the actual act of cross-dressing may not necessarily intervene in online practices), and the time and part of their life that they invest in the practice may vary widely. They come from different backgrounds, know different sexual orientations and experience their sex and gender in different ways. When some claim that being a woman does not imply rejecting their identity as a man (it is then a matter of speaking with one's other voice, or voicing one's other self),[7] others feel that nature made a mistake, that they should, in their own words, have been born women (a condition sometimes described under the medical term of *gender dysphoria*). By cross-dressing or transitioning, they are correcting this mistake – i.e. repairing nature. In these cases, individuals believe that they are not expressing another self but their *real* self and often confide in how good it feels to express *this true identity*. This desire translates in expressing a femininity (i.e. a set of attributes, behaviours, and linguistic variants generally associated with girls and women) that they feel as being quintessential to being a woman. It is not a simple matter of copying women as some male-to-female transgender individuals argue that they are *more woman* than women (reminding us of Agnes' famous statement of being '120% female' – Garfinkel 1967). What they perform is an idealized and ostensible version of what they see as being a woman: donning women's clothing such as skirts and tights, wearing make-up and jewellery, and adopting a stylized voice. With regard to the latter, individuals make use of symbolic linguistic traits such as phonologic features (i.e. high pitch, breathiness, wide-range melody, etc.), as well as feminine terms of address and the referential pronoun 'she'. These traits are linked to shared assumptions on what a feminine voice is. The explanations given in videos found over the Internet on transgender vocal performances are straightforward: 'Men talk like …'. vs. 'Women talk like …'.

It has been argued (for example in the case of drag-queens) that such performances are playful, and that they are a means to negotiate/deconstruct rigid gendered roles. Considering the fact that most of the transvestites that I studied mention that their goal is to pass, I wonder to what extent the freedom to be playful is relevant. Moreover, it is worth bearing in mind that depending on the context, and for different reasons such as to avoid verbal or physical aggression from homophobic individuals (or to be arrested by the police in countries where transgender practices are forbidden), the need to pass may be felt with a varying sense of urgency.

The media often present traditional representations of gendered voices. Gendered roles and rituals contribute to maintain the firmly established representations of gendered voices that prevail in society (even when emblematic features that index masculinity and feminine voice differ from one culture to the other). If some have argued that performers are purposefully/playfully exaggerating conventional notions of femininity and challenging man/woman binarity, the recent Conchita Wurst phenomenon, put aside its gender-bending twist (the 'bearded lady'), appears to be based on performances of a stylized female voice (verging on the girly: higher pitch, emphatic intonations linked to enthusiasm and emotional investment, breathiness, etc.), as well as on a codified body language (wide hand gestures and contact with one's own body – hair and face), that also reinforces traditional representations of women's verbal behaviour as light, voluble and emotional.

The voices that I studied in my corpus are textual voices. They do not therefore use the same salient features as *audible* voices. The process is however similar as transgender individuals borrow among semantic resources such as referential indexes (the use of the feminine pronoun and in French the use of feminine forms of adjectives or feminine forms of verb agreement) or discursive practices with high indexical values (i.e. positive politeness, expression of solidarity, etc.) to express their femininity. By doing so, transvestites and transsexuals claim their legitimacy to access such resources in order to express their gendered identity.

Finally, one should not forget that the chosen context of study is one among others where the implications of performing gendered voices vary widely. In a social media context (where participants remain for the most part anonymous and where threatening voices may be silenced by moderators), men-to-women transvestites feel a sense of security and are therefore empowered to express a feminine voice that they would otherwise keep silent. In other contexts, expressing a feminine voice is to speak in the voice of the weak (the French speak of the 'feeble' sex), the oppressed, that is, in a voice that sounds less authoritative (see Susanna's testimony in Arnold 2015) or that is often silenced, hence the need to create a new space where voices do not fully belong to one gender category or another. The fact that some male-to-female transgender individuals do not claim to don the identity of a woman but that of a lady (this is Conchita Wurst's case) highlights such desire for prestige and respect (as linked to the social category).

In any case, such performances are complex social phenomena and there is no doubt that more studies of gendered voices in general, and more studies of gendered voices in the media in particular, are needed in order to reconcile the expression of genre with individual agency.

4

Performances of Ethnic Voices in French Films

People of my generation would remember a time when one saw little problem in making fun of the *ethnic other* and of his/her *peculiar* way of speaking. Next to the traditional Belgian- and Swiss-accented jokes, French humorists and impersonators seemed to have a preference for the stylized African,[1] Arabic[2] and Chinese accents. However, stand-up comedians' ethnic performances are not a French speciality, and to this day, humorous ethnic stylizations remain a favourite among worldwide audiences (a stock-in-trade for comedians such as the well-known Russell Peters). If yesteryear's outrageous stylizations and caricatures have given way to more nuanced and diverse representations of ethnic communities found on a multiplicity of stages (theatres, music, as well as cinemas), French films still offer to this day few alternatives to the mainly *white* and standardized voices that occupy France's screens.

In this chapter, I study representations of *ethnic voices* in French films, basing my analysis on films as well as on testimonies from black actors who have been asked to stylize black varieties (i.e. Caribbean- or African-accented French) or have been discriminated by the 'colour' (Modestine, in Toscer 2008) of their voice. What I call in this chapter *ethnic voices* comprise stylizations (such as the accented voices found in comedies), alongside voices that are presented as realistic (and may also bear linguistic marks such as code-switching). The second type of voice is most often found in films directed by second-generation immigrants from North African countries, what Higbee (2013) calls *post-beur cinema* – this is the cinema of directors Yamina Benguigui (*Inch'Allah Dimanche* 2001), Abdellatif Kechiche (*The Secret of the Grain* 2007) and Ameur-Zaïmeche (*Dernier Maquis* 2008), to name but a few.

This chapter attempts to show that race is a 'floating signifier' (Hall 1997) – that is, a discursive construct. In media performances of ethnic voices, meaning is not only constructed and, by the means of indexicalities, given to the people they depict; it is also produced and reproduced. Through performances of ethnic voices, the concept of Otherness is maintained and, in the politics of difference, race is consumed and commodified as a cultural and political product (hooks 1992).

4.1 *Coloured* voices: Prejudices and discrimination in the lip-synching industry

In 2007, the mixed-race French actress Yasmine Modestine, accompanied by a colleague who was also mixed-race, was refused a part in the lip-synchronization of a recently released American TV series. The casting director gave the explanation that there were no people '*like them*' (understand *black*) in the series and that they could not do the job because of the fact that they had 'special voices' (in Toscer 2009). Maik Darah, the French voice of Whoopi Goldberg who also dubbed Madonna, Courtney Cox and Michelle Pfeifer, once stated that voices do not have any colour;[3] Modestine offers the opposite, albeit tongue-in-cheek statement:

> One needs to know that for the lip-sync industry, 'black actors have black low voices' and Asian actors have 'high-pitched Asian' voices. White actors are lucky enough to possess a wide enough vocal range to allow them to dub Blacks and Asians as well as Whites. This belief is such that it is not rare to hear a white actress assure that she has 'a black voice', without having the least feeling of being racist – quite the opposite since she dubs black actresses.[4]
> Modestine 2008

Modestine (2008) describes having felt stunned (*sonnée*) at the brutal reminder that she was *different* in a society where whiteness is held as the norm. In their book, Dubet et al. (2013) describe, among the different reactions to the experience of discrimination, the shock of the sudden awareness, a shock as intense as the feeling of injustice that comes into conflict with beliefs that were held as self-evident (i.e. equal opportunities despite diverse racial origins – see also Ndiaye 2008: chapter 5). The researchers, supported by nearly 200 interviews that they conducted through the DISCRI project,[5] documented the feelings of humiliation and shame that follow such shock. Modestine explains that after what she experienced as an act of racial discrimination, she realized that even though her parents had taught her to be proud, she was suddenly facing the fact that for some people, being black means 'you are a different human being than us, you come from Blackland'[6] (in Toscer 2009). Her experience reminds me of Hall's depiction of the traumatic character of 'the colonial experience':

The ways in which black people, black experiences, were positioned and subjected in the dominant regimes of representation were the effects of a critical exercise of cultural power and normalisation. Not only, in Said's 'Orientalist' sense, were we constructed as different and other within the categories of knowledge of the West by those regimes. They had the power to make us see and experience ourselves as 'Other'.... It is one thing to position a subject or set of peoples as the Other of a dominant discourse. It is quite another thing to subject them to that 'knowledge', not only as a matter of imposed will and domination, by the power of inner compulsion and subjective conformation to the norm.

Hall 1990: 225–226

Dubet et al. (2013) note that feelings of discrimination may vary according to the situation of integration and the social class, according to the work market, the nature of the institution or the way the latter integrates diversity. Whereas migrants may have suffered more from discrimination than their children, it is often those children who come forward to denounce prejudices. If it seems that attitudes towards diversity have evolved in the last two decades, especially in the media, one has never heard so much of the stigmatization suffered by ethnic minorities in the film industry – the latter often having the feeling of being constantly reduced to their *differences*.

Dubet et al. (2013) highlight the different techniques that those discriminated against use to get by or cope with such feelings: strategies of indifference (such as discrediting the discriminator, or generalizing one's case to make it the result of a social tendency to racism or sexism) or decisions to fight. Dubet et al. argue that for discriminated individuals, what matters most is to escape the double trap of hatred and discrimination[7] (2013: 112). Following Modestine's 2007 incident, she alerted the media and submitted the case to the HALDE (High Authority for the fight against Discrimination and for Equality), which initially refused to handle it. Later, following a few red flags raised by the press, the commission made an inquiry and concluded that racial prejudices[8] prevailed in the profession – prejudices of the sort that would prevent black actors being chosen to dub a white character. In an article published on 29 December 2008, the commission stated that the choice of an actor to dub a voice should not be made on racial grounds, but should be based on the quality of a voice or the competence to do a job.[9] A small victory – some may say that it was too little, too late. Modestine was not the first one to denounce the racial discrimination that was commonly taking place in the French film industry. Actors from ethnic minorities routinely suffered such prejudices. Kechiche hated being confined to stereotypical roles by narrow-minded casting directors because of his North

African origin (in Lalanne 2007,[10] Morice 2007). The black comedian and voice talent Jacques Martial (who, as it happens, dubs mainly black actors, such as Denzel Washington, Wesley Snipes and Samuel L. Jackson) described having to learn what it meant to play a black character for a mainly white audience.[11] He referred to the CSA (Conseil Supérieur de l'Audiovisuel) to denounce the racist acts committed for years by the French channels that persisted in rejecting black actors for parts other than African or Caribbean archetypes.[12] The already-mentioned Maik Darah explained that she would have loved to play leading roles in films, but that it never happened because 'we do not exist in the French repertoire'.[13] More recently, Omar Sy, a popular French actor of Senegalese origin, played a main part in a blockbuster (*The Intouchables* 2011) that was accused by an American journalist of displaying 'the kind of Uncle Tom racism one hopes has permanently exited American screens' (Weissberg 2011). If the French filmmakers were stunned by the vituperative review, Omar Sy seemed aware of the existence of ethnic stereotyping in the French film industry, as he mentioned in the press that he did not want to be the next fashionable black actor (Carrière 2012), and said that he felt a responsibility not to fall into the usual suburban stereotypes (Odicino 2011). These varied testimonies show that the media displays of race often function as a genre, and Hall (1997: 15) argues that 'the very obviousness of the visibility of race is what persuades me that it functions because it is signifying something; it is a text, which we can read'. Black voices have been commodified for the needs of a market that is mainly ruled by ideologies of white hegemony, according to which concepts of race are linked to narratives of norm vs. difference/deviance:

> [P]opular culture, commodified and stereotyped as it often is, is not at all, as we sometimes think of it, the arena where we find who we really are, the truth of our experience. It is an arena that is *profoundly* mythic. It is a theatre of popular desires, a theatre of popular fantasies. It is where we discover and play with the identifications of ourselves, where we are imagined, where we are represented, not only to audiences out there who do not get the message, but to ourselves for the first time.
>
> Hall 1996: 474

4.2 Commodification of ethnic voices on a mainly white market

In the history of performances, performances of ethnic voices were often promoted according to linguistic ideologies of deviance from a norm, exoticization of difference.[14] Time has passed since the early depictions of race in films[15] and the heyday of Orientalism when Arabs were depicted as exotic but also as backward, uncivilized and at times dangerous (Said 1978); however, testimonies of actors and directors, such as those quoted above, indicate that the matter of media representations of race cannot be buried. Indeed, one may want to study carefully the evolution of these representations since the time when the cultural theorists Stuart Hall and bell hooks warned against the commodification of black voices, in particular in rap music (hooks 1997, Hall 1996) and, as bell hooks put it, the 'white consumption of the dark Other' (hooks 1992: 30):

> Opening a magazine or book, turning on the television set, watching a film, or looking at photographs in public spaces, we are most likely to see images of black people that reinforce and reinscribe white supremacy. Those images may be constructed by white people who have not divested of racism, or by people of color/black people who may see the world through the lens of white supremacy – internalized racism.
>
> hooks 1992: 1

In the 1980s, French films seemed to give more visibility to black actors than they ever did before. In particular, Claire Denis' films gave major roles to French-African actor Isaac de Bankolé (*Chocolat* 1988) and French-Caribbean actor Alex Decas (*S'en fout la mort* 1990). In 1983, French-Caribbean filmmaker Euzhan Palcy's *Rue Case-Nègre* was awarded the César for Best First Film. These were the days of *SOS Racisme*, the French anti-racist NGO with its motto *Touche pas à mon pote* ('Hands off my buddy'), whose main goals were to fight racial discrimination and to give a voice to second-generation immigrants. However, one should also note that very soon the parts played by black actors in films were often restricted to stereotypical characters. For example, *Romuald and Juliette* (Serreau 1988), a light comedy and a big success of the period, was built around the interracial romance between Daniel Auteuil and Firmine Richard, a larger-than-life French-Caribbean woman with a strong accent who struggles between her night job as a cleaner and her daily occupation as a single-mom with five kids. After this golden age, black actors lost some of their visibility and in the 1990s, after having told the media how much black actors were confined to stigmatized parts ('when this character speaks, it is written [in the script] "The Black". He is not a human being, he is just a stereotype'[16] – Bankolé, in Dubois 2012: 117), Isaac de Bankolé left the country to pursue an American career. After *Romuald and Juliette*, Firmine Richard did not get another substantial part for the following twelve years. According to Dubois (2012: 111):

> The matter of the stereotypical parts reserved to the Black is not a fancy of the mind but it is well and truly real. To be convinced of it, it would suffice to read testimonies from actors themselves or to observe that for her second big role in movies (sort of her 'come-back') in Ozon's *Eight women*, Firmine Richard is given the part of a ... housekeeper.[17]
>
> Dubois 2012: 111

Richard's part may also appear to some viewers as a strong reminder of famous Hattie McDaniel's Mammy from *Gone with the Wind*, released in 1939. Closer to us and according to Dubois (2012: 112), Omar Sy's performance in *The Intouchables* presented all the usual black stereotypes rolled up in one role: the nanny, the thug and the fun guy.[18] It appears that, against the actor's wish to break with the common stereotypes, Omar Sy's Idrissa, the second-generation Senegalese from the projects, was yet another example of a commodified voice.

On a more optimistic note, one may note that hegemonic power may also give rise to resistance and standardized voices to alternative ones. If for Duchêne and Heller (2012), '[there are] complex ways in which older nationalist ideologies which invest language with value as a source of pride get bound up with newer neoliberal ideologies which invest language with value as a source of profit', voices that were commodified as a source of profit may be claimed by stigmatized minorities and become a source of profit ... and pride. Why are these new voices important? According to Hall (1990: 225): 'They are resources of resistance and identity, with which to confront the fragmented and pathological ways in which [the] experience [of the black/colonized/Caribbean] has been reconstructed within the dominant regimes of cinematic and visual representation of the West.'

However, with regards to African-French cinema, Darah (2007) taking the example of African-American professionals such as Whoopi Goldberg, has regretted the lack of black directors or producers in the French film industry.[19] And in an interview given at the Cannes Festival in 2011 where he was presenting his second film (in Pochon 2011), the French-Caribbean director Jean-Claude Flamand Barny went a step further by deploring a lack of black actors[20] – a surprising statement when one considers that a film directed in 2008 (*Aide-toi, le ciel t'aidera*, Dupeyron 2008) had an almost entirely black cast. However, in an article entitled 'French cinema: where are the Blacks?' (De Bruyn 2008), its producer, Michèle Halberstadt, remembers the obstacles that she encountered in her quest to fund the film:

> I heard everything: 'Black people don't interest anyone', 'I did my quota of films with ethnic minorities this year', 'this story is too frivolous for blacks' ... There

was a big problem because the project would not fit any box. It was not a stereotypical comedy such as *Black Mic-Mac* or an emotional drama. As if, with black characters, one had to stick to the wretched or the farcical.[21]

Halberstadt, in De Bruyn 2008

It is true to say that even today (apart from a few 'bankable' exceptions), black actors' presence on French screen is scarce. If a black French cinema is lacking, it is in the new wave of directors and actors of North African descent that one has to look for the reappropriation of ethnic voices from stigmatized groups.

4.3 Ethnic voices in French cinema: What voices in what films?

In 2005, Gaertner stated bluntly that quite often 'the Arabic character is the lazy employee whom is addressed with *tu* and that the hero does not hesitate to tell off harshly. If this tendency is on the decrease, examples are not lacking ... it would take too long to make the list of the productions that still use abundant colonial images'[22] (2005: 194). It is true to say that, for a while, French films often depicted two sorts of Arab characters: the bad guy, or the good guy who's perhaps a bit naive (an echo of the bipolar repertoires used for black characters: the nice if childish infantry man vs. the dangerous heathen[23] – Ndiaye 2008: chapter 4). However, there is no doubt that the cinematic representations of North African migrants have evolved since the 1980s and the heyday of *beur* cinema. From the end of the 1990s, with the release of films directed by North African-French filmmakers, Gaertner (2005: 199) notes the coexistence of two tendencies: the films that still make use of worn-out stereotypical Arabic characters (often in comedies)[24] and the films that offer a new visibility as well as new representations of North African second-generation immigrants. Since the first decade of this century, French actors of North African descent, such as Roschdy Zem, Sami Bouajila, Sami Naceri, Jamel Debbouze, and, more recently, actresses such as Hafsia Herzi, Leïla Bekhti, Sabrina Ouazani or the Belgian Lubna Azabal, have taken centre stage and been seen in French films as well as North African cinema. Contemporary films present more complex characters as well as more varied linguistic practices. For example, *Inch'Allah Dimanche* (Benguigui 2001) offers dialogue in French and in Algerian Arabic, as well as instances of code-switching between the two (Planchenault 2010), and a famous scene of *The Secret of the Grain* (Kechiche 2007) shows a family meal where characters from different origins (the family is from Tunisia and the son-in-law is French) switch between French and Arabic. If films that depict the life in France and challenges of North African ageing immigrants and their children, such as the recent *Cheba Louisa* (Charpiat 2013) and *Né quelque part* (Hamidi 2013), are released at regular intervals, one would be right to question why ethnic voices are still relatively rare in mainstream cinema. But first of all, one will need to ask, following Stuart Hall: 'Who is this emergent, new subject of the cinema? From where does he/she speak?' (1990: 222).

Most of the North African-French directors of this new wave have grown up in working-class, ethnically diverse neighbourhoods (housing projects situated in the suburbs of big cities such as Nice, Lille or Paris). For this reason, spectators may be under the impression that the directors' first intention is to bear witness to a social reality that they have experienced. Some of them do claim such a responsibility. For example, in a television interview (2008), Kechiche argues that to represent diversity in films is a positive and necessary action, because this population is most often underrepresented in films.[25] In the same tone, the director of *Dernier Maquis* (2008), Ameur-Zaïmeche, said: '[Films] are studies for me. They are an extension of the studies I did in sociology at university. We keep on searching, deconstructing social facts, structures of domination, exploitation, what is the most revolting and that we want to denounce in each of our films'[26] (in Pasquier 2008). Both statements highlight the directors' political commitments. These directors and their actors also declared a desire to depart from commonly held stereotypes, such as those affecting the representations of North African women in films:

> The female characters were inspired by the women I know and I love: my mother, my sisters ... But there is also the will to show them differently than the idea that one has in France of the Arabic woman ... I wanted to break this representation that I find a bit oppressive.
>
> Kechiche, in Lalanne and Fevret 2007[27]

> When I see some films where the Maghrebi woman has no sexuality, sensuality, or body, it annoys me.
>
> Herzi 2007[28]

In order to break with the traditional representations of female migrants who can hardly express themselves in French, and to provide new representations of individuals that were often silent (if not silenced), North African-French directors have constructed stronger and more *audible* voices. With this objective in mind, some of them have chosen to downplay the foreign language as well as the non-native accent. For example, in *Inch'Allah Dimanche* (2001), Zouina, the main character, speaks little Arabic and when she speaks in French, it is with a near-native accent (Planchenault 2010). For some actors and directors, this willingness to go against stereotypes means distantiating themselves from the old-fashioned stylizations and having characters speak unaccented French. However, one should also consider the fact that actors who are second-generation migrants may not have an accent,[29] or would have worked to erase it.[30] This is particularly true when an ethnic accent may be confused with a social origin and consequently becomes a source of discrimination. Some directors and actors who grew up in the projects of major French cities want to escape the stigma attached to their origins. For example, Debbouze (2011) admitted having been ashamed of his curly hair and having dreamt of owning the mane of the (presumably white) men who pose for shampoo bottles (in Ferenczi 2011). Other artists confided in sharing such feelings:

> I had a complex because of my social origin. I was hiding myself, shutting out myself by fear to be excluded by others. I grew up confined in my neighborhood, my mental ghetto; we were telling ourselves that the rest wasn't for us.... My profession taught me to accept myself.[31]
>
> Bouajila, in Mairesse 2010

> I became a filmmaker with the fear to be caught by my social status. I have to provide more efforts to acquire my freedom as an artist.[32]
>
> Kechiche, in Morice 2007

In the same way that some artists had refused the label *beur* or to be told that they were making *beur* films, today's North African-French directors do not want to be confined to one type of cinema. Since his first features, Kechiche has been working on a variety of subjects (slavery in *Black Venus*, 2010; female homosexuality in *Blue is the Warmest Colour*, 2013) that, albeit related to matters of race and social origins, do not focus primarily on working-class immigrants from the suburbs.

Going back to the presence of ethnic voices in films, I note that if some directors show a desire to break free from stereotypical voices, the traditional ethnic stylizations endure and serve unexpected functions. The study of a concrete example will allow me to explain this argument further. In the film *Né quelque part* (Hamidi 2013), I note three types of ethnic voices: Algerian-accented French (spoken by members of the family who live in Algeria), native French (spoken by the hero and his siblings, born and brought up in France) and stylized Algerian French. The exercise of stylization occurs in a single scene, at the beginning of the film, when the brother of the hero makes fun of their dad by mimicking his Arabic-accented French ([ʒi] [di][33] *travailler pour mes enfants*, [ʒi] [si] *pas là pour m'amuser* – 'I had to work for my children, I am not here to have fun'). In sketches performed by stand-up comedians (such as the previously mentioned Margaret Cho's skit, or Russell Peters' *How to become a Canadian citizen*), impersonating the non-native parent is an emblematic exercise. Demonstrated by British-born teenagers who perform the accented language of their immigrant parents (Rampton 1995, Saeed 2008), it is a way to deny affiliation and to 'display this desire to be like the dominant group, particularly because they go to such extremes to set themselves apart from the "other"' (Saeed 2008). I argue that cinematic performances of stylized languages allow second-generation migrants to distantiate themselves, while presenting the member of the older generation (i.e. the migrant) as an ethnic Other.[34] Therefore, the process of distantiation is to be found through two realizations: stylizations and accent-free performances. Hall (1990: 226–227) defined Caribbean identities as '"framed" by two axes or vectors, simultaneously operative: the vector of similarity and continuity; and the vector of difference and rupture ... one that is giving some grounding and continuity with the past, the second focusing on a profound discontinuity'. I argue that there are similar influences in the identity construction of the French second-generation migrants who may exacerbate their difference from the *Français de souche* when at the same time experiencing a feeling of disconnection from the land of their parents[35] (and maybe even more intensely with the wars and popular upheavals that have shaken Africa and Maghreb in the last decades). Actors from hyphenated cultures claim hybrid identities, but may also want to find roles that would not be defined by their ethnic characteristics – that is, they want to be visible, but they want their ethnic origin to be inconspicuous at the same time.

Throughout recent centuries, black people and Arabs have been represented in arts in opposite ways, and although Sub-Saharan Africans and North Africans experienced different histories of migration and lived different stories of integration in France (see Ndiaye 2008), they have also experienced similar discrimination. Their cases are treated in films through similar representations of a common social reality: the experience of the *black blanc beur* youth from the projects. In this vein, French-Caribbean director Jean-Claude Flamand Barny (in Pochon 2011), referring to a new wave of young filmmakers from the suburbs, argued that the 'new multicultural and urban generation' were more active and loud than the past generation of filmmakers from ethnic minorities[36] (note that the word multicultural makes no ethnic distinction). I argue that there is a very similar convergence in the choice to select a black actor in *The Intouchables* to play a character using the true story of Abdel Selou, a man of Algerian origin. The filmmakers explained that they wrote the part with Omar Sy in mind, as they had already worked with the actor of Senegalese origin, and most journalists saw no problem in this personal choice. However, it is also very probable that the French directors felt that since both individuals had been brought up in the projects by parents who were African migrants, being *black* or *beur* made no difference. However, Dubois (2012: 107–115) argues that, at a period when there is such an array of very good North African-French actors, the choice remains a surprising one. An Algerian news website (Soltane 2012) questioned the directors' intentions by asking whether the voice of an Algerian actor would have been less credible for the film.[37] Another argument developed in the sarcastic article written by French journalist Yannick Rolandeau is a reminder that one should not ignore the history of commodification of the black Other and the representations of the black body as an object whose main attractive features is strength and virility: 'The choice of a black man, obviously a good-looking one, well-built, and bowing and scraping (instead of the original character of the carer who was Algerian, the Algerians as one knows do not dance as well and are less humorous).'[38] To add another argument to these, I would like to question whether, at a time when actors of North African origin aim at constructing roles which are not ethnically defined, black remains the *visible* ethnic Other. According to Ndiaye (2008: 17), although black people in France remain invisible as a social category, they are always visible as individuals.

4.4 Conclusion

In this chapter, I have strived to demonstrate that performances of ethnic voices in films construct a genre whose practice contributes to maintain politics of ethnic difference. According to Taguieff's argument (1988: 29–48), there is a tension in racist as well as anti-racist discourses between two poles: heterophobia (which rejects the difference) and heterophilia (which exacerbates it). As a result, practices of ethnic voices hinge on such tendencies by contrasting or conforming to the linguistic norm and presenting voices that are at turns accented and accent-free. I also discussed the extent to which ethnic voices are reclaimed by discriminated communities – questioning the leeway between artistic agency and the necessity to fulfil an audience's expectations. While some actors from discriminated visible minorities claim that they are free to be/perform their own hybrid identity (such as Omar Sy, who affirms that he picks what he likes from the French and African cultures,[39] in Odicino 2011), others have acknowledged that hegemonic discourses of race maintain rigid ethnic archetypes in the film industry. Taking into account cultural change, and the active work and political commitment of French filmmakers of North African origin, one can be reminded of Hall's (1990: 225) words: 'Cultural identity, in this second sense, is a matter of "becoming" as well as of "being". It belongs to the future as much as to the past. It is not something which already exists, transcending place, time, history and culture. Cultural identities come from somewhere, have histories. But, like everything which is historical, they undergo constant transformation.' This diachronic approach to cultural identities does not prevent the analyst from focusing actively on current discourses of race. Dick and Wirtz (2011) argue that 'to examine racializing discourses is to confront a truth about race as a social imaginary in contexts where it is a significant form of social difference: it is unavoidable, all-pervading, even as we try to disengage from it. The circulation of even the most blatant stereotypes and slurs illustrates this pervasiveness'. Studying ethnic voices in films is a way to highlight the ideologies of race that are at play in very specific contexts, as well as to show that these ideologies may be negotiated between the diverse individuals involved in the production and consumption of such media products.

Part Two

Voices in French-accented English

As significant as the dialogue's words or syntax, performed accents play a crucial part in the meaning that is delivered during performances of voice. This meaning relates to attitudes and beliefs towards accents. When speaking in a second language, individuals are faced with two options: to sound or not to sound native. In the second case, the kind of foreign accent that they have may influence hearers' reception of their speech. However, one would be right to wonder, in Moyer's words (2013: i), whether a 'foreign accent [is] inevitably associated with stigma'. In the case of films, foreign accents are to be interpreted according to a specific context, and a particular accent will be received differently in a given media stage. But however familiar it may be to audiences, and as the following excerpt comically demonstrates, a foreign accent will nevertheless sound *strange* (i.e. different/marked):

– I'm French! Why do you think I've got this outrageous accent ...?
– ... What a strange person!

Monty Python and the Holy Grail, Gilliam and Jones 1975

In this second part of the book, I study performances of French-accented English in fiction (American films and British television) as well as bilingual practices on the Internet. More specifically, phonological, lexical and syntactic features, as well as instances of written code-switching, are analysed in order to demonstrate that these language displays (Eastman and Stein 1993) are fashioned for monolingual English-speaking audiences and that, similar to the performances in French studied in the first part of the book, they too index specific persons and/or signal ideologies of Frenchness as well as of linguistic otherness.

While focusing mainly on English-speaking countries (England, the United States and Canada), this part of the book intends to analyse the ideologies that relate to French culture, as well as to show how linguistic practices in French in these countries' media (films, TV and the Internet) contribute to maintain these ideologies. For this, I focus on performances that take place in different forms of media (films, cartoons, and websites) and show that they share common traits, symbols, linguistic practices and assumptions with regards to French culture and the values that came to be associated with it. The linguistic samples studied in the following chapters are instances of French taking place in discourses that are otherwise in English. They are words or short sentences in French that are often chosen for their *accessibility* to non-French speakers: 'Whether a word is a loan word, an internationalism, or a domesticated foreign word depends on a great number of factors ... Usage, spelling, phonology and other factors all combine to make a word more or less "foreign"' (Kelly-Holmes 2005: 14).

As well as foreign words in French, the following chapters will highlight other linguistic traces left on the English language to index personae and linguistic differentiation. I shall, for example, study a discursive genre that I call French-accented English and its varied forms: real or stylized, performed by native speakers of French or by British/American actors, with the goal of being as credible as possible or with the least preoccupation for realism. If performances of French-accented English are often encountered in films, such performed voices index values that do not only prevail there. Kelly-Holmes has argued that a 'French Linguistic fetish' (2005: 54) is firmly established in English-speaking countries, as one would find frequent occurrences of French words (what Kelly-Holmes calls 'domesticated words') in commercials that relate to cosmetics, food or cars.[1] In one case (2005: 55), she explains that an advertisement for French wine functions thanks to a combination of visual symbols (in her example, the picture of two lovers in a French café) as well as linguistic symbols (a few words in French used as a spectacular fragment and amplified by the accompanying text in the quoted slogan)[2] that depict France as romantic. Other commercials draw on varied values that relate to France and its culture, but all of these are restricted to a few domains: food and wine, women and fashion, arts and lifestyle. Among many examples collected throughout the years, let me quote a few:

> Oh la la Crème
> > *Danone*, 2000
>
> Le Sac Dress
> > *American Apparel*, 2007
>
> Le Antibacterial Spray
> > *Cif*, 2007

If these commercials combine visual symbols (the Danone commercial involves a British housewife dressed up as a French maid) and linguistic practices (emblematic words such as interjections, definite articles or rituals), a simple display of French language may summon associated values. As an example, in a 1996 cultish episode of *Dexter's Laboratory* (Cartoon Network), and without any further explanation or any intended display of charm from the young nerdy character, the only pronunciation of the few words in French – *Omelette du fromage* (grammatical mistake intended?) – is enough to make girls swoon. This fragment draws on emblematic values related to French culture (food, language and romance) that are so common to the American audience that they do not need much explanation. A search on 'what is French ...' on Google generated the automated responses based on the most common inquiries shown in Figure 1.

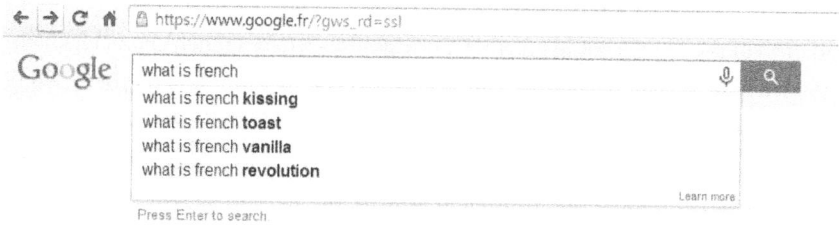

Figure 1 Google search on 'what is French ...'

There is, however, more to the representations of French culture in England and America than the otherwise positive stereotypes relating to romance, food and history.

In 2007, a *Time* magazine article entitled 'The death of French culture' (Morrison 2007) provoked the ire of France. French nationals (including a few ministers, intellectuals and artists), as well as Francophiles from around the world, went online to declare their indignation in the face of such an attack. More than the article's actual argument (i.e. the fact that after centuries of being considered as a world beacon for all things cultural and despite considerable state subventions, France had lost its prominence), what is interesting here is how the whole event (the article as well as the reactions it provoked) embodies the long love–hate relationship between France and the United States with regards to culture. If there is no doubt that the Americans have always had a strong esteem for French culture, the French attitude has also been a strong source of irritation.

In her study of accents in Walt Disney's cartoons, Lippi-Green (1997) quotes this portrait of French people as drawn by a manual whose aim is to teach actors about foreign dialects (Herman and Herman 1943: 143):

> Despite, or possibly because of, their civilized natures, the French people retain a childish eagerness for fun and frivolity as well as for knowledge. There is an impishness about many of them which is captivating. They are curious, like most children, and this curiosity leads them into experimenting with such things as piquant sauces for food... it can be said of the French... that when they are good, they are very, very good – but when they are bad, they are – Apaches.
> Herman and Herman 1943: 143

In this excerpt, the authors draw two opposite types: the French people are light and childish, yet deep and educated. Such negative associations can be found in current expressions such as 'Pardon my French' (reminding us of the emblematic rudeness of the French) or in recent American films where French characters have a tendency to put their wit and intellect to bad use.[3] In this vein, Ferber (2008) presented a list of the French stereotypes in the American media to undergraduate students for examination – a list from which I draw a selection, from the highly expected clichés to the most absurd and downright hilarious statements:

> The French are romantic ... The French think they are superior ... The French believe that if God lived on Earth, He would live in France; The French smell bad; French women do not shave; The French have a different idea of personal hygiene; The French have discussions without making decisions ... The French are temperamental ... The French have no respect for rules, procedures, or deadlines ... The French are artistic ... immoral ... All French know how to speak English, they just refuse to do so; French chefs are the best in the world; The French know proper etiquette better than other cultures; The French are ... are fashionable; The French eat sugary and rich foods constantly, yet remain slim; The French smoke and drink excessively.
> Ferber 2008

Based on this list as well as on my own studies (as presented in the next chapters), Table 1 presents a summary of the values attached to French culture and people, which are represented in the American media (note that, along with a few local specificities, similar values are found in the English as well as the Canadian media).

Table 1 Summary of the values attached to French culture and people in the American media

French culture	Authenticity; tradition; romance; arts; gastronomy; fashion
The French	(+) Passionate, sensual, hedonist, romantic, intellectuals and artists, elegant, proud
	(−) Arrogant, big mouth, quick-tempered, philanderer, inconstant
	Two types: – urban, intellectual, educated, cultured – rural, unsophisticated (wearing beret and baguette)

It has been said with a touch of sarcasm that French artistic endeavours that succeeded in America were either silent (Mime Marceau, Cousteau's silent sea world or the more recent *The Artist* – Hazanavicius 2011) or in English (Maurice Chevalier, or the more recent Daft Punk). However, this part of the book shows that French voices are commodified products of value in the film industry as well as in the restaurant industry.

Finally, the following chapters will bring to the forefront issues of *voice appropriation* (a part of what is known as 'cultural appropriation'), a topic that has occupied a prominent position in literary studies in Canada and North America since the 1990s, in particular with regard to books that portray aboriginal people but are not written by members of these communities. Most of the films studied in the book have avoided such controversies and accusations of lack of legitimacy or authority by overtly stylizing French voices in comedic and mystery genres. I will argue that these stylized voices nonetheless raise ethical issues by contributing to the beliefs that the ventriloquized communities are voiceless and not able to speak for themselves.

5

Performances of French-accented English in Hollywood Films

In the *Lion King*'s (1994) sequence when the grown Simba is reunited with his childhood friend Nala, Timon the meerkat (voiced by the comedian Nathan Lane),[1] despairing of the fact that his friend looks so infatuated with the lioness, speaks-sings on the first notes of *Can you feel the love tonight* (John and Rice 1994):

> I can see what's happening, they don't have a clue, they'll fall in love and here's the bottom line: our trio's down to two. [Adopting a stylized French accent, in the style of Maurice Chevalier] *The sweet caress of twilight*, there's magic in the air! And with this romantic atmosphere, disaster's in the air.
>
> *The Lion King*, 1994

The display of French-accented English is remarkably short. In this case, in a fraction of second, the audience is required to select among the semantic associations attached to the use of a French accent in the media (and in films in particular), the few traits relevant to the scene: romance, love, seduction – a few values traditionally attached to what the Americans know as 'French lover'. Interestingly, there is no mention of anything French in the characters present in the scene or no real reason in the narrative that would explain why Timon suddenly expresses himself with a French accent. The reason for the switch lays in the American language ideologies that link French language with romance and romanticism. It is difficult to date precisely the origin of the myth but one reason behind this association may be found in the heydays of French actors in Hollywood such as Maurice Chevalier, Charles Boyer[2] or Louis Jourdan. But who among the 4- to 12-year-old children (Disney's main target audience) could associate the accented voice with actors whose careers date back to the 1930s and 1940s? If they are not able to do so, it is however probable that some of the young spectators are able (or are learning) to identify the performed voice as similar to previously heard voices for the reason that French stylizations are frequently displayed in the English-speaking media under the form of faked French accents or performed personae. For a start, French-accented voices have always been commonly heard in Disney's cartoons (*The Aristocats*, 1970; *The Beauty and the Beast*, 1991; *Ratatouille*, 2007; to name but a few) and Lippi-Green (1997: 98–100), in her seminal study of non-standard-English accents in Disney's films, dedicates a whole section to the phenomenon under the evocative title 'Francophilia Limited'. The use of a French accent in English-speaking films comes with an array of connotations. For example, American audiences are familiar with the male depiction of the French *bon vivant* who loves good food, red wine and pretty women. In this chapter, I analyse the phonological salient features of such performances and study the processes by which French-accented voices are marked alongside standard American or British voices, and therefore enregistered. I finally show that the stylized French accent is a commodified genre that can henceforth be performed, especially in comedies, without the least preoccupation for realism (Steve Martin's performance in the 2006 opus of the *Pink Panther* is an example of such practices).

5.1 Characters speaking French-accented English in Hollywood films: Types and linguistic practices

French accents are not the only accent to be heard in American films as there is a long history of representations of the linguistic *Others* in films in general and in Hollywood films in particular. This history predates sound as silent films already made use of eye dialects to transcribe non-standard varieties of English (see note 15 in chapter 4). In the last decades, numerous academic studies have been published on the subject of accented English in films and popular culture (sometimes defined as stylized and mock languages). They focus particularly on performances of Native American English (*Hollywood Injun English* – Churchill 1998, Meek 2006, Buscombe 2013), Spanish English (*mock Spanish* – Hill 1993, 1995), African American English (*Hollywood AAE, mock Ebonics* – Bucholtz 2011, Bucholtz and Lopez 2011), or Asian English (i.e. *mock Asian* or *yellow English* – see Yuen 2004, Chun 2009, Chung 2013). In films, these stereotypical accented varieties of English are always used as tools of differentiation (i.e. 'they are not like us') but carry negative as well as positive values. As was the case in the depictions of North African and African characters (see chapter 4), they function on binary systems of opposition which are built around simplistic dichotomic representations (e.g. the 'dragon lady/lotus blossom dichotomy' of the Asian female characters – Reyes

2009: 44 – and the 'below-human', incomprehensible and kind of dumb vs. the really bright/'super human' Asian male – Yuen 2004: 254). Most of these studies demonstrate that these representations actually reflect more on the society that produce them than on the linguistic communities that they portray. Moreover, these studies generally focus on stigmatized groups and visible minorities, but not as much on other less stigmatized groups. Other studies (such as Lippi-Green's 1997 chapter) that analyse film renderings of such accents or ways of speaking English do so from a more general perspective to demonstrate how the concept of race governs the characterization of non-white/foreign characters. And more recently, Bleichenbacher's book also chooses to deal with multilingualism and linguicism (i.e. linguistic discrimination) in Hollywood films without dedicating more space to one language or culture over another. By focusing on French, I intend to show that seemingly innocuous (i.e. not obviously racist) linguistic practices may also participate in practices of linguistic differentiation.

5.1.1 Types of French characters

The characters who speak French-accented English in American films present different levels of connection with French nationality and culture, as well as different levels of authenticity with regards to this connection (i.e. authenticity may be minimal in the case of performances played by well-known American actors, questioning the extent spectators are willing to go with regards to suspension of disbelief). They express their *Frenchness* through varied use of the French language (accent, syntactic calques or lexicon) and affiliate with French characteristics or *essence* to varied degrees. The eighteen films selected for the data set involve the use of French-accented English. These films vary in genres and release dates (although most of the selected films are from the 1990s to the 2000s) but share similar linguistic and semiotic features in their representations of French characters. The following list provides an overview of these types of characters:

I. **The character is French. There are two case scenarios:**

   i. The character is played by a French actor
      E.g. Gerard Depardieu's Georges in *Green Card* (1990), Juliette Binoche's Vianne Rocher in *Chocolat* (2000), Lambert Wilson's Merovingian in *Matrix Reloaded* (2003), Audrey Tautou's Sophie Neveu in *The Da Vinci Code* (2006), Vincent Cassel's François Toulour in *Ocean's Thirteen* (2007), Jean Dujardin's Jean-Jacques Saurel in *The Wolf of Wall Street* (2013).

ii. The character is played by an English actor
E.g. Peter Sellers' and Steve Martin's Inspecteur Clouseau in the earlier and later film series of *the Pink Panther* (1976, 1978, 1982–2006, 2009), Bronson Pinchot's Serge in *Beverly Hills Cop* (1984), Patrick Stewart's Jean-Luc Picard in *Star Trek* (1987), Kevin Kline's Luke in *French Kiss* (1995), Frances McDormand's Chantel DuBois in *Madagascar 3* (2012).

II. **The character is not a French national, but has French as an L1**
E.g. Vincent Cassel's Monsieur Hood in *Shrek* (2001).[3]

III. **The character is not French, but pretends to speak French and imitates/stylizes a French person**
E.g. Bill Murray in *Groundhog Day* (1993).

IV. **There is no connection to French nationality or culture in the story** and nothing is said about why the switch to a French voice is made (the accent's interpretation relies mainly on spectators' familiarity with the cinematic genre):
E.g. Nathan Lane's Timon in *The Lion King* (1994).

In this corpus, actors and actresses perform a wide range of French accents (in leading and supporting roles, bit parts or cameos): from realistic slight foreign accents to heavily stylized French-accented English (that I shall later call French-stylized English or cod-French accents).[4] Note, however, that in the case of French actors and actresses it remains difficult to appreciate fully whether a French accent is emphasized or if one would naturally speak that way. For English actors, apart from the rare cases where there is no attempt whatsoever to perform a French accent (Patrick Stewart in *Star Trek*), performances often lean on the heavily stylized accent. Most of the listed movies are comedies, romantic comedies or action-comedies. In other films, the French characters present comic features or, at the very least, the particular moment when they display a French-accented English is meant to be light-hearted. Irrespective of the intensity of the accent, these performances present similarities in their indexical field ('stereotypical rude, romantic, seductive, and artistic French men and women' – Ferber 2008) as well as in the way they are realized (i.e. in their use of salient linguistic features).

5.1.2 French characters' general features

Why dedicate a whole section on dramatic features in a chapter that is mainly about language? When actors and actresses prepare for a part, they often work on where their character *is coming from*, who he or she is (his or her identity, personality, mood, etc.): they *envisage* him or her (from the French that literally means 'to put a face on'). At the same time, they give a voice to this character or *envoice* him or her (this is even more noticeable with animation where it is literally the case and where animated characters are given a voice),[5] as the work that is done on a character's speech is rooted in the work that is done on the character's dramatic features. Moreover, for many, French language is intricately attached to French culture and identity. Speaking French (or speaking English with a French accent) goes hand in hand with a specific Gallic demeanour and poise: an attitude to life that is perceived as quintessentially French. In this way, a manual for American actors (Blumenfeld 2002) opens the chapter dedicated to French accents with a whole paragraph on literature and drinking coffee as a way of life. Despite – or because of – this, 'the domain of life for things French is narrow' (Lippi-Green 1997: 100) and the professions occupied by French characters in films are limited: these often have to do with food or wine (cooks, chefs or waiters), arts (composers or art dealers) or are one side or the other of the law (small crooks, bandits, evil masterminds, *inspecteurs*, *capitaines* or police cryptographers). Other dramatic features vary according to the sex of the character.

5.1.2.1 *Male parts*

According to Lippi-Green's (1997: 100) study of French characters in Disney's cartoons: 'If a personality is established at all, there are two basic personality types available to them: irascible (the chef in *The Little Mermaid*, and his counterpart in *The Aristocats*); and the sensual rascal.' In the latter case, the tendency to depict Frenchmen as womanizers predates *The Aristocats*' (1970) alley cat, as the well-known Looney Tunes' character, Pepe Le Pew (created in 1945),[6] was itself inspired by Charles Boyer's seductive Pepe le Moko (*Algiers*, 1938). As an example, Pepe Le Pew's pick-up line from the 1954 cartoon *The Cat's Bah* refers directly to a famous quote from the pre-war film: '*You do not have to come with me to the Casbah*, we are already here, so *mon chéri*, we can do away without all preliminaries and make love right away, we can spend the rest of our lives making love' (my emphasis).[7] This anecdote is a clear example of how the discursive tradition of the Frenchman as a philanderer has been carried over from film to film throughout the years.

But French men as displayed by American films not only love women, they have the know-how to seduce them (or, as Lippi-Green puts it, 'a special talent for light-hearted sexual bantering' – 1997: 100). Indeed it seems that just speaking French is enough to have women melt, especially when the right words are being said. In this way, French language in films is found associated with art and seduction. For example, in the two following films, male characters recite poetry in French in order to seduce the educated female lead-roles played by Andie MacDowell. In *Green Card* (1990), Georges (Gérard Depardieu) recites a poem that he just made up and gets the enthralled attention of a public of snobs. In *Groundhog Day* (1993), Phil (Bill Murray) pretends that he studied nineteenth-century French poetry in college and recites: '*La fille que j'aimera sera comme un vin qui se bonifiera un peu chaque matin*' (a line which is actually from a Jacques Brel song and is not very romantic at all). Note that in both cases directors take an ironical standpoint on the stereotype that links French language to refinement and romanticism. *Green Card* makes fun of the snobbishness of upper-class Americans who delight in the reading of a poem, which content is ludicrous, merely for the fact that it is in French.

Another specificity of the French men as portrayed in Hollywood films is a stylishness that is generally excessive and may sometimes verge on mannerism (Merovingian in *Matrix Reloaded*) or rigid sophistication (Inspecteur Clouseau, of course). In relation to this, French characters' masculinity is often out of the norm: by lack of it (i.e. effeminate characters such as Serge in *Beverly Hills' Cop*) or an excess of it (in the case of womanizers). Conversely, excess of masculinity may also be represented as a form of crudeness and through other sorts of excesses: 'You snore and your manners are atrocious' says Bronte about Georges (*Green Card*, 1990) and Kate describes Luc as 'hygiene-deficient' and 'nicotine-saturated' (*French Kiss*, 1995). It is interesting to note that excess of manners (i.e. the Frenchman seen as the epitome of gallantry) may easily shift towards a complete absence of them. This draws the binary system of French characterization of which many American spectators came to be accustomed to: refined if rigid vs. sensual but coarse. This dichotomy is linked to symbolic linguistic practices, to which I shall return in the next section. Note also that rudeness, though often represented as more typical of the French male behaviour, may also be displayed by French women, as when Colette abruptly interrupts Linguini's interview (*Ratatouille*, 2007) with this line: 'We hate to be rude but we're French'.

A final comment should be added on the names that are often chosen for the French male characters. *Serge, Georges, Luc, Jean-Luc, Jacques, François* are all but very traditional French names, if somewhat old-fashioned. They are also unmistakably French for their use of sounds that are typically French (/r/, /y/, nasal vowels, etc.).

5.1.2.2 Female parts

French women in American films are often sophisticated and alluring, if not ingénue. One thinks of the days of Leslie Caron in Hollywood (Lise in *An American in Paris* (Minnelli 1951) or *Gigi* – Minnelli 1958). The tradition seems to have lasted to these days with actresses such as Audrey Tautou, Juliette Binoche or Marion Cotillard (a few examples among the French actresses popular in Hollywood). The characters that they play are often impulsive, excessively sincere and uncompromising. They are also quite intense, in temper as well as in the way they speak (too loud and too much – Julie Delpy's Céline in Richard Linklater's trilogy *Before Sunrise / Before Sunset / Before Midnight* is a perfect example of this). Despite this intensity, French actresses generally present lighter accents, especially when they are in the lead roles (would that be due to the popular belief that, unlike men, strong accents are not sexy for women? Compare, for example, Depardieu in *Green Card* and Juliette Binoche in *Chocolat*).

If male and female characters have accents that vary in intensity, the linguistic features that they display present similarities. These features are described in the following section.

5.1.3 French characters' linguistic features

This is how the stand-up comedian and voice talent Janeane Garofalo explains the formation of Colette's accent (*Ratatouille*, 2007):

> I had a CD of a French gentleman speaking English. And then I lost it. And then I watched CNN International. There's a French anchor who speaks English ... so I just mimicked some of the things that he was doing, not pluralizing certain things. I would think of the word 'ce-re-mony' instead of 'ceremony'. ... But I didn't take French in high school or anything, so I was sort of flying blind and hoping for the best.
>
> Garofalo 2007[8]

Finding such voice can be a long process. Some of the best testimonies on this process come from the British actor David Suchet who explained a few times how he worked on Poirot's accent (see note 2 in chapter 6 as well as other television interviews).[9] However, not every actor improvises his or her own way of speaking French-accented English or work for months on developing an accented voice. Numerous books on the market are aimed at actors who would like to perform the most convincing accent as possible. These books often have a separate section on French accents. A relatively recent edition of the already mentioned Herman and Herman (1997) dedicates more than twenty pages to the subject in a chapter entitled 'The French dialect' (understand 'the French accent'), which opens with these lines:

> The French language is spoken in a pitch that is the highest of all the Romance languages. Italian and Spanish both have the same excitable quality which makes the voice shrill – but they possess certain other features which soften them ... The French use none of these softening features. Consequently, the French dialect is brisk and sharp and is spoken with almost staccato effect.
>
> Herman and Herman 1997: 123

For Herman and Herman (1997), a *dialect* is 'a sort of second language that has been superimposed on the natural American language of the actor' (p. 16), a genre that they describe as a set of rules (I shall come back to the numerous ones given by the writers for the French dialect). Table 2 presents my own study of the linguistic features displayed by characters who speak French-accented English in Hollywood films. Note that the list of linguistic features is not exhaustive and that some features are more emblematic than others and for this reason may be performed more frequently (i.e. some features are found in the English actors' performances more readily than in those of the French actors).

Table 2 The linguistic features of French-accented English

Description of features	Films and examples
Phonological features	
/r/ is pronounced /ʀ/ or /ʁ/ or /x/ or /w/	Ii. *Green Card; Da Vinci Code; Matrix Reloaded; The Wolf of Wall Street* Iii. *Pink Panther; Beverly Hill Cops; French Kiss; Ratatouille; Madagascar 3;* *Mark my words François, sinister forces are at work* (Inspecteur Clouseau, *Pink Panther* 1976) II. *Shrek* *How rude* [ʁud] *oh la la* (Monsieur Hood, *Shrek* 2001)
Interdental fricative /θ/ is pronounced /z/ or /s/	*She die in Africa ... killed by* [zi] *elephants* (Georges, *Green Card* 1990) *It was never about* [zi] *money, it was about* [zi] *lion!* (Chantel DuBois, *Madagascar 3* 2012) *We know nothing* [nosin], *you are now up to speed* (Inspecteur Clouseau, *Pink Panther* 2009)
/h/ is not pronounced	*'amburger* (Inspecteur Clouseau, *Pink Panther* 2006) *Still I'm 'ere, 'ow did this 'appen?* (Colette, *Ratatouille* 2007)

[u] is more rounded, emphasized	I'm the [zØ] 'usband, that's **who** [u]! (Georges, *Green Card* 1990)
/oʊ/ is pronounced /o/ or /ɔ/	*One moment* (Serge, *Beverly Hills Cop* 1984) *I would like to take a closer look at your bowls* [bȯlz] (Inspecteur Clouseau, *Pink Panther* 2006)
/ɒ/ is pronounced /ɔ/	*Bob!... Like* [bɔb] *Dylan!* (Luc, *French Kiss* 1995)
/ɪ/ and /iː/ become /i/ or /a/	*Do you have for me the* [meːsaːʒ] (Inspecteur Clouseau, *Pink Panther* 1982)
Words are pronounced phonetically	*Maybe you give me your* [naːm] (Serge, *Beverly Hills Cop*)
Stops' VOT are anticipated (no aspiration after the release of p, t, k)	*Please let me introduce myself* (Monsieur Hood, *Shrek* 2001)
Schwa is pronounced /ø/ or /œ/	*What exactly is this specific temperature?* (Inspecteur Clouseau, *Pink Panther* 1982) *I don't trust* [pipœl] (Georges, *Green Card* 1990) *Can't you see I'm a* [litœl] *busy?* (Monsieur Hood, *Shrek* 2001)
Insertion of /œ/ in past participles	*Until we meet again and the case is* [sɔlvœd] (Inspecteur Clouseau, *Pink Panther* 1975)
Word stress is moved to the last syllable of words	Very common especially in French actors' performances (*Green Card*, etc.)
The voice consonant at the end of a word is pronounced at the beginning of a following word that starts with a vowel	*This is a ba' d-idea* (Inspecteur Clouseau, *Pink Panther* 2009)
English words are pronounced in French or as their French cognate	*This is* **New York** (*Green Card* 1990) *The* **parallel** *bars. My* **speciality**. (*Pink Panther* 1976) *The soup was a* **révélation**, *a spicy yet subtle taste* **expérience** (*Ratatouille* 2007)

Syntactic/morphological features

Syntactic calques (transfer from L1)	*Him you really love, huh?* (Georges, *Green Card* 1990)
Syntactic incongruities (the interference is not due to L1 transfer)	*And Steven wanted to marriage you* (Georges, *Green Card* 1990)
Deletion of inflexion (conjugations – such as preterit –ed, third person –s, etc.)	A regular feature in Georges' speech (*Green Card* 1990) and in Colette's speech (*Ratatouille* 2007)

(*continued*)

Table 2 Continued

Description of features	Films and examples
Pragmatic features	
Register incongruities	*And what it's pertaining?* (Serge, *Beverly Hills Cop* 1984)
Characters break the maxim of quantity (i.e. they speak too much)	Merovingian (*Matrix Reloaded* 2003), Colette (*Ratatouille* 2007)
Lexical features	
Swear words	*Merde!* (Inspecteur Clouseau, *Pink Panther* 1982) *Merde!* (Jean-Luc Picard, *Star Trek* 1987) *J'en ai marre... merde!* (Luc, *French Kiss* 1995) *Nom de Dieu de putain de bordel de merde*, etc. (Merovingian, *Matrix Reloaded* 2003) *Oh les petits fils de pute!* (François Toulour, *Ocean's Thirteen* 2007)
Interjections	*Oh la la* (Monsieur Hood, *Shrek* 2001) *Nan! You listen.* (*Ratatouille* 2007)
Spectacular fragments	*Coïncidence, exactement.* (*Green Card* 1990) *When are you coming, chérie?* (*Green Card* 1990) *Be still, mon chéri* (Monsieur Hood, *Shrek* 2001) *Do you speak French? – Oui!* (Phil, *Groundhog Day* 1993) *You are one of us now, oui?* (*Ratatouille* 2007) *Ça dépend, oui* (Jean-Jacques Saurel, *The Wolf of Wall Street* 2013) *Ouh la mer... bon! Voilà he's clean* (Jacques the Shrimp, *Finding Nemo* 2003) *Vive la France!* (Chantel DuBois, *Madagascar 3*, 2012)

Most often these features are combined, as this short excerpt from Vincent Cassel's performance (Monsieur Hood, *Shrek* 2001) shows:

Be still, **mon chéri***, for* **I am** [fɔ' ʁa jam] *your saviour* [sevjœːːʁ] ...

Can't [kãt] *you see I'm a little* [litœl] **busy** [bizi] *here* ...

Of course how [a] *rude* [ʁud] **oh la la***, please let me introduce* [intʁodus] *myself*, etc.

Table 2 presents a selective overview of the possible linguistic variants adopted by actors in their performance of French-accented English. Blumenfeld (2002), however, gives six basic rules that should guide the actors' work (last-syllable stress; uvular /r/; raised tongue /l/; dropped /h/; softer consonants; *th* pronounced as /z/, /s/ or /d/): Herman and Herman's (1997) manual lists no less than thirty-one rules for vowels (pp. 125–134), twenty-three for consonants (pp. 135–138) as well as a whole section dedicated to 'the French glide' (pp. 139–140).

Among the phonological features common to most performances of French-accented English, some are more emblematic than others and the uvular /r/ is certainly one of these (often considered by students of French as a second language as the cornerstone of a good French accent). It seems that this phonological feature alone would suffice to epitomize the French sound. The elision of /h/ and the pronunciation of /th/ as /z/ are two other examples of such emblematic features. For Herman and Herman (1997: 137), '[actors] merely have to say "zee man ovair zair", and presto chango, they have become Gaston Duval'. But the authors also warn against overdoing it (as 'too much seasoning in a good French soup can spoil the effect' – Herman and Herman 1997:138). They note the possible variations that make accented speech sound more natural and comment that /th/ may also be pronounced as /d/ and that /h/'s are not always dropped but may sometimes be produced with much emphasis. Herman and Herman (1997) describe the resulting accent as 'sharp', French sounds should be treated more 'clearly' or 'cleanly', produced with 'tensed lips' or lips which are more pursed or more retracted. If Blumenfeld (2002) also notes that lips should be slightly more forward, corners of the mouth more taut,[10] his five categories (from slight to very heavy accent) have the merit to allow for more variability. One should note that if most English actors tend to stylize 'heavy' French accents, in recent films, French actresses have been heard to adopt lighter accents.

As for the presence of French words in scripts that are for the most part in English, Bleichenbacher's (2008: 24) taxonomy makes a difference between a mere evocation (by the use of an accent, instances of code-switching and other sorts of interferences such as syntactic or structural calques) and the actual presence of the language (i.e. when it is spoken for more than a few words or a few lines). The latter case is rare in Hollywood films. In our corpus, a couple of exceptions were found in a scene in *Green Card* when Gerard Depardieu recites a poem that he created and that is synchronously translated by a character in the scene, and in a scene in *Madagascar 3* when Chantel DuBois sings Edith Piaf's song *Je ne regrette rien*. These may be explained by the fact that both cases are instances of artistic work and that the tolerance of an American audience for foreign linguistic material would be greater when presented in such contexts. Apart from these exceptions, I argue that for most cases, films do not present cases of code-switching (i.e. natural occurrences of French in the discourse of a person who speaks both languages), but *spectacular fragments* (Rampton 1999: 423) that frame sentences in English. These are words (terms of address, salutations, swearwords or cognates) that are familiar to American audiences and whose use would not impede a full comprehension of the actors' lines. Herman and Herman (1997: 142–143) list thirteen typical expressions and interjections (*eh!; eh bien!; zut!; oui!; non!; n'est-ce pas; chéri, chérie; chic; c'est la vie; bien!; madame; mademoiselle; monsieur*). Some of these words (such as *oui* or *chéri*) were found in our corpus and are among the favoured spectacular fragments in French that one finds in American films. One should add *voilà, oh la la* and, in order to modernize the list, a few swearwords such as *merde*. Note, however, that swearwords are not always used appropriately and would sound pragmatically incongruous to a native French speaker. This is the case in a hilarious video from YouTube[11] which documents the dubbing in French of a few lines of dialogue from *Star Trek* (1987). A line of the original dialogue, in which the captain Jean-Luc Picard mumbles a bothered *Merde*, is not translated with the French swearword but dubbed with 'C'est pas vrai!' ('That's not possible'). This example shows that, more than for their meaning or pragmatic function, spectacular fragments are used for their symbolic function. This is made possible by the fact that films constantly re-use semiotic resources that have been widely circulated in previous cultural texts.

5.2 The French-accented voice of Inspecteur Clouseau

Like other mock accents (Asian or Latino), the French-accented English displayed in Hollywood films is often an object of fun and ridicule, and the misunderstandings and confusions that it causes are sources of gags. In *French Kiss* (1995), Luke is unable to pronounce the name Bob and, in the *Pink Panther* films, the word *message* is pronounced as *massage* (*Pink Panther*, 1976), *bowls* as *balls* (*Pink Panther*, 2006), giving in the two latter cases a sexual innuendo that makes the scenes humorous. Note, however, that even if the French accent causes diegetic confusion (i.e. the characters who speak English as an L1 misunderstand what Luke and Inspecteur Clouseau are saying), most spectators are able to understand the words that the French characters are trying to pronounce as well as the pun that is intended with the words resulting from their mispronunciation (showing therefore that spectators are familiar with the rules followed in the performances of French-accented English). As I mentioned previously, pleasure comes not only from being able to understand the puns, but also from recognizing a well-known genre. Consequently, spectators may appraise performers' ability to play with emblematic features such as phonological traits or spectacular fragments. They may also judge the result as a success or a failure. For example, in the case of *Ratatouille* (2007), the performed accents were evaluated by some as more Italian than French.[12] Being able to perform accented varieties of English is not always the result of a competent application of the rules. Performers do not only choose among a variety of features, they are also given some leeway in repeating well-known linguistic features or creating new ones. For Bell and Gibson (2011: 561):

> Performers recontextualize cultural texts, with meaning emerging and being reworked in each new context, and *a constant tension between the pre-given and the new*. Culture can be seen as a kind of collective memory that exists through its re-reading, re-performance, and re-contextualization.
>
> Bell and Gibson 2011: 561, my emphasis

It is, however, a fine line between a performance that is original and a performance that is simply not recognizable. Indeed, Herman and Herman (1997) insist on the fact that '[i]t is the actor's job to communicate. If his speech is incomprehensible to his audience, his artistry is wasted' (p. 16). This is what makes the difference between the simple executor, the imitator of imitators, or the talented artist. This is also what makes the genius of the actor Peter Sellers, who was able to perform a dialect that was more his own than a realistic French idiolect: an idiosyncratic semi-lingua that was at the centre of cult scenes nearing Beckettian absurd. Clouseau's accent was Peter Sellers' creation (Walker 1982) and the British comedian explained that at first he did not spend much time creating an accent that he wanted to perform spontaneously:

> I thought that one of the things that some Frenchmen have is this sort of ostentatious virility. So I think Clouseau will have a nice moustache and I shall play him with great dignity because I feel that he thinks he is probably one of the greatest detectives in the world.
>
> Sellers, in Starr 1991: 89

However, for the second opus of the *Pink Panther* (*A Shot in the Dark*, 1964), Peters Sellers changed his accent:

> It is not pure French because you have to be careful with the French accent, apart from Maurice Chevalier's. I wanted to get some other sound. You'll find, if you look at the original Panther, that the sound changed for *A Shot in the Dark*, and

he started to say a word like 'bump' in a pursed way, similar to speech patterns based on the actual French language.

Sellers, in Starr 1991: 111

In the 1970s *Pink Panther* films, he performed this accent by using well-known rules (the pronunciation of /r/'s and /th/'s) as well as by following consistently a few rules that he created for the character, adopting a 'twisted French accent far removed from Clouseau's previous diction ... It was humorous exaggeration that eventually grew laborious and highlighted the film's cartoonish dimensions' (Starr 1991). By the end of the 1970s, Peter Sellers was taking more and more phonetic liberties in the creation of an accent that would remain his trademark. After the release of the last *Pink Panther* film in which appears an already very sick Peter Sellers[13] (*The Revenge of the Pink Panther*, 1978), a film reviewer wrote: 'Sellers has achieved a rich comic creation, down to the least quiver of the haughty Clouseau nostril. The ripeness of his accent in this new film almost defies phonetic reproduction' (*Saturday Review*, in Starr 1991: 202). And yet it is the very same rules that are taken on by Steve Martin in the 2000s *Pink Panther* films. Most characteristic is the treatment given to vowels:

Back vowels are given a front-pronunciation treatment (contributing without doubt to the stiff pursed-lips effect):

- 'o': pronounced /oʊ/ or /ɔ/ in American English, and which Herman and Herman (1997) suggest to pronounce /o/ in French dialect, is pronounced /œ/:[14]

  – *Does your dog* [dœg] *bite?* (*Pink Panther*, 1976)
  – *The phone* [fœn] *is ringing* (*Pink Panther*, 1976)
  – *This is chief inspecteur* Clouseau [klyzœ]*'s speaking on the phone* [fœːn] (*Pink Panther*, 1976)
  – *Inspecteur Jacques Clouseau* [klyzœ] (*Pink Panther*, 2006)

  Note how the exact same pronunciation of the name Clouseau (in 1976 and 2006) is performed with a thirty-year interval and by two different actors (Peter Sellers in the first one, Steve Martin in the second).

- 'oo', 'ou': pronounced /ʊ/ or /u/ in American English and which Herman and Herman (1997) suggest to pronounce /u/ with pursed and tensed lips, are pronounced as a cross between /ø/ and /y/:

  – *Do you have a room* [rym]? (*Pink Panther*, 1976)
  – *I would* [wyd] *like to buy a hamburger* (*Pink Panther*, 2006)
  – *It only looks* [lyks] *like a tape recorder* (*Pink Panther*, 2009)

– 'i' when pronounced /aj/ in American English and which Herman and Herman (1997) suggest to pronounce as /a+i/, is pronounced as /aː/

– *Does your dog bite* [baːt]? (*Pink Panther*, 1976)
– *I would like* [laːk] etc. (*Pink Panther*, 2006)

Even though these examples remain recognizable as performances of a French accent, they are also recognized as just so: *performances*. For this reason, there is little doubt that most spectators would know that this is not the kind of accent displayed *naturally* by French actors speaking in English. Spectators are not only aware of the fact that they are watching English-speaking actors who are pretending to be French, they also know that these actors are engaged in an act of parody. According to Bucholtz and Lopez (2011), performances of mock accents are processes of de-authentification because they are 'exposed to the viewing audience as false' (p. 685). Because of the fact that a performance 'deliberately misses the linguistic target' (2011: 685) – as it is, for example, the case in the famous scene of the *Pink Panther* (2006) where Steve Martin is simply incapable of pronouncing the word *hamburger*, the performance is viewed as a sham. However, if Clouseau's accent has often been described as ludicrous or idiosyncratic (for Blumenfeld, it is a 'hilarious fake French accent' –2002: 196), it is nevertheless recognizable as French. I personally believe that fake accents and the genre that they contribute to maintain have far-reaching influences. As I tried to demonstrate in the introductory chapter of this book, such performances are never created on a blank slate as nothing may ever be said that does not connect in one way or another to previous voices. The commonalities found between the linguistic features of French actors' performances and American comedians' stylizations bring to light their complex relationship with authenticity, especially when they are about performing linguistic otherness.

Hollywood's commodification of French-accented voices surely benefits French actors and actresses who work in North America (including voice-over professionals). However, one would be right to ask who really benefits from commodification of accented voices. Going back to Bourdieu's argument on legitimate speakers (and the fact that it is them who have the power to set the rates on definite markets and to obtain the highest benefits for their productions), I would like to ask: who are the legitimate speakers on such markets? Are they the native French actors or rather the actors who can perform the required genre? The testimonies from Asian American actors in Hollywood could bring the beginning of a response. Very much like African actors in France (see chapter 4), these claim that they are often asked to perform an accent that is closer to what producers expect rather than the one that they know to be realistic (let alone the one that they would naturally perform – Yuen 2004, Chung 2013). But actors have to work and even though 'there's always this moral side battling with the artistic side' as the actress Ann (quoted in Yuen 2004) confides, actors have no other choice but to accept to 'put on a verbal act' (Chung 2013: 175) and to perform yellow voices. Therefore, Chung (2013) notes the 'complicity of Asian and Asian American actors in the construction of Oriental imagery in the US popular culture'. I admit that I did not find such testimonies from French actors. However, considering the fact that 'L2 speakers often aspire to native standards of speech' (Dewaele and McCloskey 2014: 3)[15] and that most actors can access the services of a speech/accent coach, I would not be surprised to hear that some actors were chosen for their L1 accent, or were even encouraged to keep it.

Stereotypes are circulating resources (Reyes 2009) that can be used by different players and for Hill (2009: 85), if discriminated actors can *recruit* and *reshape* semiotic resources for pragmatic purposes, these resources are still articulated within a white-hegemonic framework and constrained by a racist world (Hill 2009).

Other examples that will confirm this argument, and the fact that French-accented English is merely an instrument among others in the process of linguistic differentiation, are the cases of French characters who speak English with an accent that is not French: Captain Haddock's Scottish accent in *Tintin* or Gavroche's cockney accent in *Les Misérables*. According to Bleichenbacher's taxonomy, both are cases of signalization (2008: 24): i.e. films where the characters do not use the L2 or give any hint about their real origin (such as a French accent or spectacular fragments), but where other linguistic hints of differentiation are given to audiences. Next to characters who speak English with a British accent (which is already a case of differentiation in an American market where British accents are often used to create distance – in time or in narration – in historical dramas and fairy tales movies), characters who speak English with an accent evoke difference.[16] In these cases, what is indexed is not Frenchness or French values; rather it is plain *otherness* (in terms of time, space, language or fictional format).

5.3 Conclusion

In this chapter, I studied a wide range of French-accented voices that, albeit varying in intensity, also presented important commonalities with regard to their form as well as to the cultural and dramatic values that they index. Next to voices that are heard as French actors and actresses' authentic voices, other voices present themselves as crafted exercises of stylizations. I have argued that the latter are practices of enregisterment (Agha 2005) and commodification. First of all, these parodies of accents belong to genres (*fake accents, stylized languages, mock languages,* etc.) that present the performed voices as unauthentic while (due to the long history of development of such genres) still indexing Frenchness and French associated values. Like any accented voice (see, for example, Yuen 2004 on Mock Asian English), there is an important economic factor in being able to rely on established genres. It allows precious time to be saved: not only for actors, but also for scriptwriters who can get around characterization quicker, and therefore for filmmakers and the studios that can save minutes of the film if they can rely on the fact that such assumptions are shared by audiences. As Lippi-Green (1997) argued, if the values that are associated with Frenchness are not all negative (there are no French criminals and no French harming any child in Disney's films), French characters generally do not occupy prestigious status. She concludes: 'The cultural stereotypes for specific national origin groups are perpetuated in a systematic way in these stories created for, and viewed primarily by children' (Lippi-Green 1997: 100). I would like to add that they are also viewed by adults. Politically, such practices are not innocuous as they participate in processes of differentiation and discriminations (Hill 1995). As Bourdieu reminds his readers in an article written on Kafka's Trial, 'The word *kathègoresthai*, from which derives our categories means to accuse publicly'[17] (1984a: 268–270). Categorizing is also discriminating.

6

The Case of Poirot's Voice[1]

In the opening of a recent commercial for Heineken, a narrator displaying a cod-French accent, declares: 'You British have always struggled to the concept of killing what you eat.' What follows in this hilarious advertisement deals with gastronomy and adultery – themes traditionally linked by the British with the French. In order to evoke imagined continental values, this commercial uses complex layers of representation of the foreign language and culture for a mainly monolingual audience. According to Androutsopoulos (2007: 219), it is a matter of 'styling ethnic otherness for majority audiences'. French is not only present in advertisements but can be found on British TV and in English-speaking dramas under the form of favoured linguistic tokens or familiar excerpts from the foreign language. There are styles of discourse that are conceived, produced and released by the mass media in order to provoke a certain kind of reading or recognition (Rampton 1999). French words in the media are used as spectacular fragments of language (Rampton 1999) or tokens of French fetish (Kelly-Holmes 2005), stylization (Coupland 2001) and ethnosymbolism (Haarmann 1986) whose role is to convey specific values to the audience.

In this chapter, I would like to consider the way French language is used in the British media and how speakers of French are portrayed in fictions particularly. I shall argue that these personifications are meant for a supposedly monolingual audience and are not a re-enactment of a real linguistic behaviour. I shall then relate the staging of salient linguistic traits to folk linguistics, which deals with the beliefs that a speech community has about itself as well as about other speech communities and their ways of speaking. For this purpose I shall focus on a famous example of French stylization: Agatha Christie's character, Hercule Poirot. By analysing the detective's lines in an episode of the British televised adaptation Agatha Christie's *Poirot*, broadcast on the ITV channel, I propose to explain that representations of a foreign speaker's accent, code-switching and choice of lexical items and syntactic forms are accounts of bilingual behaviours according to monolinguals. In order to do this, I shall examine the number of

French words used throughout the film as well as their place amongst lines in English and their pragmatic functions. I shall then show that the French words used in the dialogue are forms of language display, and that their actual meaning is less important than the symbols they stand for. I shall finally argue that the recurring forms and idiosyncrasies of speech are meant to create a familiarity between the audience and the TV series, before concluding on the construction of foreignness that Poirot's dialogues embody.

6.1 Folk linguistics and stylized French English

Throughout the reading of this chapter, it is important to bear in mind that this study is based on fictional creations, dealing therefore with the authors' expectations of the audience's assumptions regarding speakers of English as a foreign language. In this kind of movie two levels of representation are intertwined: a representation of foreignness as well as a representation of the British audience and its beliefs.

Moreover, in the analysis of Hercule Poirot's speech, there will be two separate frames to consider:

- First frame: the audience is watching a character displaying typical traits of a French speaker of English as a Foreign Language.
- Second frame: film viewers are aware of the fact that this character is actually played by a British actor only pretending to be a Belgian person speaking in English.

I believe this performance deals with shared representations about the way the French use English language, therefore with folk linguistics.

6.1.1 Folk linguistics

According to Preston (2004), folk linguistics is a metalanguage; it is language about language. A member of a speech community engages in folk linguistics when he/she comments on the pronunciation, the choice of lexicon or the register of his/her own or another speech community. This comment can be either positive or negative but he/she does it consciously. The variety of comments ranges from very specific remarks on a particular person's single utterance to broad generalizations on dialects and languages such as 'Inuits have more than fifty words to speak about snow', 'French is the language of love', 'Italian is very melodious', etc. Folk linguistics seems to draw on a shared cultural knowledge about languages and different groups' linguistic identity. According to Kramsch (1998: 67): 'Group identity is not a natural fact, but a cultural perception ... What we perceive about a person's culture and language is what we have been conditioned by our culture to see.' Folk linguistics relates to a common awareness of what the *norm* is, an awareness of how a language should be spoken and how dialects deviate from this norm, as well as an awareness that other people can speak differently than one does. Houdebine-Gravaud (2002) speaks of 'imaginaire linguistique' to designate the speech of the everyday layman on languages, verbal behaviours and choices of registers. According to the concept of 'imaginaire linguistique', what people say about language is either an 'auto-evaluation' (speaking about their own dialect) or an 'allo-evaluation' (speaking about others' language).

If folk linguistics is to be found in the four forms described by Preston (2004: 88) as: 'What people say about: 1) what is said 2) how it is done 3) how they react to it 4) why they say what they say', then one can argue that analysing film dialogues would not allow access to what Bloomfield calls secondary responses to language (or 'utterances about language', 1944: 45). However, considering that these dialogues have been written with a specific audience in mind, the linguistic forms used by Poirot's character are a representation of their 'imaginaire linguistique', Frenchness styled for the British TV audience (or for what the creators of the series consider as a typically monolingual audience, which is disputable). For Meinhof (2004: 276), they are 'metadiscourses of foreignness' and 're-representations' or representations of representations. Developing the concept of 'Styling the other' within his 'Audience Design Framework', Bell (1999) introduced the term of 'referee design' to define situations when a media text focuses on an absent referee group by adopting a non-native accent rather than the present addressee, as is the case when Poirot imitates a French accent for a British audience. The form of speech that results is surely not representative of the way a Belgian would speak but it is representative of the expectations of a spectator listening to a French speaker of English as a Foreign Language. In a similar way that Rampton (1995) used the denomination 'Stylized Asian English' to refer to some forms of speech spoken by British youth, it seems one could speak in this case of stylized French English.

6.1.2 Stylized French English

The practice of stylization of French speakers of English as a Foreign Language has a long history in the English-speaking film industry. With regard to American cinema, different characters come to mind such as, for example, the famous Inspecteur Clouseau played by Peter Sellers in the different episodes of the *Pink Panther*. As for British television, one may remember the series *'Allo 'Allo!*, which played heavily with stylization of British, German and French characters. In these cases, the actors are typical performers of what is called a 'cod-French accent'. Their accent relies on highly symbolic phonological traits such as the pronunciation of r's in a trilled mode and th's as [z] or the non-pronunciation of h's in order to give the immediate impression of English as spoken by the French. The staged accent is immediately recognizable by the audience and there is an unquestionable pleasure in the identification of performed accents, the viewers 'rejoicing in [their] own semiotic competence' (Meinhof 2004: 277). Stylization is not only used in the performing arts; the telling of jokes with imitated accents (e.g. Belgian jokes for the French, Irish jokes for the British) is a very common and widely shared cultural script. The exercise relies on the Bakhtinian concept of *heteroglossia* or 'multiple voicing' as it introduces the speech of others in one's discourse. According to Coupland (2001: 345), 'stylization is the knowing deployment of culturally familiar styles and identities that are marked as deviating from those predictably associated with the current speaking context'. In Agatha Christie's *Poirot*, most of the characters are British or speak in English, and the fact that the detective is Belgian and a foreigner is regularly emphasized on a serious or humorous note.

Coupland (2001: 346) distinguishes stylization from styling as stylization deals with performance in a theatrical way: 'it brings into play stereotyped semiotic and ideological values associated with other groups.' The stylized French discourse has become a genre of its own with its own norms and codes of reading. For Coupland, stylization has a complex relation with authenticity – claiming to represent reality but being a blatant pastiche at the same time and hence a strong de-authentifier. It is artificial since the actors put on a voice. A cod-French accent is an obvious caricature. In the case of the British TV programme, even though the French accent of the actor playing Poirot is not so dramatically caricatured, viewers can trace David Suchet's assumed accent to what it stands for through the salience of a few traits distinguishing Poirot's speech from that of the other characters (in the pronunciation of French words as well as in his lines in English): guttural pronunciation of r's, non-aspirated voiceless consonants, voiced consonants' VOT closer to the French one and, in prosody, stress falling regularly on the last syllable of rhythmic groups. One has to admit that it gives a fair imitation of the hybrid accent of a foreigner. In a recent 'behind the scenes' interview, the actor David Suchet explained how he adopted what he called 'a voice' when rehearsing Poirot's character: 'That voice took me three months of really hard work and research to find, I mean now I can [*switching to Poirot's accent*] put it on almost immediately. But it was a difficult find.'² On the viewer's side, there is a complex system of readings and interpretations. It is true to say that the audience is not completely unaware of the fact that they are watching someone only pretending to be a French-speaking Belgian. However, in order for the suspension of disbelief to function, viewers are willing to relinquish this knowledge temporarily. A French accent can be enough to reinforce a French aesthetic in the media. For Meinhof (2004), French and French sonority came to signify sensuality and hedonism: 'The use of French or of French accentuated speech in perfumes and chocolate ads ... where the sounds of French simply set out to enhance the sensuous appeal of the product' (Meinhof 2004: 282). Other commercials like the ones for Stella Artois are mainly in French and do not bear any subtitle, a practice that Kelly-Holmes (2005: 186) calls '"language as soundtrack" approach'. It will be shown that the scriptwriters of Agatha Christie's *Poirot* use a similar device.

Finally, apart from speech, bodily gestures can be stylized and artificial. There is some mannerism in Poirot's behaviour but his attitude is an embodiment of his character: rigidity tinted with bonhomie. Some specific traits of the physique of the detective are overdrawn: i.e. the handlebar moustache that Poirot wears proudly and which acts as a synecdoche. Here in the same way r's and th's embody the French style, parts of the character such as a moustache, a walking style or a cane stand for a whole persona: a mix of arrogance and elegance, symbolizing a Gallic attitude.

6.2 French stylization in Hercule Poirot's *The Mystery of the Blue Train*

6.2.1 Data and method

Agatha Christie's screen adaptations of Hercule Poirot and Miss Marple are a much loved part of the British televisual landscape. I chose to work on ITV's adaptation of Agatha Christie's *Poirot* as it has been a huge popular success and quite a TV phenomenon (its viewings have been repeated on an ongoing basis for more than fifteen years and the series sold to more than a hundred countries throughout the world).

In the following analysis, I examine the use of French utterances and syntactic turns of Poirot's speech in one episode of the series entitled *The Mystery of the*

Blue Train and broadcast for the first time on UK's ITV channel on 11 December 2005. I chose this particular episode because of the fact that most of its action is set in France (the murder occurs in a train travelling between Calais and Nice). In this episode, the forms of code-switching in French are more prominent than in other episodes of the detective series. Here Poirot is not the only character using French and the other French-speaking characters use the local language in a similar fashion. In the analysis I first examine the number of French words used throughout the film as well as their place amongst lines in English and their pragmatic function, and then go on to look at specific syntactic forms used in the detective's speech. Excerpts 1 and 2 present typical examples of the film's dialogues:

(1) **Poirot and Katherine**

1 P: so you travel by what? The Blue Train?
2 K: yes I do. Tomorrow
3 P: so do I!
4 K: no?!
5 P: *mais oui*. Ah you know it is beyond measure delightful *mademoiselle* that I may have *en route* the pleasure of your company ... I shall be your avuncular
6 K: oh yes an avuncular. That's exactly what I need!
7 P: *alors papa Poirot* he is at your disposal

(2) **Poirot and Mr Kettering in the Police station**

1 Ket.: I knocked on Ruth's door and had a blazing row with her
2 P: *alors* you must celebrate order the *champagne*
3 Ket.: what are you talking about?
4 P: Mr Van Alden informed me that your wife she made no will *alors* you are richer by two million pounds your wife she dies intestate so the money it is yours *je vous félicite*

In these excerpts, French words are framing the text in English (for example, turns 5 and 7 in excerpt (1) and turn 3 in excerpt (2)). In the *Poirot* TV series, French is quasi-systematically placed next to sentences in English, in bilingual text. According to Coupland (2001), short excerpts from the foreign language act as a 'framing device', which means that linguistic tokens at the start or the end of a sentence are enough to refer to the linguistic and cultural identity of the language evoked. Monolingual texts in French are rare, short and mainly reserved to concise speech acts (e.g. *'Un cassis s'il vous plaît'*).³ Haarmann (1986) uses the terms 'impersonal bilingualism' and 'ethnosymbolism' to designate the use of foreign languages to symbolize other ethnic groups and their culture. In his study on the use of English and French words in Japanese commercials, he shows how some words like 'élégance' (for luxury cars), 'amour' (for lingerie) or complete sentences such as 'C'est magnifique!' came to be used for their particular connotations and the way they relate to the image conveyed of France, its fashion world and lifestyle. In a similar way, French words in *Poirot* are often related to the stereotypes commonly conveyed on French culture (gastronomy, romance and *savoir-vivre*).

6.2.2 French lexicon and code-switching into French

In the film *The Mystery of the Blue Train* (Andrews 2005), I counted 126 occurrences of French in the English dialogue (including thirty-two in the final scene). In a length of 1 hour 35 minutes, and taking into account the fact that Poirot is a very talkative character, it is a minimal presence. It is important to stress that in the film all the characters speak in English most of the time, even when they are French. For example, in one sequence where the characters are all native French speakers, the dialogue opens with Comte de La Roche stating to the Inspector and Poirot: '*Toujours aussi raffinée et douce, une femme bien élevée*' (a sentence which actually does not make any syntactic sense) but the sudden arrival of Mr. Kettering has Poirot say 'Continue but in English', an excuse to make the switch to English. In another sequence we have yet again two French speakers, the *Inspecteur* and Poirot, speaking in English to each other, but this time viewers are not given any logical reason for this linguistic behaviour. Finally it is interesting to note that most French characters are bilingual without any justification or reason as if it is a standard practice for anyone to speak fluent English (see also Petrucci 2008). The few tokens of bilingualism are a reflection of the supposed minimal knowledge of the audience in the foreign language. As I shall explain shortly, they use the symbolic function of the language rather than the referential one (Androutsopoulos 2007: 214).

Among these 126 occurrences of French, I counted seventy different words. There are in fact two possibilities regarding the viewers' reception of the French language: either they understand the linguistic tokens and feel flattered by their own linguistic competence (in this case a minimal bilingualism is enough),⁴ or they do not understand them and the sonorities of the French language serve mainly to create a local decor or a sound ambiance. In *The Mystery of the Blue*

Table 3 French words in *The Mystery of the Blue Train* (ITV adaptation, 2005)

Addresses	44
Names	11
Politeness markers and greetings	15
Pragmatic markers	26
Discursive markers	7
Qualifying terms (placed after a noun)	5
Locations	7
Swear word and interjection	2
Speech acts	4
Other linguistic tokens	5

Train, comprehension of the French words is often supported by visual context and pragmatic force of the utterance. This is why I decided to categorize the utterances according to their pragmatic functions in the dialogues (see Table 3).

Looking at Table 3, one will notice first the major use of addresses in French (e.g. *mademoiselle, mon ami*, etc.) as well as politeness markers (e.g. *merci, bonjour*, etc.). As mentioned previously, this is one of the defining personality traits of Poirot's character, and in the novel *The Mystery of the Blue Train*, published in 1928, Christie described Poirot as 'full of the Gallic politeness' (2003: 337).

The significance of the terms 'pragmatic markers' and 'discursive markers' is the following: Pragmatic markers such as '*hein*', '*c'est ça*' and '*d'accord*' in excerpts 3 and 4 play a role in the interaction; they occur in reaction to what the interlocutor has just said, or are cues to have the interlocutor react or participate.

(3) **Poirot and Dolores Valesi**

1 P: *Mais quel cauchemar*! The plan it fails **hein**? /Monsieur Kettering proves immune to her powerful charm because he has a secret that nobody knows ...
2 D: He loves his wife.
3 P: *C'est ça*!

(4) **Poirot, Dolores Valesi and Van Alden**

1 P: you had the desire the *passion nécessaire* to commit a crime of such atrocity *et ça c'est la vérité*!
2 D: nevertheless i did not do it
3 Va: finished with the lady Poirot? Feel like picking on someone your own size?

4 P: *d'accord*. The conduct of your daughter monsieur it humiliates you **hein**? Her *mariage catastrophique* her *liaison ridicule* with La Roche

In the film, pragmatic markers are often emphasized by prosodic features and specific gestures of the eyes or of the hands (for example, '*c'est ça!*' is accompanied by a pointing forefinger). On the other hand, discursive markers are used to organize the different sections of the discourse, such as '*alors*' in excerpt (5). It is most often found between two segments of Poirot's speech and serves to coordinate several parts of his argument.

(5) **Poirot**

1 P: Mr Van Alden informed me that your wife she made no will **alors** you are richer by two million pounds your wife she dies intestate so the money it is yours *je vous félicite*

In excerpt (4), one can note similarities in sound between English and French words that do not get visual redundancies in the film or do not have the sort of pragmatic force just mentioned (words like *nécessaire, catastrophique* and *ridicule*). In the same excerpt pronunciation was enough for an English word to become French (i.e. *the passion* pronounced [paːsjɔ̃]; *liaison* pronounced [liezɔ̃]). In a couple of cases however, lexical inventions have been noticed: *The compartement* (instead of the French '*compartiment*'), *The Rivière* (referring to the Riviera).

Kelly-Holmes (2005: 14) identifies different categories of lexical borrowings of foreign words and transferences, internationalisms or domesticated foreign words. Defining 'internationalisms' (2005: 61–2), she explains: 'a word or a phrase, which with minor spelling amendments is similar in a number of languages due either to a common root or origin or the fact that it is a new word that has been borrowed into a number of languages with only minor modification.' This could be the case for the qualifying terms or some of the other linguistic tokens (i.e. '*personne*' or '*passion*') in *Poirot*. But what about other words used by the scriptwriter like '*mademoiselle*', '*je vous en prie*' or '*s'il vous plaît*'? These words seem to be part of a global cultural knowledge of French; which would come along minimal lists of words known in foreign languages such as *hasta la vista* in Spanish, *ciao* in Italian or even *sushi* and *hara-kiri* in Japanese, most of them having to do with greetings, gastronomy or cultural oddities. This knowledge is widely shared throughout the world, with a few variations according to the relations maintained between the country displaying the foreign words and the country of origin, 'provid[ing] a paradigm within which a type of linguistic fetish operates' (Kelly-Holmes 2005: xi). With regard to Europe, there is certainly a commonly shared linguistic knowledge, or more precisely what Trim (2002) calls a 'European lexicon', even though connotations surrounding specific words may vary from one country to another. The French words found in international movies are recurrent 'language displays' (Eastman and Stein 1993) used in commercials or films making them 'entirely familiar and appropriately exotic' (Kelly-Holmes 2005: 62).

In *Poirot*, most of the French terms intervene in code-switching between French and English. I argue that popular media texts of this kind permit us to delve into the folk linguistics of code-switching and to understand how the general public might envisage such linguistic practices. A common description of code-switching portrays a confused bilingual, often with a weak competence in the second language, mixing codes or borrowing from the L1 when words in the L2 are missing. One can now question whether code-switching in *Poirot* is due to a weakness in the foreign language, to a lack of English vocabulary or to a communication breakdown. However, it is obvious to any viewer that Hercule Poirot is a fluent speaker of English. In his speech one notes intersentential switches,[5] such as excerpt (1) turn 5 ('*Mais oui!*'), excerpt (2) turn 4 ('*Je vous félicite*'), excerpt (3) turn 1 ('*Mais quel cauchemar!*') as well as intrasentential switches, such as excerpt (1) turn 7 ('*alors papa Poirot* he is at your disposal'), excerpt (2) turn 2 ('*alors* you must celebrate order the *champagne*') and excerpt (4) turn 1 ('you had the desire the *passion nécessaire* to commit a crime of such atrocity'). In the two last examples, it is interesting to note the use of English articles with nouns in French. Other similar examples have been found in Poirot's lines, such as 'her *mariage catastrophique*', 'a *cauchemar*' or 'this *mauvais moment*'. Those intersentential and intrasentential switches are common practices in bilingual speech. However, contrary to bilingual practices, the film's dialogues sometimes violate grammatical rules of the language. In the second turn of excerpt (6), the singular article *le* is used with the plural form of the noun:

(6) Poirot and Katherine in the Blue Train

1 K: where are we? It seems it keeps stopping and starting
2 P: at the moment we travel around Paris on the *ceinture le* suburbs

Referring to Myers-Scotton's *Markedness Model of Code-switching* (1988), it seems that Poirot does not make any unmarked choices of switching because he does not switch more with French speakers but uses as much English with them as he does with English speakers. So is it true to suggest that his choices of switching are all marked? For Myers-Scotton, this would mean they would be disruptive and would be used to increase or narrow a social distance or to exclude by using a language not known by all participants. However, this is not the case since in the beginning of the century many members of the aristocracy or the upper class (most of Poirot's characters) had a minimal French competence (elite bilingualism). Overall though, the linguistic behaviour of Poirot is not credible and it remains difficult to logically explain why the detective keeps on code-switching into French with non-French speakers when he seems to be fluent in English and persists with English when talking to French speakers. An interesting display of code-switching is found in the final scene where Poirot seems to use more French due possibly to loss of self-control. There is a crescendo in the movie for which the last scene appears to be the climax. All the characters are gathered in the Blue Train listening to Poirot's final revelations. One could relate this to a popular representation of code-switching and expression of emotions (for example, in films, foreign characters often code-switch into their L1 when swearing – unfortunately, even though this linguistic attitude is very common in the series, I noted only two examples in this particular episode).

(7) **Poirot, Dolores Valesi and Van Alden**

1 P: all this is the work of an *intelligence* formidable and it moves amongst us now. Sinora Valesi you are forty years of age so it is not unreasonable that you should wish that Mr Rufus Van Alden should formalise your relation which you could yet provide him with an heir ...
2 Va: look here god dammit!
3 P (raising his voice, imperious): *s'il vous plaît* this *mauvais moment* can only be prolonged by your interruption I advise against it / (calming down:) And yet he makes no move to do so ...

In the film, words in French never hinder the general comprehension. This could have been a fine line to tread but, as was previously mentioned, it was permitted by the pragmatic force of most of French utterances as well as their visual support in the film. Moreover code-switching is similar to a figure of speech, it symbolizes the ethnic identity of Poirot or stands for his foreignness. The French words are at the same time representative of stereotypes of the culture and are linked to Poirot's persona, his bon-vivant lifestyle, his love of good food and his hyper-politeness.

6.2.3 Syntactic forms

Listening to the movie, it is noticeable that the English spoken by Poirot is very rigid. Even though he is a fluent speaker of the foreign language, he seems confined to one register whoever his interlocutor is, and that is a formal register. One could argue that these register choices are made by a character that has a stiff-necked attitude. However, other syntactic extravagances are more surprising, such as a repetitive left dislocation with resumptive pronoun (examples 1 and 2).

(1) '**The numbers they** are odd and I prefer them to be even... **The odd numbers they** make me...'

(2) '**Your wife she** made no will... **Your wife she** dies. **The money *it*** is yours.'

These are just a few examples of the phenomenon and I collected more than thirty dislocations, occurring on a regular basis throughout the movie. In French generally, this stylistic device is used to put an emphasis on the subject or the object of a sentence such as in examples 3a and 3b.

(3) (a) *Ton frère il m'a dit que t'étais parti* (Your brother he told me that you left)
   (b) *Des fruits, j'en mange tous les jours* (Fruit, I eat some everyday)

It serves to focus on the important information given by the speaker or to avoid any ambiguity from the anaphoric pronoun. It does not seem that it is the case in Poirot's lines, as the prosodic features do not indicate any disconnection of the segment. It appears rather that there is in this case a redundant anaphora of the agent.

Moreover, dislocations characterize colloquial speech and once again Poirot's, in both English and French, are rather formal. Therefore these specific syntactic forms are not credible transfers from the French but are used to exoticize the foreigner's speech. One would argue that these forms could be Poirot's linguistic idiosyncrasies, particularities of a character that is not only foreign but also formal and very rigid.

Another distinctive feature of Poirot's speech is the way he constantly refers to himself by using his own name and the third person pronoun, such as in example 4.

(4) 'May Poirot sit? He wishes to tell you a little story.'

The form is often accompanied by a redundant anaphora (examples 5, 6 and 7).

(5) 'Poirot he left the dining car at 10 o'clock. He saw Madame Kettering.'
(6) 'Even Poirot he was deceived.'
(7) 'Poirot he marvelled at the strength and the audacity of the murderer.'

At this point of the analysis it has become clear that the recurrent syntactic oddities were meant to be interpreted by the viewers as interference in English from a foreign language. Yet research in SLA has shown that speakers of foreign languages do not systematically transfer syntactic forms from the L1 as it was commonly thought before. Auer (2007: 319–320), recalling the way scientists at the turn of the century became interested in the presence of languages in contact, describes interferences in those terms:

> On the level of the individual, the coexistence of two languages only started to become a topic some time later, when linguists became interested in speakers with a foreign 'accent', or in those who 'wrongly' used the grammar of their second language because their 'mother tongue' had a different structure and the acquisition of the second language had not been fully successful.

Once again, these idiosyncrasies of speech are more to do with the assumptions of the series' creators who are anticipating viewers' expectations in order to create for them enjoyment in the deciphering of these shared representations of French speakers of English as a foreign language.

6.3 Conclusion

In this chapter, I have tried to demonstrate that the way Poirot expresses himself contributes to the stereotypical images widely conveyed of foreign users of English. In the movie analysed here, forms of code-switching are regular and appear as verbal tics. The lexical and syntactic idiosyncrasies are as important as the detective's moustache in the construction of his character and persona. Peppering the dialogues with these forms, moviemakers establish a playful interaction between Poirot and the film viewers who, by being able to 'read' the verbal cues as cultural symbols (even when not 'understanding' them), become acquainted members of the series. However, I argued that the viewers should be aware of the televised archetypes of users of English as a foreign language. Besides, it is important to bear in mind the ongoing debate on the potentially racist or sectarian comments unearthed in Christie's novels. There are some undoubtedly controversial remarks to be found in her novels: on religions (i.e. Judaic), races and social classes. In *The Mystery of the Blue Train* (Christie 2003: 228), the first description of Poirot portrays 'a small man distinctly foreign in appearance'. Even if the commonly shared view on the ITV channel adaptation is that scriptwriters mellowed the xenophobic views, there are in the movie some remaining stereotypes of French culture. The use of stylized English French and the staged accent depict a man who is closer to the French cliché than the Belgian one (whatever this cliché may be), and this stylization categorizes foreigners as users of English with unconventional syntaxes and funny accents. In a chapter of her book on English, Lippi-Green (1997) showed how the use of accented English by some characters of Walt Disney cartoons taught discriminative and simplistic views on foreign cultures to children's malleable minds.

It is, by now, clear that film viewers are dealing with representations of bilingualism constructed for a majority monolingual audience. Some would argue that the exposure of languages other than English on TV should be seen as a promotion of foreign languages through the media and according to Androutsopoulos (2007: 207): 'These observations indicate a gradual shift in the sociolinguistic condition of a domain that has traditionally been dominated by ideologies and practices of monolingualism.' However, I argued throughout this chapter that *Poirot*'s words in French are rather tokens of bilingualism and address viewers with no French competence at all or a minimal competence. For Hill (1995, 1999), with regards to the use of Spanish in American commercials and films, the performance of mixed forms of language and culture (what she calls 'mock Spanish') is discriminatory and denigrating because 'it cannot be understood without knowing about the stereotypes that such indexes presuppose and entail' (Hill 1999), and affirms linguistic stereotypes by stylizing foreign ways of speaking. As Anderson (2007: 178) clearly demonstrated in her article, it is obvious that this sort of 'speech relies on available discourses of differentiation'. The staged forms of stylized French English have nothing to do with real English as spoken by a French speaker; it is what Kelly-Holmes (2005: 173) calls 'paradoxical or fake multilingualism'. She adds further that it is 'exploiting difference, accentuating or hyperbolising it against a monolingual norm' (2005: 173). The created bilingual speech delivers views on correctness and discourse ideologies. Being a fluent speaker of English and using minimal and understandable code-switches in French, Poirot brings a comforting representation of foreignness that does not endanger the monolithic and monolingual popular vision of British society.

7

Performances in French on Vancouver's Dining Scene: The Case of French Restaurants' Menus

According to popular wisdom, *you are what you eat*. A French version of the saying is the oft-cited quote from Brillat-Savarin: '*Dis moi ce que tu manges, je te dirai qui tu es*' ('tell me what you eat and I will tell you who you are'). However, for Bourdieu (1984b), people's tastes are not those of individuals, but they are shaped by the values of the classes in which they are socialized. With regards to food rituals, culinary practices or emblematic dishes contribute to a sense of shared values that goes beyond the class system (see Barthes 1951 on the French consumption of beefsteak and fries) and, for the culinary historian Massimo Montanari, everything that has to do with food (being its capture, cultivation, preparation, or consumption) is a cultural act (2006). Therefore, the choice and patronage of specific restaurants are also cultural practices and can inform the researcher on individuals' affiliation to a group (social or cultural), as well as on individuals' shared beliefs on foreign cultures (in the case of *ethnic* cuisine – see Elliott 2008). Furthermore, as a special issue of *Le Monde*, dedicated to gastronomy, daringly puts it in its introduction, 'a meal would be nothing much without the discourses that are produced before, during and after.'[1] It is true to say that discourses that surround food rituals (i.e. recipes, menus, comments during meals, etc.) play a major part in the maintenance of culinary traditions and cultures:

> By fixing the individual gestures that would otherwise remain buried among the pots and pans, cuisine pushes culinary practice out of the kitchen into the culture beyond. There, in that larger culture, cuisine reaches beyond the food that supplies its raw material; it outperforms the cooks by whom it is produced; it outshines even the consumers who justify the cycle of production. All this is possible because cuisine is not merely a culinary code that anchors custom. It is as well a panoply of narratives that sustain praxis. Cuisine constructs and upholds a community of discourse
>
> Ferguson 2004: 8

This chapter endeavours to show that analysing the discourses produced by restaurants helps to understand how linguistic practices contribute to ideologies related to food, language and culture. Among these discourses, media performances are sites of reproduction of cultural ideologies as well as of *enregistered* discourses. In order to highlight these, after a preliminary section on how the 'French language culinary fetish' (Kelly-Holmes 2005) emerged in English-speaking countries (and in particular in North America), the current chapter focuses on the Internet media texts published by Vancouver's French restaurants (a city where English is the dominant language), and more specifically on their menus – whose role is defined by Seaberg (1991) as follows:

> When customers are seated at a table in your restaurant, they are given a menu – the primary communications, sales, and public relations tool of your restaurant.... A menu is a piece of paper on which words and illustrations are printed. It should be colourful, attractive, clean, and reflective of the quality, appearance, and style of the restaurant.... The average Customer does not always come to your restaurant knowing exactly what he or she wants, unless yours is a very limited fast-food operation. Instead the menu guides the decision of what to order, and the right words and pictures appropriately arranged determine both what and how much the customer orders.
>
> Seaberg 1991: vii

My premise is that the use of French language in Vancouver's haute-cuisine and bistro-style restaurants' menus is mostly designed for monolingual English-speaking customers and contribute to a ritualized *mise-en-scène* that includes pictures of small-portion and meticulously designed dishes (for the latter, see Bourdieu 1979). As an example, *Le Crocodile*'s online menu offers a 'Terrine de Fois Gras, Gelée au Sauterne' (followed by an English translation in italics), but other restaurants propose bilingual variations and in some cases, names of dishes appear in mixed versions of French and English (e.g. 'Chicken Coq Au Vin'). This chapter provides textual analysis of such menus, in terms of structure and use (registers, rituals, etc.), and most of all in terms of semantics (indexicality). After describing and analysing their contextualized use, I argue that these displays of bilingualism are spectacular fragments (Rampton 1999) where French is not used for its meaning but rather serves as a form of ethnosymbolism. By using French, restaurants display a posture of authority in gastronomic culture and prompt their clients to a feeling of belonging: not to a linguistic or social group, but rather to a community of taste. In effect, for clients, to understand the genre is not only to display a sociocultural status (*connaisseurship*) as well as a linguistic competence (in French or in the lexicon of gastronomy), but also to *distinguish* oneself (Bourdieu 1984b).

The study finally ponders whether the French language that is displayed in Vancouver's French restaurants is the same as the one used in the French restaurants of major English-speaking cities in North America (such as New York, Chicago or Los Angeles). More precisely, does the fact that French is one of the official languages of Canada makes any difference in terms of linguistic structure or use of French words in menus? Since French is a part of Vancouver's linguistic landscape, its presence in restaurants would be felt as less *exotic* than in New York or Sydney's French restaurants. However, I show that the word French in *French cuisine* relates to a mythological France (the projection of a North American collective imagination), rather than to a French-Canadian culinary experience.

7.1 Menus, French gastronomy and French language in English-speaking restaurants

7.1.1 Menus as a genre: Structure and function

> Menus are the Pavlov's bell of eating out. They are a literature of control. Menu language, with its hyphens, quotation marks, and random outbursts of foreign words, serves less to describe food than to manage your expectations.
>
> Dickerman 2003

Although a great deal has been published on food in the last decade (especially in the relatively new field of *Food studies*), there still exists few textual studies of restaurant menus. Among these, Zwicky and Zwicky's (1980) study of American menus intends to show the 'conventions that govern its form, and to investigate the menu register as a solution to conflicts between the diverse aims of menus' (1980: 83). Restaurant menu is a textual genre that needs to be recognized at first glance for customers to review them with maximal efficiency. Indeed, patrons are required to navigate the proposed options and make their choices in a short space of time and without becoming confused by the format or the order of the items on the document. For this purpose, people who conceive menus (chefs or restaurants owners) follow a set of specific rules with regards to their form as well as to their content. For Seaberg (1991):

> Like a novel or a symphony, a meal has a beginning, a middle, and an end, and this sequence indicates how a menu should be designed. Regardless of the size of

the menu, the fold of the pages, and the number of pages, the menu layout should follow the meal sequence. The usual order of reading is from the outside of the pages, from top to bottom, and from left to right.

Seaberg 1991: 23

Figure 2 presents an example of the sorts of bilingual menus that can be found in Vancouver's French restaurants. Note that whereas it provides full sentences in French followed by a translation in English, other menus limit their French to a few words.

Menus involve a 'compression of content' (Zwicky and Zwicky 1980: 86) that is due to the fact that the physical space dedicated to dishes is limited, and the extent of the compression is variable: from a single page to a small booklet. The allocated space or the laconicism of style (from bistro simplicity, to chic sobriety, and to verbose pomp) varies according to the restaurant's desired communicational intent (to inform or to impress).[2] For each dish, a binary presentation is common in many restaurants' menus where the names of the dishes are followed by a description:

ESCARGOTS EN COCOTTE
Mushrooms, Confit Garlic, Tarragon Cream

Le Parisien, Vancouver[3]

Escargots Maison
Snails[4] baked in Pastry "Shells" with Garlic Butter

Le Crocodile, Vancouver

Other restaurants present the dish followed by a succinct explanation on the way it is prepared on the same line. Some choose a more laconic list of dishes and limit themselves to their name only.

Escargots Bourguignonne,[5] Garlic and Parsley Butter

Jules, Vancouver

Escargot à l'aïl

Salade de fruit, Vancouver

As in the given examples, the names of the dishes are not preceded by articles[6] and the descriptions do rarely include verbs (except for a few past participles: baked, served, seared, scented, etc.).

In order to analyse restaurants' menus as a textual genre, Zwicky and Zwicky (1980: 85) enumerate five dimensions relevant to the study of registers: (1) the medium of communication; (2) the number of persons addressed; (3) the relationship between participants in time and space; (4) the social dimensions

Le Crocodile

HOME ABOUT MENUS WINE GALLERY AWARDS RESERVATIONS GIFT CARDS CONTACT

| Chef's Menu | Lunch | Dinner | Set Menus | Dessert |

Entrées Froides

Salade Panachée de Tomates et d'Avocat au Crabe du Pacifique 16.50
Composed Tomato and Avocado Salad with Dungeness Crabmeat

Salade de Betteraves et Fromage "Buffala" 19.50
Vinaigrette à la Moutarde et Miel
Beet Salad and Fresh Buffala Cheese served with Honey & Mustard Dressing

Fromage de Chèvre Poêlé servi sur un lit de Salade Frisée 16.50
Pan-Fried Goat Cheese served over Curly Endive Salad

Asperges Vertes Grillées, Arugula, Vinaigrette 14.50
aux Truffes et Parmesan
Grilled Asparagus served with Arugula Salad, Truffle Oil Dressing and Parmesan Shavings

Filet de Boeuf Tartare préparé à la minute 18.00
Beef Tenderloin Steak Tartar, made to order, served with Classic Garnishes

Terrine de Foie-Gras et Crème Brûlée au Foie-Gras, ... 29.00
Gelée au Sauterne, Toasts
Duo of Foie-Gras Tasting, Foie-Gras Terrine, Foie-Gras Crème

Figure 2 Excerpt from *Le Crocodile*'s online Dinner menu

involved; and (5) the 'point' or intended effect. If compared with Biber and Conrad's (2009) framework of register analysis, these appear to be rather simplified criteria. In the case of our study, however, they pinpoint a few elements of importance. Taking that menus' medium of communication is print (i.e. on paper) and digital (on the Internet), the second dimension brings to light the fact that, in cities where English is the dominant language, French restaurants present one single version for all customers.[7] It is crucial to bear in mind that in the case of Canadian cities where there may be a remote possibility that patrons speak French, an English translation is provided in cases where French is used. When studying such menus, the analyst therefore deals with cases of bilingual practices mostly designed for an audience that is largely monolingual. With regard to the third dimension and in the case of online menus, the relations between participants are asynchronous, as people consulting the restaurant's website may not ever go there and take part in the ritual in which the menus participate. Note that the menus presented on restaurants' websites may not be strictly the same as the ones presented in restaurants, but may also appear in a more elaborate web version (as slide shows, for example).[8] It is, however, interesting to note that few restaurants fully use the audiovisual potential of the digital media and choose a traditional approach to the genre. The fourth dimension will be developed largely throughout this chapter. Finally, the intended effect is to 'create a positive attitude ... and encourage people to take up the offer' (Zwicky and Zwicky 1980: 86). Menus participate in the *mise-en-scène* of emblematic French dishes: exotic because they differ from the usual daily fare (such as snails, frog legs or raw beef meat served *tartare*),[9] yet familiar for being commonly viewed as the canon of French restaurants' offerings, true symbols of French cuisine.

7.1.2 French gastronomy outside France: The value of French food in America

> For generations of English speakers, *gourmand* and *gourmet* were wicked French words, and no post-Cromwellian Anglo-Saxon has ever found an equivalent expression for "bon appétit." Thus, French language hegemony: our prominent food magazines today include *Saveur*, *Bon Appétit*, and *Gourmet*. The inaugural (January 1941) issue of the latter featured columns entitled "Bouquet de France", "Gastronomie sans Argent", and "Spécialités de la Maison" as well as culinary lingo quiz asking for definitions of *bisque, sauté, ragoût, petits fours*, and *à la* just about anything, enough to send us all posthaste to sign up a Linguaphone course!
>
> Sonnenfeld, in: Pitte 2002: ix

At the turn of the twentieth century, elite American food culture was dominated by French haute cuisine (Johnston and Baumann 2007, Trubek 2000). If it is undeniable that an American culinary tradition has since carved its way to the realm of high-end gastronomic restaurants, French cuisine has conserved to this day its reputation for exceptional and refined cooking. Different reasons have been given to explain this predominance. Some scholars give French people the merit. For Ferguson (2004: 4), 'The French, as we all "know" are culinary masters – so much so that to modern ears, gastronomy sounds far more like a French enterprise than the original Greek word on which it is based.' The French are seen as the creators of a gastronomic tradition of excellence or, as Child's famous *Mastering the Art of French Cooking* put it in its opening dedication, 'through generations of inventive and loving concentration [French peasants, fishermen, housewives, princes and chefs] have created one of the world's great arts' (Child et al. 1971). Trubek (2000) and Ferguson (2004) also highlight the role played by the people (chefs as well as intellectuals) who contributed to the codification of the French culinary art through their writings (as one may note that the same preoccupation for codification was also to be found with regards to language as well as the arts – theatre, painting, etc.). Other scholars give priority to the country's geographical and historical assets. Pitte (2002) describes France's geography as having an undisputable advantage: it is a land of Cockaigne where fresh, diverse and tasteful products come in abundance. Furthermore, there is no doubt that the geopolitical influence of the French colonial empire over nineteenth and twentieth-century Europe and the New World also played an important part in the diffusion of a French culinary model throughout the world. If the French 'believe themselves to be the enlightened eater, the gourmets' (Pitte 2002: xv), there is still something of the old colonial spirit in the French culinary endeavour that sees itself as bringing civilization to *unenlightened* palates. If people, geography and history all contributed to give French cuisine its status of refinement and excellence in gastronomy, the following comment from a Canadian patron shows that in America it is also synonymous with *out-of-the-ordinary*:

> **Realy dis-appointed** . . . . Being a Franch restaurant the food supose to be good. Not at all. It just like a normal restuarant
> *Dined on 1/31/2014 (Opentable.com – spelling mistakes included)*

If *authenticity* and *exoticism* are two important values that serve to valorize food in the media (Johnston and Bauman 2007), it seems that the offering and consumption of French food in America go beyond these. In this chapter, I argue that the predominance of French cuisine is maintained by beliefs that may have little to do with France or the French themselves, but that rather relate to an American mythology about French culture and lifestyle. Ferguson underlies the common myth that 'French cuisine offers French culture' (2004: 9).[10] What is sold with French food? What values are commodified on Vancouver's French-dining scene? The first words of a press article on *Chez Mémé Baguette Bistro*, a French eatery of the Vancouver suburb may give the beginning of an explanation:

> French culture has always been looked up to as a way of life that many North Americans would love to follow. With a passion for high fashion, art, and fine food, it has a lifestyle that takes personal enjoyment as seriously as work.
>
> The Heights Merchants Association[11]

Looking at the way French food has been presented by the North American media, it appears that French cooking is for the *gourmand*, the *bon-vivant* who enjoys life to the full, as well as for the *refined* who love arts and the *gourmet* who appreciates fine food made with the best ingredients. Julia Child's book (*Mastering the Art of French Cooking*) and TV Programs (*The French Chef* with its famous *Bon Appétit!* closure) played a part in bringing French cuisine to the American public or, to be precise, to a larger audience than was previously the case. In the words of the DVD that was produced from her TV shows (WGBH Boston Video 2005), her mission was not only to bring French food to an American audience, but also to enlighten a 'nation fed on Shake'n Bake and Tang'. She was herself a bigger-than-life, cheerful, sensual (the title of her biography is *Appetite for Life*), albeit sophisticated, woman: some characteristics that matched the American vision of the French approach to food and cooking that she embodied as a balance between savoir-faire (i.e. a know-how, as she held that French cuisine was a matter of knowing the right techniques) and savoir-vivre.

French cuisine in America does not refer to just one type of cooking; one could count up to three sub-categories of French cuisine on the American dining scene: French bistro fare (casual), traditional/regional French cooking (hearty, comfort-food, homey French) and haute/grande/classic cuisine (formal, fine dining). Similar values commonly associated with French culture and French culinary tradition may be found in all three styles (see Figure 3), but they also present important variations. For example, chance is that one's best choice for a romantic[12] dinner would be a French restaurant (if not an Italian one). However, the style of the chosen restaurant may deliver different messages to the loved one. The same association between the consumption of French food, the use of French language, ways of life (savoir-vivre) and values such as romance, will be found in different instances in the studied corpus (on restaurants' websites or in customers' evaluations).

Two films played a part in maintaining such reputation. In 1987, *Babette's Feast* (a cult film for the American foodies – Ferguson 2004: 192) inaugurated the genre of the food film and offered a good illustration of what would stand as the epitome of French cuisine, a work of art realized through the combination of savoir-faire

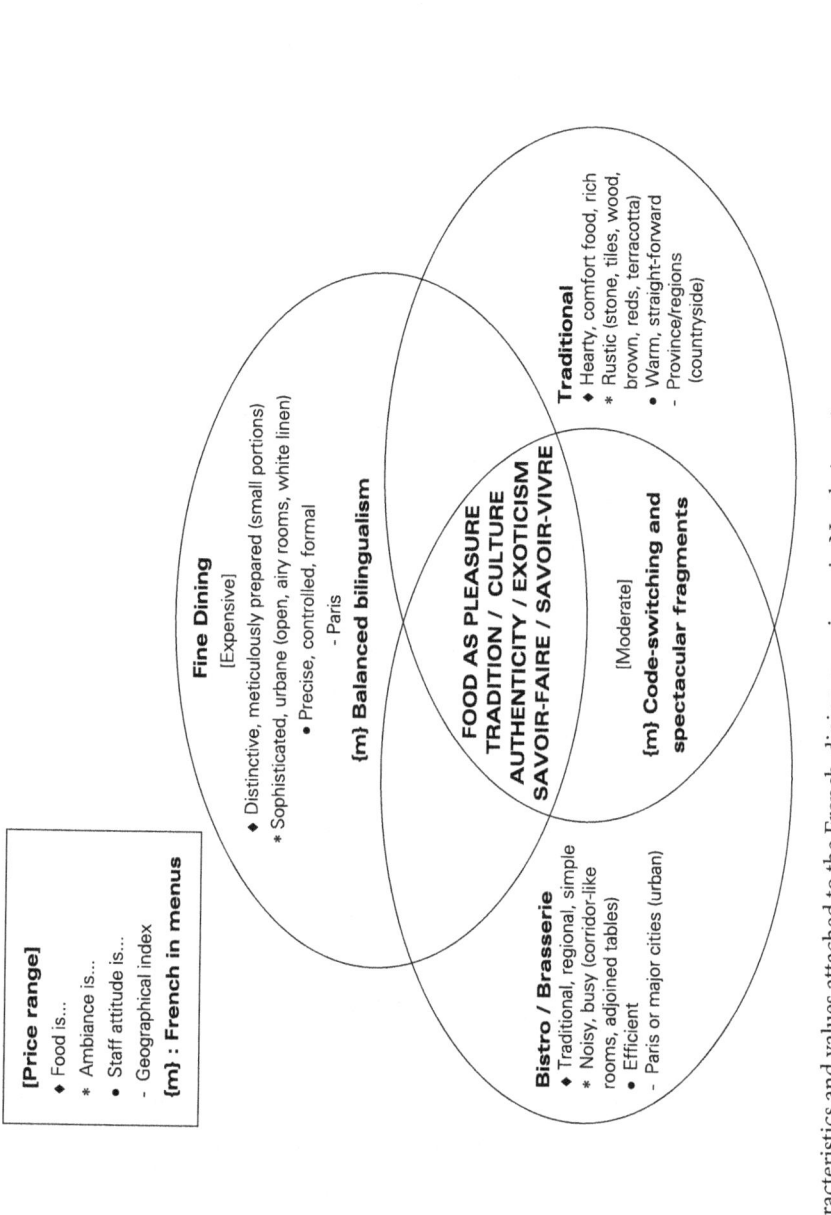

Figure 3 Characteristics and values attached to the French-dining experience in North America

(that lingers on artistry) and savoir-vivre ('I made them happy' says Babette talking about her customers at the *Café Anglais*). More recently, *Chocolat* (2000)[13] exploited the same values by presenting the role of food in French culture as a way to rediscover earthly pleasures and true feelings.[14] French food does not only address the palate, it is a full-body experience that requires the participation of all senses. For example, since Carême's elaborate *pièces montées* and nouvelle cuisine's artistically designed small portions, the dishes' presentation is capital. Moreover, French food is also described as food for the mind: in this vein, Child described her first French meal in Normandy (oysters, *sole meunière* and fine wine) to *The New York Times* as 'an opening up of the soul and spirit' (Child, in Mellowes 2005).

Figure 3 presents the characteristics, settings, and values that came to be associated with the three sub-categories of French gastronomy in the American context. These shared representations of French cuisine relate to concepts of food as pleasure, tradition and culture, authenticity and exoticism, savoir-faire and savoir-vivre.

If some values are familiar to restaurants' patrons in France, others are characteristic of an American take on French culinary culture (that goes with restaurants' prominent displays of French emblems, such as the Eiffel Tower or the fleur-de-lis). These may also be troped upon in order to yield hybrid/fusion versions (i.e. fine-dining with a relaxed, bistro-like atmosphere).

The genres' specific discursive practices will be developed later. In the meanwhile, the next section shows that the use of French in menus is linked to distinction. Menus bear economical value: their aim is to guide restaurants' patrons in their purchase, but also to impress and to flatter. Being able to recognize or read into these coded values is to distinguish oneself as a *connoisseur*. Zwicky and Zwicky (1980: 87) define connoisseurship as 'the sharing of special knowledge about an art or craft' and add that '[it] is certainly the point of some menus, as is evidenced by the frequent use of French in menus' (1980: 87).

7.1.3 The use of French words on menus

> French is the language of great cuisine. Listing items in French, therefore, gives the menu authenticity and panache. A French restaurant at the bottom of its ice cream and sherbet listing says: 'Fabrication artisanale traditionnelle', which translates as 'Made in the traditional manner'. The customer can be sure that there is a French chef out in the kitchen preparing the special, not just ordinary, food.
>
> Seaberg 1991: 160

Finding French words on restaurants' menus is nothing of a new trend as in most restaurants (even restaurants that do not serve French cooking), parts of the meal were traditionally in French (*hors-d'oeuvres, entrées*, etc.). With time French language came to be used to distinguish sophisticated food and fine-dining from the common fare ('plain English and fancy French' – Zwicky and Zwicky 1980: 89) and some words found their way into the English language with and without spelling or morphological changes (terrine, puree, sautéed, etc.). In modern menus, French words may not be distinguished from the English language: they are used as borrowings rather than instances of code-switching or spectacular fragments (ex: frites instead of French fries, printed without italics, no translation given). Among other emblematic borrowings, *le* is the French word par excellence. 'Sometimes just a French word is enough ... It need not even be the right article' (Zwicky and Zwicky 1980: 89). Indeed, the French language that is used in menus does not need to be *real* French: looking French or sounding French will suffice, as long as the hybrid forms are understood by English-speaking patrons (for example, 'Pomme purée' instead of *purée de pommes de terre*). In other cases, French words are most often signalled one way or another (a different font or typesetting, a specific place allocated in the menu) and carry a distinctive flavour. For French-restaurants patrons, to be able to understand them is to demonstrate 'educated connoisseurship' (Silverstein 2003). In his study on *oinoglossia* (wine talk), Silverstein (2003) shows that the use of technical vocabulary is a second-order indexicality: a '"life-style" variable or emblematized speaker-defining index' (2003: 222). Providing 'identity-by-visible-consumption' (2003: 227), it indexes social register. Wine-tasting and the discursive practices that go with it are 'culturally eucharistic':

> [B]y using the lingo in context, the lingo has the indexically entailing effect or creative power to index consubstantial traits in the speaker. As we consume the wine and properly (ritually) denote that consumption, we become, in performative realtime, the well-bred, characterologically interesting (subtle, balanced, intriguing, winning, etc.) person iconically corresponding to the metaphorical 'fashion of speaking' of the perceived register's figurations of the aesthetic object of connoisseurship, wine. The eucharistic exercise is a powerful microcontext of higher-order indexical authorization.
>
> Silverstein 2003: 226

In the case of French restaurants, the necessary competence in French may be limited to written (and little oral) comprehension as customers can get away without ever saying the name of the dishes.

Finally, as this anecdote narrated by the BBC reminds us,[15] one cannot ignore that the use of a minority language always takes place in a context with a political agenda. In 2003, in order to protest against France's opposition to the war on Iraq, the American House of Representatives renamed their French fries and French toast 'Freedom fries' and 'Freedom toast'. However, the fact that the political institution was one of the few places where such linguistic measures were taken shows that cultural practices can also be detached from very local preoccupations.

7.2 French restaurants in Vancouver

There is no doubt that Vancouver prides itself in having an exceptionally diverse dining scene. Among ethnically-varied restaurants, the city benefits from a fair number of French restaurants (my corpus counts sixteen although I acknowledge that some could have escaped my careful search). Most of them (fourteen) define themselves as belonging to the bistro category, either by including the noun in their name (*Bistro Pastis*; *Chez mémé Baguette Bistro*), by bearing it prominently on their signboard or on their website ('French bistro'), or by mentioning it in the description of their establishment ('in a bistro setting' – *Salade de Fruits*). The two other restaurants are haute-cuisine and traditional. Even though *Le Crocodile* restaurant presents itself as belonging to the traditional category ('Le Crocodile blends traditional French cooking with innovative Westcoast style'), Vancouverites would argue that, after the closure of the restaurant *Lumière*, *Le Crocodile* is the last place in town (the restaurant has been in Vancouver for thirty years) where French fine-dining can be found. As for the French-cooking label, if the names of the restaurants is a definitive clue (most of them bear French names), where some highlight a French affiliation on their website (on its home page, the *Left Bank* states: 'vancouver french kissed'), others choose to downplay the category in which the reviewers place them, by not using French on their websites or by not indicating clearly that they serve French cuisine (but, for example, signal a mere 'French influence'). It is worth bearing in mind that restaurants which are not French may use spectacular fragments or borrowings in French in their menus (where one may also find Italian or Spanish words). Note also that if for most restaurants the word French relates to France's cooking, other restaurants present themselves as belonging to the French-speaking world (i.e. *Francophonie*): Belgian (*Chambar*), North African (*Café d'Afrique, Carthage Cafe*), Lebanese (*Nuba*) and of course French-Canadian (*La belle patate*).

Focusing on the bilingual discursive practices of the French restaurants in Vancouver, one will first notice that their menus present important variations on the theme of the French-English menu. These range from the nearly all-in-English menus to the all-in-French menus. I present these variations under four categories: (i) spectacular fragments; (ii) code-switching; (iii) balanced bilingualism; and (vi) in French, without English translation.

7.2.1 Spectacular fragments (*Absinthe Bistro; La Brasserie; L'Abattoir; Left Bank; Le Parisien; Pied-à-Terre; Tableau; The French table*)

In these restaurants' menus, most dishes are presented in English. However, on a closer examination, one finds that French words pepper the text. These spectacular fragments are often limited to emblematic dishes – that is, dishes that would be perceived as iconic in French cuisine (viz. *escargots, soupe à l'oignon, foie gras, cassoulet, bouillabaisse, crème brûlée, millefeuille,* etc.). One also reads more obscure terms, such as sauces (*rouille, gribiche,* etc.) that could require translations and/or explanations (one would argue that a sauce would generally require a few words of explanation on the part of the waiter), as well as other words that may be common to the cosmopolitan restaurant goer (*confiture*). It is true that it is always a fine line between words that may be understood by customers, words that would need explanations from the waiter, and words whose opacity may dishearten. There is a variation in the amount of spectacular fragments that are displayed: whereas some restaurants present hardly any, others choose to place them prominently. For example, *Pied-à-Terre* and *La Brasserie*'s menus present sections in French ('Les Aperitifs', 'Hors d'Oeuvres', 'A la Carte') and by doing so emphasize their European identity (*La Brasserie* defines itself as Franco-German).

Among emblematic French words that can be found in restaurants' menus is the already mentioned French article '*le*'. For example, the Lebanese restaurant *Nuba* (in a menu that is otherwise in English) has a few dishes that make use of a French article: 'Le Petite Feast', 'La Feast' and 'Le Grand Feast'.[16] In these instances, the French article may be used to emphasize the out-of-the-ordinary, uniqueness of a dish, rather than its Frenchness.

7.2.2 Code-switching (*Faux-Bourgeois; Jules; La Cigale French Bistro; La Régalade; Pastis; Chez Mémé Baguette Bistro*)

In these restaurants (mainly bistros), most dishes are in French. These are classic dishes of the bistro fare but the use of French is limited to a few words (ingredients and explanations in English follow): *Steak frites; Moules frites; steak tartare; salade* niçoise; queue de boeuf; omelette basquaise; Sandwish Jambon-Brie; croque-monsieur, etc. In 2014, the front page of *Pastis'* website displayed a video in which the restaurant owner presented the restaurant (with a noticeable French accent and syntax) in these words: '*Pastis* for me is an elegant French Bistro ... the menu is also items that are easy to understand, *very classical dishes that we have*. Also as a host, I want to make sure that people feel warm, at ease' (John Blakeley, my emphasis). If this is the desired effect, how does French language participate in it? More than in the previous category, such linguistic practices do not only index French cooking but they also participate in a French ambiance that says to the customers that what they see is the kind of menus that they would find in France. The sense of authenticity (authentic language indexing authentic cooking) and the feeling to be there[17] is an important part of the culinary experience. Note, however, that the dishes have been carefully selected not to confuse, as John Blakeley's (*Pastis*) statement to his customers would confirm: 'It is food *that you will understand*' (my emphasis). This is an important difference that separates this category from the next where linguistic and culinary creativity is more prominent.

7.2.3 Balanced bilingualism (*Le Crocodile, Pastis*)

In *Le Crocodile*'s dinner menus,[18] the names of the dishes are given in French in short sentences that include the mode of cooking and/or the way the dish is served. A translation in English is provided on the following line:

> **Os à la Moelle au four servi avec Salade de Saison, Fondant de Tomates, petites Tranches de Pain grillées et Fleur de Sel**
> Oven-Roasted Beef Bone Marrow, Served with Seasonal Salad, Fresh Tomato "Fondant", Toasts and Fresh Sea Salt

The sentences in French are rather long and may include a verb (past participles such as *servi, préparé, parfumé,* etc.). The wording is more elaborate than in the previous category and is not restricted to classic dishes. The crafted sentences give a sense of lexical virtuosity, if not poetry. Restaurants following this type of discursive practices are higher-end restaurants. Unlike the model followed by bistros (where ingredients, the way of cooking and serving are usually given in English only), the translation gives the same amount of information and would be redundant to any bilingual speaker. Note that French may also appear in the translation. In this kind of menu, French is not an addition or a decoration, but is central to the text.

Bistros may punctually adopt a similar version. By choosing to be linguistically creative (such as in *Pastis'* original wording of dishes such as 'L'omble chevalier et le quinoa' or 'Les escargots et le pastis'), they signal a form of cooking that goes beyond the simple casual bistro fare.

7.2.4 In French, without English translation (*Salade de fruits*)

Salade de fruits is the only restaurant in my corpus that presents a menu that is nearly exclusively in French. This may be explained by the restaurant's location: situated near Vancouver's French Cultural Centre and the French-speaking *Théâtre la Seizième*, it may have been intended to cater for French customers mainly. This is not the case and *Salade de fruits* is a well-known address in Vancouver where customers find that the linguistic ambiance contributes to the place's charm:

> (1) FlavorBudz, 07/16/13
>
> This restaurant has great ambience and authenticity. The French servers speak in trusting accents, you can hear their voices float as they speak the language of love. The feeling is also very homey, but you know that they mean only the best.
>
> Urbanspoon

Note that, once again, the association between food, language and other values (authenticity, romance, tradition, etc.) is evocative of the American take on French culture.

7.3 French language and the French dining experience in Vancouver

As mentioned before, language is part of a culinary experience. French is not only found in menus, but may be used in restaurants (by waiters as well as customers). By ways of influence, symbolic uses of French language also appear in restaurant reviews (some of them published on *Le Crocodile*'s website) and in customers' comments:

> There's no shortage of great little French bistros in town but this one's particularly and bodaciously rustic, delicious, and *vrai* French. It's also got a convincingly French atmosphere with French as the first language.
>
> *Vancouver Sun* – Top 20 Vancouver Restaurants[19]

> Le Crocodile doesn't have the attitude that if you have to ask about the price, then, *mes cheries*, you can't afford it.
>
> Mia Stainsby, *The Vancouver Sun*

Chef Michel Jacob deserves knighthood for the impeccable styling of his superior cuisine at this top-notch Classic French restaurant, where the rich and indulgent food is always a great experience; such perfection includes wine to match and superb service and if some lack a sense of humility that's dangerous close to pretentious, the majority just swoons 'magnifique!'

Zagat Survey[20]

The French words are not chosen randomly as they too index French values such as authenticity (*vrai*), romance (*chéri*) and artistic appreciation (*magnifique*). For customers, French language plays an important part in the pleasure of a French experience. For some, this goes beyond a passive knowledge of the language:

(2) Simplement parfait! Diner Review Feb 21, 2014

After passing Chez Meme so many times on the busride up to school, I FINALLY got to try it! To my surprise, I was greeted in the french the moment I walked in. The whole time I was there I noticed all the employees speaking french (even if it was just simple expressions to customers). It was refreshing to go to a French cafe where French is actually spoken!! I had the Brioche French Toast and wow c'était DELICIEUX! ... Merci beaucoup Chez Meme! Tous les choses étaient géniale, je retournerai! :)

Urbanspoon – spelling mistakes included

The fact that in this particular case the reviewer appears to be proficient in French incites me to come back to my premise that menus are mainly designed with monolinguals (i.e. English speakers) in mind. Having shown that French language plays a part in the culinary experience of a monolingual audience and that the linguistic practices vary according to restaurants' styles, I wish now to consider that practices in a minority language occur in local contexts where they may bear political implications. According to Androutsopoulos (2007: 213): 'the staging of "mixed forms of language and culture" in performance arts can be "in itself" a form of legitimation of everyday bilingual practice when addressed to a local bilingual audience (Jaffe 2000: 43); but it can also reaffirm cultural stereotypes by stylizing linguistic minorities for the sake of a monolingual audience (Hill 1995).' In the studied cases and to unveil whether the practices in French address local (i.e. potentially bilingual)[21] speakers, the first question that I would like to raise concerns the meaning of French in *French cuisine*. Regarding what they call *Canadian culinary identities*, Charron and Desjardins (2011) argue that: 'Language and food define and shape collective identities. This is true especially in Canada, a country where collective identities seem disparate and fragmented' (Charron and Desjardins 2011). In the case of French-Canadian culinary identity, one finds that the values that are usually attached to food and cooking differ significantly from the ones that I listed previously. Desjardins (2011) argues that for Quebecois culture, cuisine is about *'bonne bouffe'* (popular French for good food – the cooking of/for the working class) and the comfort-food *poutine* is an emblematic example of such cuisine. If there are numerous restaurants in Montreal or Québec where fine and inventive French-Canadian gastronomy can be found, it is not the case in Vancouver and the only places where Québécois cuisine is claimed to be served are in fast-food outlets such as *Frenchies Diner* and *La Belle Patate*. For example, the latter advertises 'Authentic Québécois Cuisine' on the front page of its website. Apart from the name of the restaurant and the word Québécois, the website does not display a word in French as all dishes (even fries) are presented in English. *Frenchies Diner* uses a few spectacular fragments (Le Classic Poutine, Poutine L'Italienne), as well as the French-Canadian English borrowing 'steamé'.

If culinary values are fundamentally different, however, note that the association with authenticity remains fundamental. *La Belle Patate*'s owner is a Montreal native, employs French Canadians and plays Québécois music in the background of his restaurant. As for *Frenchies Diner*, a reviewer describes the restaurant's setting and cooking with enthusiasm: 'It could be the fleur-de-lys flags, the Montreal Canadiens memorabilia, or the fact that it is designed to look like an old-school 50's diner, but there's something about Frenchies that just screams, "QUEBEC!" and makes it my favourite spot for poutine in Vancouver … take your tastebuds on a trip to La Belle Province' (Marshand 2013). Note finally that restaurant reviews and travel websites (*Urbanfood*, *Yelp* or *TripAdvisor*) do not place the restaurants under the French category but under 'Fast Food' or 'Poutineries'. It appears therefore that in Vancouver the word 'French' in *French cuisine* relates to France's cooking only.

Considering the fact that French is an official language of Canada and as such is a part of Vancouver's bilingual landscape, I would like now to question whether restaurants' menus in the west-coast Canadian city present noticeable differences with the menus that are handed out elsewhere in North American restaurants. Note firstly that in the case of Vancouver no bilingual French-English menus are found outside of French restaurants. Secondly, in the case of French restaurants, Zwicky and Zwicky's (1980) study on American as well as Canadian restaurants found that 'regional variation is negligible' (p. 83). A review of French restaurants' online menus in New York, Chicago and Los Angeles reveals the same types of linguistic practices in French: from spectacular fragments in Bistro restaurants (with the typical classic dishes: *Escargots, Steak frites, Moules Marinières, Coq au vin, Foie gras*, etc.) to bilingual displays. Interestingly, high-end restaurants in these cities offer a different linguistic behaviour, and most of them appear now to prefer an English version for their menus (with a few spectacular fragments in French). In these cases, it appears that French language does not index refined and exceptional cooking anymore. As for Vancouver, it is difficult to draw specific conclusions from such variation as the fine-dining category in our corpus is represented by a unique case (*Le Crocodile*). However, I am hopeful that a future ethnographic study in different locations will shed more light on the matter.

7.4 Conclusion

> When he buys an item of food, consumes it, or serves it, modern man does not manipulate a simple object in a purely transitive fashion; this item of food sums up and transmits a situation; it constitutes an information; it signifies.
>
> Barthes 2013 [1961]: 24

If the patronage of high-end French restaurants used to signify high status based on social position, distinction as well as *connaisseurship* and familiarity with French culture and language, Johnston and Baumann (2007: 165) also believe that the 'boundaries between highbrow and lowbrow cultures' are eroding. They also note that 'cuisine is a cultural realm where individuals can effectively engage in status displays' (p. 168). Moreover, considering that spectacular fragments in foreign languages are common encounters on the Vancouver dining scene (in the case of Japanese, Lebanese, Indian, Mexican restaurant menus), and that 'the language of food might actually be a more apt *lingua franca* than English or French' (Charron and Desjardins 2011), one may question to what extent the use of French language to indicate distinction has endured.

The display of the Other's language is entextualized (according to genres, such as bistro or high-end restaurant menus), contextualized within a local frame (Vancouver, Canada), and to be *read* firstly by the local's eye (monolingual/bilingual). In such contexts, old categories (French) may intersect with new ones ('locavore' as some restaurants claim to offer a blend of French cuisine with *a West Coast style*). As the *exotic* does not necessarily come from the *outside*, the limits between *here* (the local) and *there* (the French) cannot be restricted to national or regional borders any more.

Conclusion

In this book, I have endeavoured to show that media performances of voice participate in processes of linguistic differentiation, and most importantly that these practices are constrained by clusters of conventions known as genres. Most chapters focused on performances of discriminated voices (social, ethnic, sexual), and highlighted the fact that such performances contribute to maintain ideologies of linguistic differentiation as well as prejudices (linguistic patterns being linked in turn to social attributes and behaviour) that are consequently conjured to justify discriminations. As an example, what is seen as a 'loose' pronunciation is associated with a lack of control or morals (see Introduction and chapter 2), heavy accents with strong appetites and sexual looseness (chapters 4 and 5), performed with such excess that it sounds grotesque (such as the cod-French accent which in films is often the attribute of the fool – chapter 5). Performers' comments on their own vocal productions highlight the performances' physicality as well as the symbolism of such practices. In some cases, the voice is said to be *brought from the chest to the head*. Men-to-women transvestites is an obvious example, but David Suchet, for example, stated that he used a similar technique when performing Poirot,[1] symbolizing on the one hand women's voice pitch and lightness of speech and, on the other, Poirot's cerebral output.

The ability to modulate one's voice to speak like another person is a characteristic that makes us fundamentally human and social, as it is by styling the other that one defines who one is and where one belongs (see Bell 1999). It is a practice that is learned early, as young children start mimicking very soon after they pronounce their first sentences and then never really cease to perform other voices (and others' voices). The competence to perform such voices relies on processes of socialization and on the learning of categorizations that guide children to discriminate the characteristics to be used to *envoice* the Other. Such categorizations are based on social conventions that link ways of speaking to ways of being (fathers vs. mothers, men vs. women, adults vs. children, heroes vs. victims, the strong vs. the weak, etc.). Performances of voices in the media not only make use of such social conventions, they rely on others that are more specific to the medium. With regard to films, Chion (1999: 125) reminds his readers of the technical 'split' that separates the voice from the body, as image and sound used to be recorded separately. In the early days of the film industry, and in a time when movie cameras were very noisy, actors had to dub their own performances (and sometimes were dubbed by other actors, as *Singing in the Rain*'s plot shows). For Chion (1999: 126), *grafting voices* on particular bodies or bringing elements that from the start do not necessarily *stick together* depend on arbitrary conventions: 'The process of "embodying" a voice is not a mechanistic operation, but a symbolic one' (Chion 1999: 129). Such symbolic operations are based on social assumptions related to genders, races, social classes and their ways of speaking *in films* (i.e. working-class men speak like that, black women speak like that, etc.), therefore constructing cinematic genres.

With regards to the performances of voice that preceded them, performed voices give an illusory impression of stability. Within a given genre, the use of emblematic features contributes to maintain an illusion of continuity from one performance to another. When watching a fresh performance, spectators instinctively reduce the new to the old, the unknown to the familiar. Through their willingness to recognize established genres, they participate in the permanence of conventions.

Before bringing this book to a close, and in order to propose new paths for future research, I would like to extend my reflection to the conventions that frame the reception of plural media voices, which arguably participate in making the diversity harmonious, and the cacophony polyphonic.

Voices in the media: Multiplicity, diversity and polyphony

In literary studies, a *voice* is understood to be the distinctive style of an author. Against this reductive acceptance, Bakhtin (1981) embraces the concept in its plurality. For the Russian literary critic, the author's voice is one among many voices to be found in the novel (the narrator's as well as those of various characters). The author is akin to a ventriloquist or a choir conductor: 'Heteroglossia, once incorporated into the novel (whatever the forms for its incorporation), is *another's speech* in *another's language,* serving to express authorial intentions but in a refracted way' (Bakhtin 1981: 324). When he uses the word *voices,* Bakhtin (1981, 1984) is concerned with the means by which utterances index typified speaking characters. However, these voices are not merely the expressions of the individuals' points of view; they are also class-based varieties. The novel's polyphony reflects society's *heteroglossia* (i.e. the 'internal stratification of any single national language into social dialects' – Bakhtin 1981: 260). Voices are perceivable through *voicing contrasts*: 'No figure of personhood is typifiable as a discrete voice (of whatever type) unless it is differentiable from its surround' (Agha 2005: 40). In the media, heteroglossia is performed through processes of linguistic othering. Diversity emerges from the plurality of media voices, as well as within each individual voice.

Although the term *media* is used in a form that, by hiding its plurality behind a Latin flexion, seems to reduce the concept to one collective entity (i.e. the media, the mass media, the social media, etc.), one generally conceives of it as the sum of local, national and international/transnational voices. Familiar representations of such proliferation of voices are found in collages of news headlines, mingled TV voices, walls of TV screens and edited Internet windows. Media voices include not only those of celebrities as well as lesser-known voices of legitimate speakers (journalists and officials of various status), but also the voices of the nameless masses, for whom the new media, and particularly the social media, arguably provide a stage.[2] To scholars, this plurality leads to a few questions: How is one to evaluate such diversity of voices? How should the *space* given to these voices be compared (should scholars even try to compare the *audibility* of such voices)? Should one deal with these voices separately or, bearing in mind to mistrust the false impression of polyphony or organized choir these voices give (including the lead voices of hegemonic ideologies as well as the contrapuntal voices of resistance), should one address the diverse ways they have to co-exist? In front of the gargantuan task, scholars have often homogenized this diversity in order to grasp it better. Appadurai who highlighted the complexity of addressing voices' diversity (1988), speaks in terms of 'flows' and 'scapes' and describes *mediascape* (1996: 35)[3] as part of *global cultural flows*, which has the merit of partly avoiding the fixing in place and time of such discourses. Indeed, to capture what is essentially ever-changing, complex and fluid, the language phenomena were first transcribed and analysed, before being reduced to structures and functions, categorized into systems and oppositions, pinned down like the entomologist's butterflies. In this book, I have myself categorized performances of voices in terms of *marked* and *unmarked* voices, evaluating the borders between them by what I assumed to be voice contrasts (Figure 4).

If such processes of categorizations enable scholars to highlight symbolic associations and unearth hidden mechanisms and practices, it is nevertheless important neither to reduce complex social phenomena to constructed grids,

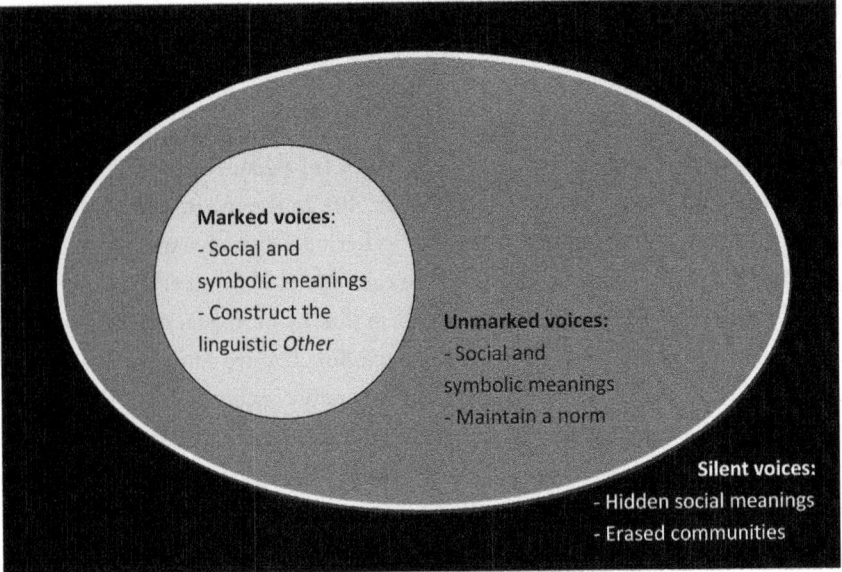

Figure 4 Marked, unmarked and silent voices in the media

nor to lose from sight the limitations of such frameworks. For example, what may appear to fit neatly in given categories should be considered in time as *unseizable*. 'Silent voices' (Figure 4) provide a good example of such a phenomenon. By 'silent voices', I mean voices that, at a given time, are not audible/visible in the media for different reasons: they may not be of current media interest (when some regional or social accents are favoured such as Scottish, British, Russian or French accents in US films, others are not heard in the media),[4] or were but are not performed any more (because they are not in fashion, or are considered inappropriate – for being racist or sexist, etc.), or are not performed in the way they used to be (ethnic voices may be toned down to the extent that they disappear altogether). For all of these reasons, silent voices may move in and out of media silence. In the same way, unmarked voices present variability in their *unmarkedness*. Boundaries between what appears to be marked and unmarked in the media are fuzzy: features that appear as marked for some may not be for others, or may lose salience in different contexts (i.e. the contrast between the performance and the norm is perceived with less intensity). Furthermore, markers may at turns be perceived as stigmas, signs of distinction or emblems of affiliation. In the case of transvestites, such variations in the performance's interpretative frame cause the performed voices to be received with completely opposite reactions (the contrasted but always passionate comments posted on Conchita Wurst's YouTube videos provide a good example of such a phenomenon).

In this book, I aimed to demonstrate that media voices perpetuate discourses that are previously circulated in and out of the media (by conforming to them or opposing them). For Bakhtin (1981), due to a phenomenon that he calls *dialogism*, any pronounced utterance is charged with value, surrounded:

> ...by the 'light' of alien words that have already been spoken about it. It is entangled, shot through with shared thoughts, points of view, alien value judgments and accents. The word, directed towards its object, enters a dialogically agitated and tension-filled environment of alien words, value judgments and accents, weaves in and out of complex interrelationships, merges with some, recoils from others, intersects with yet a third group: and all this may crucially shape discourse, may leave a trace in all its semantic layers, may complicate its expression and influence its entire stylistic profile.
>
> Bakhtin 1981: 276

The 'living utterance' activates and organizes existing socio-ideological consciousness and any artistic representation is at turn 'penetrated by this dialogic play of verbal intentions that meet and are interwoven in it' (Bakhtin 1981: 277). When such intertextuality functions by means of reiteration, in the case of performed voices, repetition of features co-exists with innovation, and individual agency may develop within the practice of a given genre.

Hegemonic ideologies and individual agency

Whether media performances of voice affiliate to them or resist them, hegemonic language ideologies frame the market for such performances as well as their commodifications into genres. The analyst of performed voices should nevertheless consider agency within structure and difference within repetition (as pattern and creativity are 'two co-existent but distinct dimensions of style' – Bell 1999: 526). Difference and agency are not merely signs of resistance, but are also the rightful manifestation of individual creativity ('agentive use of language, building on the foundation of existing social meanings' – Bell and Gibson 2011: 555). Moreover, since in some of the studied cases performances of voice are the creations of artists, one should not ignore the artistic part of *verbal art*. Working with such performances, the analyst may hesitate between the desire to study the text as an 'unmediated expression of authorial individuality' (Bakhtin, 1999: 267) or a more deterministic approach to the study of style as the application of rules and genres (stylistics). Bakhtin (1999) argued that such a dilemma is 'by no means universally recognized. Most scholars are not inclined to undertake a radical revision of the fundamental philosophical conception of poetic discourse' (p. 267).

As intertwined and inseparable as a DNA double helix, difference and repetition are two fundamental aspects of artistic performances, and should be considered equally important. However, is it possible to reconcile both traditions of study and to embrace agency within repetition, individuality within diversity? As voices have ceased to belong to the bodies that utter them, to be reclaimed by other bodies, turned into valuable commodities or reified into ideological symbols, it appears that it is now time to fathom the very own agencies of performed voices.

APPENDIX

A Framework for the Study of Voices in the Media

I. Source

- What is the source of the voice? Is the source named/known? Is the voice embodied?
- Is the voice bodiless? Detached? In disjunction?
- Does the body support the voice (participate in/contribute to the performance)?

II. Performance

- Is the voice performed? If yes, how *visible* is the performance? I.e. is it realistic? Is it stylized? Is it an obvious pastiche? Etc.
- Is the identity performed by the voice coherent with the identity of the performer (in terms of belonging or affiliation to a social group)? What is the speaker's legitimacy with regards to the voice (i.e. his or her rights to perform such voice)? What is the speaker's stance?
- Is the voice supported by other props (i.e. how is it staged)? Is the voice in harmony with the props? Does it contrast with them?
- What is the creative/artistic part of the performance? Is it assumed, legitimized (such as in actors' performances) or claimed by authors (director and/or performer)?

III. Grain

- What are the voice's characteristics? Phonological features (i.e. accent, texture, etc.), lexicon, discursive features, etc.?

IV. Index

- What values are attached to the voice (social, cultural, dramatic, symbolic), both in general and in the given context?

V. Context

- How does the relation between the voice's salient features and the values that they index inform us on the context of performance, and on the values shared between the performer and the audience?
- What are the social representations, language ideologies attached to the performed identity in the particular media and/or genre? Are these coherent with the one given outside of this media and/or genre?

VI. Entext (genre)

- **Macro-genre**: what are the media means of communication (audio/visual/both)? What is the media genre (TV, radio, film, etc.)?
- **Sub-genre** (see VII. Intertext): What cluster of salient features is used in the performance of the chosen sub-genre? What features are selected and emphasized? What features are erased?
- What are the dynamics between the macro-genre and the sub-genre? (Where are the sub-genres usually found? Is the macro-genre a conventional or innovative choice?)
- **Innovation**: does the performance voluntarily break with certain conventions?

VII. Intertext

- How does the voice relate to other voices that preceded it (mentioned or not)?
- What voices are silenced?

VIII. Commodity

- How is the voice sold on the media market?
- What is its value? Is there a high demand for such voice?
- Is it new on the market? Did it previously belong to silent voices?

IX. Audience

- Is the voice reclaimed by members of the audience? Is it reused/recirculated?
- How is the voice received/appraised? (In terms of aesthetics, legitimacy, authenticity, etc.)

Notes

Introduction

1 'Il donne à la *présence vivante* une possibilite d'"être là" à nouveau sans aucun équivalent, sans aucun précédent' (Derrida 2001: 81). From here onwards, and unless stated otherwise, all quotations translated from French into English will be my own translation.
2 http://www.guardian.co.uk/commentisfree/2012/nov/27/joey-barton-french-accent-expat-fit-in [accessed 15 January 2015].
3 http://www.dailymail.co.uk/news/article-2239044/Joey-Barton-French-accent-video-Watch-football-bad-boys-hilarious-interview.html#ixzz2SW4gpTu4 [accessed 15 January 2015].
   In a similar piece, found on a website where the video of the interview was published, the journalist comments: '*Zut Alors!* Seems Joey has been watching old *Pink Panther* movies ...' http://www.whoateallthepies.tv/videos/148577/joey-barton-talks-in-hilarious-faux-french-accent-after-popping-his-marseille-cherry-video.html [accessed 15 January 2015].
4 It is arguable that, in the case of most published articles and released films, there is a linguistic consensus and that it is uncommon for readers or spectators to question openly the displayed linguistic ideologies that are central to their understanding. Note however that the recent trend of commenting on online articles permit these discussions to take place more than ever before.
5 Literally: 'Fuck Rohmer!'
6 For Conboy (2010: 7): 'These [genre] expectations form part of a shared sense of community in reading and are an important contributor to the social aspects of writing.'
7 Following the same idea, Caroline Howarth (2006) suggestively entitled her article: 'A social representation is not a quiet thing'.
8 This has changed little since and the same negative connotations prevail to this day in the French media: when writing these lines, in May 2013, a riot took place in Paris during an evening that was intended to celebrate the victory of the Paris-Saint-Germain football team. After a few hours of joyous celebration near the Eiffel Tower, violence escalated, shop windows were smashed and cars set on fire in the Trocadero's quarter. As the interviewed police representative described the

troublemakers, he settled for the laconic: '*Ces gens-là viennent de banlieue*' (These people come from the suburbs). All was supposedly said.

9 'Le degré zéro de la ville, à mille lieues d'une vraie cité. Mais cela n'était rien encore puisque le mot va servir, à partir de 1985 à peu près, désigner tout à la fois les lieux, les maux et les peurs associés à la crise de la société française née du chômage et du racisme qui aujourd'hui compromettent l'intégration d'une partie importante des enfants de migrants' (Faure 2006: 19).

10 When telling the history of the French suburb's media coverage, Fagyal (2010) notes: 'Toward the end of the 1990s, the suburban theme provokes the reappearance of the emblematic figure of the delinquent Other (*the deviant Other*), exclusively male and often of North-African descent. The traditional Parisian slang, formerly included in colloquial French, starts from this day to "index the youth from the projects of the old red belt suburbs" (Valdman, 2000: 1190)' (Fagyal 2010: 31, my translation) ['Vers la fin des années quatre-vingt-dix, le thème des banlieues fait ressurgir la figure emblématique de l'Autre délinquant (*the deviant Other*), exclusivement masculin et bien souvent maghrébin. L'argot traditionnel de la capitale, fondu auparavant dans le français parlé, devient à ce moment-là "la marque indicielle des jeunes des cités de l'ancienne ceinture des banlieues rouges" (Valdman, 2000: 1190).']

11 In French, the word *répétition* has the double meaning of *to repeat* and *to rehearse*.

12 Since the 1980s, the acronym NTM (i.e. *Nique Ta Mère*) is also known as the name of a rap band from the Parisian suburbs.

13 However, some values are not equally shared by audiences. In some cases, performers may also choose to address parts of the audience only. More importantly, one should always bear in mind that language ideologies may be understood without being *shared*.

14 According to Carrie Tarr: '*Cinéma de banlieue* emerged within French film criticism in the mid-1990s as a way of categorizing a series of independently released films set in the rundown multi-ethnic working-class estates (the *cités*) on the periphery of France's major cities (the *banlieues*), the most significant of which was Mathieu Kassovitz's *La Haine* (1995)' (Tarr 2005: 2).

15 An example of such practice is to be found in the rather serious *Sciences Humaines*, in an article entitled '"*Tu flippes ta race, bâtard!*": *Sur le langage des cités*' (Dortier 2005) ('"Now you're freaking out, bastard": on the language of the projects'), an article that is peppered with such borrowings.

16 In January 2013, the French public channel France2 broadcast in its evening news a report entitled '*Réapprendre à parler pour pouvoir travailler*' ('Re-learning to speak to be able to work') that showed young men from the Parisian suburbs who felt that their accent was an obstacle in their quest to find a job and therefore decided in a sort of linguistic rehabilitation to take a few courses to improve on their French. This is not a new argument in the news as a few years earlier, Nabila Ramdani had

reported for the *Guardian* that language was 'a barrier in the banlieue' and related an argument that opposed in 2007 Rachida Dati – who was to become spokesperson of French president Nicolas Sarkozy – and a teenager from the projects whom she reprimanded for wearing his baseball cap back to front and for using *verlan*. Interestingly, the same year, Fadela Amara, secretary of state for Sarkozy's government, used a spectacular fragment of *Banlieue* French when announcing, during a cabinet meeting, a project of reform that she had entitled '*Plan zéro glandouille*' ('No bum plan') with the need to do it '*à donf*' (verlan for *à fond* – 'in depth, to the maximum'). Note that her use of the vernacular provoked the wrath of ACLEFEU (an association created after the notorious 2005 riots), who accused her of stigmatizing the suburbs and asked her to 'speak in French' (sic). A couple of years later, Nadine Morano, junior secretary of state for family and social unity, condemned *verlan* again when she said that any youngster from a Muslim background should 'love France when he lives here . . . find a job, *not* speak verlan and *not* wear his cap back to front'. http://www.guardian.co.uk/commentisfree/belief/2009/dec/16/language-banlieue-islamophobia-france-sarkozy [accessed 15 January 2015].

17 'En revanche, l'émergence des "beurs" dans la société française, notamment depuis l'alternance politique de 1981 a permis l'éclosion d'un nouveau langage, parti des banlieues défavorisées pour rayonner jusque dans les quartiers chics de la capitale en influençant au passage même les médias et les milieux intellectuels!' http://www.dilap.com/contributions/banlieue-beur/beur-arabe.htm [accessed 15 January 2015].

18 This being said, one should acknowledge the role played by Alain Rey (the well-known editor of the French dictionary *Le Robert*) who prefaced the book and took part in media interviews during its release. Being an authoritative figure in the field of French lexicography and by ratifying the legitimacy of the work done in this unconventional dictionary, he gave authority and legitimacy to the novice lexicographers, and ultimately to the book (as well as added value to the product).

Chapter 1: The Sociolinguistic Study of Voices and Performances in the Media

1 In this book, I shall not explain the difference between media discourse and media texts. For clarification on the two concepts, see Fairclough 1992's introduction, Meinhof 1994, Wodak and Busch 2004.

2 One should never forget that a main goal of most media institutions as profit-making organizations is to attract consumers and to sell their products (Fairclough 1995, Conboy 2010, Molek-Kozakowska 2013). When broadcasting media texts that

are non-standard, abstruse or provocative, media institutions take the risk to confuse, or worse, deter readers and viewers.

3   This book will not focus on audiences' reception, and even though it will always bear in mind the eventuality of *non-reading* (resulting from resistance or non-acculturation), the analyses provided are based on the premise that there are dominant/hegemonic readings that organize production and reception. I chose to reproduce Stuart Hall's long quote not only for the way that the cultural theorist highlights media's use of semantic resources (such as social categories and representations), but most importantly for its insistence on the fact that the media select what they see as *worthy* for their audience. In narrating these news-worthy events (in processes known as *media storytelling* or *media fiction*), the media *make sense* of a complex world. The resulting media discourses participate in the construction and the maintenance of a social order – an idea that is central to my book.

4   See Irvine's (2001: 23) definition of style as 'social semiosis of distinctiveness', based on Bourdieu's concept of *distinction* (1984 [1979]).

5   This is why with regards to linguists' use of the concept of stylization, Carroll's (2013) article calls for a questioning of the meaning of 'artistic'.

6   Many of us have experienced the feeling of awe that recordings of long-dead artists and historical figures inspire (Martin Luther King's 'I have a dream' is one among many of these recordings).

7   http://www.youtube.com/watch?v=HpqjErGfJ9c [accessed 9 September 2013].

8   http://www.youtube.com/watch?v=-TdG1dDFXgQ [accessed 9 September 2013].

9   Mistakes are rare and short-lived. The few occurrences of performances passing for real, such as the famous Orson Welles hoax, have passed to posterity.

10 As an example, the first film that was labelled as *film de banlieue* (*La Haine*, Kassovitz 1995) was directed by an artist born into a family of filmmakers and brought up in the capital city of Paris.

11 The media generally target particular groups of the social classes. This is particularly obvious with the written press and in the example that I used, the magazine *The Inrockuptibles*' focus on a left-wing intellectual readership has been the object of criticism in recent years for its elitist editorial policy.

Part 1: Voices in French: Performances of Linguistic Differentiation in the French Media

1   Interviewed by A. Charon '*L'atelier intérieur*', France Culture, 7 November 2011: http://www.franceculture.fr/emission-l-atelier-interieur-numero-11-la-voix-a-rose-is-a-rose-2011-11-07 [accessed 23 May 2014].

Chapter 2: Performances of Non-standard Voices in French Films

1. This chapter was originally published under the title 'Accented French in films: performing and evaluating in-group stylizations', *Multilingua*, J. Androutsopoulos (ed.) Special Issue: Language and Society in Cinematic Discourse, 31: 253–275 (2012).
2. Alain Bentolila is a French linguist who is well-known for his mediatized stance on what he calls a 'linguistic inequality' (Bentolila 2002) or what he denounces as an affliction suffered by the youth living in underprivileged suburbs. His notorious article entitled '*Vivre avec 400 mots*' ('Living with 400 words', in Potet 2005) was published in *Le Monde* and was very much debated by journalists and linguists.
3. It is an exercise of stylization in the Bakhtinian sense as the characters who borrow the prestigious voice stylize the most.
4. http://www.commeaucinema.com/notes-de-prod/l-esquive,13129 [last accessed in July 2011].
5. http://www.migrantcinema.net/glossary/term/accented_cinema [last accessed in July 2011].
6. The main character is given the corrupt form of the word *ch'timi* at the beginning of the film – *cheutimi* is meant to sound like *châtiment* ('punishment') in a comical depiction that shows the North and its inhabitants as the chamber to Hell.
7. A well-loved French movie that previously made an important use of accented French was the two-part drama *Jean de Florette/Manon des sources* (Berri 1986), which was situated in a small rural village in the South of France.
8. Kechiche said more about the writing of the dialogues in an interview with *Cineaste*: 'The script had actually been written more than fifteen years ago. It of course became dated because of the language – this sort of argot naturally evolves over time. So as the filming approached, I had to do some work with a dialogue coach. We would, for example, go into places like McDonald's where young people gather and record their speech patterns and expressions. I had to do a great deal of work during the casting phase to get the language right. I gave the young people a great deal of freedom during the rehearsal period to explore the best way of saying certain things' (in Porton 2005: 48).
9. He said that his goal when making the film was 'to break the caricatured image that is generally given of *banlieue*: of a violent and scary youth' (in Fajardo 2004) and 'to educate the spectator's gaze' (in Lalanne 2004).
10. Bienvenue chez les Ch'tis: 'Vin dious que ch'té bin!' *L'Express*, 5 March 2008. http://www.lexpress.fr/actualite/societe/i-bienvenue-chez-les-ch-tis-i-vin-dious-quech-te-bin_470810.html [accessed in June 2011].
11. For this study, I benefited from a Press book put together by the British Film Institute.
12. The following lists are established thanks to the edited script by *L'avant-scène Cinéma* 542 (2005).

13 Among these I found: *ouf* for the standard *fou* ('mad'), *téma > matez* ('look'); *péta > taper* ('nick'), *oim > moi* ('me') *chelou> louche* ('shady'), *chantmé > méchant* ('terrific'), *vénère > énervé* ('on edge'), *à oualpé > à poil* ('naked'), *keumé > mec* ('guy'), *meuf > femme* ('women'), *vesqui > esquive* ('dodge'), *secla > classe* ('class'), *eins > sein* ('breast'), *pécho > choper* ('catch'), *noich > chinois* ('Chinese'), *guedin > dingue* ('nuts').

14 Since the publication of this article in 2012 a documentary showed that some girls from the projects had gone into the habit of behaving and talking like boys in order to protect themselves (Les Roses Noires, Milano 2012).

Chapter 3: Performances of Feminine Voices on the Internet

1 This chapter was originally published under the title 'Virtual community and politeness: the use of female markers of identity and solidarity in a transvestites' website', *Journal of Politeness Research*, M. Locher (ed.). Special issue on 'Politeness and Impoliteness in computer-mediated communication' 6(1): 83–103.

2 According to Herring (2001: 614), '[a]synchronous CMD systems do not require that users be logged on at the same time in order to send and receive messages; rather, messages are stored at the addressee's site until they can be read.'

3 The data used for this chapter has been anonymised in order to protect the individuals quoted in the analysis. However, the author is aware that using such data is ethically problematic, especially when dealing with sensitive issues (Ess and AoIR 2002, Eysenbach and Till 2001). The website and pages used for analysis are freely accessible to all and the webmasters do not mention in their pages of introduction any restriction to the access of these texts. Finally, the website has been officially inactive since November 2008.

4 It is interesting to note that this form is very unconventional since the French do not usually use a feminine form for words of English origin.

5 It actually happened to a similar website that had to close a couple of years ago since it fell victim to the harassment of a virulent outsider.

6 *The Graham Norton Show* (BBC One, 2014)

7 This may arguably be the case of Conchita Wurst who claims on her website that she has 'two hearts': i.e. Tom (described with the masculine pronoun) and Conchita (described with 'she').

Chapter 4: Performances of Ethnic Voices in French Films

1 One example of such stylizations is the still very much controversial 1980s sketch from the stand-up comedian Michel Leeb entitled *L'épicier africain* ('The African

Grocer'). The mention of one of the lines (*C'est pas des lunettes, c'est mes narines* – 'These are not sunglasses, they are my nostrils' – performed with hyperbolic rolled /r/'s) should suffice to give an idea of the tone of its humour. A look at the sketch on YouTube as well as at the commentaries following the video is enlightening and shows that representations have evolved since these days: many viewers denounce what they call a '*Banania* humour' (in reference to the cocoa commercials that represented a Senegalese Infantry man wearing a wide smile in a very colonialist fashion), but when some admit that they used to find the sketch hilarious when they were kids and would find it unacceptable coming from a contemporary comedian, others do not see any harm in still finding it very funny (even if some of the latter also feel the need to defend themselves against accusations of racism by mentioning that they are black – obviously not asking themselves, in bell hooks' words, if 'black people … have learned to cherish hateful images of [them]selves, then what process of looking allows [them] to counter the seduction of images that threatens to dehumanize and colonize?' (hooks 1992: 6).

2 See, for example, Pierre Péchin's (1975) Arabic-accented version of La Fontaine's fable *La cigale et la fourmi* ('The Grasshopper and the Ant'), which was a huge popular success.

3 'Maik Darah Interview (La voix Française de Whoopi Goldberg)' (Morgan 2007) http://www.dailymotion.com/video/x7f3rv_maik-darah-interview-la-voix-franca_shortfilms [accessed 5 January 2015].

4 'Il faut savoir que dans le doublage, "les comédiens noirs ont des voix graves de Noirs" et les comédiens asiatiques ont une voix "aigue d'asiatique". Les comédiens blancs, eux, ont la chance d'avoir une tessiture suffisamment étendue qui permet de doubler et les Noirs et les asiatiques et les Blancs. Cette croyance est telle qu'il n'est pas rare d'entendre une comédienne blanche affirmer qu'elle a "une voix de Noire" sans penser être raciste; au contraire, elle double des Noires' (Modestine 2008).

5 *Discrimination comme expérience et comme philosophie politique pratique*, funded by the ANR.

6 '[V]ous êtes "noire", cela signifie : "Vous êtes un être humain différent de nous, vous venez du Noirland"' (in Toscer 2009).

7 'Il importe avant tout aux individus d'échapper "au double piège de la haine et de la victimisation afin de rester, même partiellement, le maître du jeu"' (Dubet et al. 2013: 112).

8 It is interesting to note that the word *prejudice* was chosen in this note when in all likelihood it is an act of discrimination that took place (for the difference between the two, see Fiske 1998 and Dubet et al. 2013).

9 'Le choix d'un comédien-doubleur devait se faire en fonction de sa qualité de voix et de sa compétence, et non en raison de sa couleur de peau ou de son origine' (in *Le Monde* 2009).

10 '[L]es représentations liées à l'immigration sont souvent très stéréotypées. Quand j'étais un jeune acteur, j'ai refusé beaucoup de rôles de dealers, de délinquants' – 'Representations linked to immigration are stereotyped. As a young actor, I had to refuse many parts of drug dealers and delinquents' (Kechiche, in Lalanne 2007).

11 'Jouer un Noir, j'ai dû apprendre à le faire, j'ai dû apprendre à jouer le Noir, ne me demandez pas comment on fait, je ne sais pas, mais apparemment j'arrivais à convaincre.' ('Playing the part of a Black man is something that I had to learn, I had to learn to play the Black man, don't ask me how one does it, I don't know, but it seems that I managed to be convincing' – in Gélas and Blanchard 2012.)

12 http://www.franceinfo.fr/chroniques-itineraires-2007-11-18-jacques-martial-portrait-d-un-acteur-militant-39347-81-155.html [accessed 5 January 2015].

13 http://www.dailymotion.com/video/x7f3rv_maik-darah-interview-la-voix-franca_shortfilms [accessed 5 January 2015].

14 It was, for example, the case of the mangled English of *Blackfaces*: a stereotyped caricature of black people in minstrel shows and vaudeville in nineteenth-century American theatres (Bucholtz and Lopez 2011).

15 See Dubois' (2013: 13–14) description of a Lumière brothers' short feature entitled *Village noir au jardin d'acclimatation* (Black village in the Jardin d'acclimation) in which black children jump into a fountain to get coins thrown by tourists. In other national cinemas, *Birth of a Nation* (Griffith 1915) was an often-cited case of controversial depiction of race in films. Although silent, the film displays ethnic linguistic stylizations in the form of eye dialect used in captions such as: 'Is I yo' equal cap'n – jes like any white man?' (2:30).

16 'Quand ce personnage parle, on inscrit "le Noir". Il n'est pas un être humain, il n'est qu'un stéréotype' (Bankolé, in Dubois 2012: 117).

17 'Cette question des rôles stéréotypés réservés aux Noirs n'est pas une vue de l'esprit mais bien une réalité. Il suffit pour s'en convaincre de lire les témoignages des acteurs eux-mêmes ou simplement de constater que pour son deuxième grand rôle au cinéma (son "come-back" en quelque sorte) dans Huit Femmes de François Ozon, Firmine Richard se voit confier un rôle de … gouvernante' (Dubois 2012: 111).

18 'Noir tout à la fois nounou, voyou et drôle' (Dubois 2012: 112).

19 'Il nous manque la productrice noire que notre communauté attend' (Darah, in Morgan 2007) http://www.dailymotion.com/video/x7f3rv_maik-darah-interview-la-voix-franca_shortfilms [accessed 5 January 2015].

20 '[C]'est vrai que le cinéma noir, pour l'instant en France, n'a pas d'écho. Il n'y a pas d'acteurs noirs, de producteurs noirs' (Barny 2011) http://www.clapnoir.org/spip.php?article737 [accessed 5 January 2015].

21 'J'ai tout entendu: "les noirs n'intéressent personne", "j'ai déjà produit mon quota de films avec des minorités cette année", "cette histoire est trop futile pour des noirs"… Il y avait un problème, un gros problème. En fait, le projet ne rentrait dans aucune

22 '[L]'Arabe est encore l'employé fainéant qu'on tutoie et que le héros n'hésite pas à tancer vertement. Si cette tendance est à la baisse, les exemples ne manquent toujours pas... il serait trop long de dresser la liste des productions qui utilisent abondamment l'imagerie coloniale' (Gaertner 2005: 194).
23 'Celui du brave tirailleur (enfantin) et celui du sauvage (dangereux)' (Ndiaye 2008: 215).
24 In this vein, it is disconcerting to read in the otherwise serious magazine *Télérama* the comedian actor Djamel Debbouze being described first with the banlieue slang *rebeu* ('Arab') and later on in the article the actor calling himself 'the most fortunate Arab in France' ('Sa tchatche et son regard perçant sur la société ont fait du "rebeu" de Trappes, "l'Arabe le mieux loti de France"'): www.telerama.fr/scenes/jamel-debbouze-les-francais-ont-peur-de-leur-immigration-c-est-normal-c-est-tf1-qui-a-fait-les-presentations,64722.php#zgXRdHtwCeZWsDo6.99 [accessed 5 January 2015].
25 'C'est bien qu'il y ait cette diversité dans le cinéma français [...] une population qui est très peu représentée dans le cinéma'. France 2 Evening News (with Abdellatif Kechiche and Hafsia Herzi, 2008) http://www.ina.fr/video/3562871001030 [accessed 5 January 2015].
26 'Ce sont des études pour moi, je prolonge mes études universitaires de sociologie, on continue à chercher, à démonter les faits sociaux, les structures de domination, d'exploitation, c'est ça qui est le plus révoltant et qu'on dénonce dans chacun de nos films' (Ameur-Zaïmeche, in Pasquier 2008).
27 'Les personnages féminins sont inspirés de femmes que je connais et que j'aime, ma mère, mes sœurs... Mais il y a aussi la volonté de les montrer autrement que selon l'idée qu'on se fait en France de la femme arabe... Je voulais casser cette représentation que je trouve un peu pesante.'
28 'Quand je vois certains films où la femme maghrébine n'a pas de sexualité, de sensualité, de corps, ça m'agace'. Interview with Hafsia Herzi about *The Secret of the Grain* (published in the Press book, 2007) http://www.cinemotions.com/interview/11953 [accessed 5 January 2015].
29 To the extent that in order to find *authentic* ethnic voices, directors such as Abdellatif Kechiche or Ameur-Zaïmeche resort to North-African or amateur actors.
30 This is also the case of actors who have regional and social accents. For example, Ariane Ascaride and Hafsia Herzi have explained how difficult it is to have a career while displaying a strong regional accent, and the latter confessed to having used drama training in order to *lose* her accent (Weck 2008).
31 'J'ai été très complexé par ma provenance sociale. Je me cachais presque, je m'excluais de peur d'être exclu par les autres. J'ai grandi enfermé dans mon quartier, mon ghetto mental, on se disait que le reste n'était pas pour nous. Mais ce n'est pas plus dramatique que ça. Mon métier m'a appris à m'accepter' (Bouajila, in Mairesse 2010).

32 'Je suis devenu cinéaste avec la peur d'être rattrapé par ma condition sociale. Il me faut fournir plus d'efforts pour acquérir ma liberté d'artiste' (Kechiche, in Morice 2007).

33 In performed stylizations of Arabic-accented French, French vowels (such as [ə], [e], [y] or [ɔ̃]) are systematically replaced with [i]. *Je* and *j'ai* are therefore pronounced [ʒi] and 'du' is pronounced [di].

34 In the case of the United States, Gal (2009: 328) argues that '[e]thnicity in the United States is often a matter of commodification: the claim to "ownership" of voices, accents, and images that, because of social distance, provide authenticity but not stigma.' A recent American film (*The Book of Life*, Gutierrez 2014) gives an interesting example of such variations in the performances of accents across generations: while the grandparents and parents speak English with a non-native accent (the grandparents display the strongest Spanish accent), the children speak unaccented American English.

35 This feeling of disconnection is central to the story of recent films such as *Né quelque part* (Hamidi 2013) or *Paris à tout prix* (Kherici 2013) where a trip to Algeria or Morocco becomes a series of ordeals for the main characters who struggle to go back to France, the country that they see as their home.

36 'Et il y a une génération multiculturelle urbaine qui pousse les portes de manière plus violente. Ce n'est une question de caractère. Ils poussent les portes pour qu'on leur permette de s'exprimer' (Barny, in Pochon 2011).

37 'Pourquoi alors les deux réalisateurs ont décidé d'exclure l'arabe pour mettre en valeur un aide-soignant d'origine africaine? L'Algérien était-il moins crédible? Un acteur d'origine algérienne ou maghrébine serait-il nocif pour le succès du film? Omar Sy star de Canal+ correspond-il mieux au rôle d'Abdel? On n'en saura rien, car curieusement, aucun journaliste ou critique n'a osé soulever ce dilemme ou dénoncer cette «discrimination» artistique' (Soltane 2012).

38 'Le choix d'un noir, évidemment d'un beau noir, bien bâti et faisant des ronds de jambe (en lieu et place du personnage original de l'aide de vie qui était Algérien, ces derniers comme on sait dansent moins bien et ont moins d'humour)' (Rolandeau 2011 [personal blog]) http://yrol.free.fr/CINEMA/critiques/intouchables.htm [accessed 5 January 2015].

39 'Entre la culture française et la culture africaine, je glane ce qui me plaît' (Sy, in Odicino 2011).

Part 2: Voices in French-accented English

1 Conversely, I note a recent tendency to use foreign languages in French commercials for cars. In 2011, a series of TV commercials for Renault advertised '*La qualité*

version française' and made use of French-accented German interspersed with code-switching into French. These commercials were in fact parodies of the French commercials for German cars, and their well-known slogans in German (i.e. VW's *Das Auto* – 'the car' – and Opel's *Deutsche Qualität* – 'German quality').

2 'It's so easy to fall in love. And when it happens, you'll know it's for real. By the familiar French names of the famous French grapes. By the warmth of the reds, the freshness of the whites. By the three little words that signify so much. *Vin de Pays*' (in Kelly-Holmes 2005: 55).

3 See, for example, Lambert Wilson's character in *The Matrix Reloaded* (Wachowski and Wachowski 2003) or Vincent Cassel's in *Ocean Thirteen* (Soderbergh 2007). More will be said on these characters' French-accented English in the following chapter.

Chapter 5: Performances of French-accented English in Hollywood Films

1 Nathan Lane is a well-known stand-up comedian, well-rehearsed in the sort of vocal stylizations.

2 Who famously said: 'In America, when you have an accent, in the mind of the people they associate you with kissing hands and being gallant. I think that has harmed me' http://www.tcm.com/this-month/article.html?isPreview=&id=139158%7C121579&name=Algiers [accessed 7 January 2015].

3 To a spectator writing about his astonishment at hearing a well-known character of the English folklore express himself with a French accent, an internet user gave this plausible explanation: 'The Normans (French) conquered the Saxons (native English) in 1066 AD. Nearly everyone of importance was French speaking. Richard the Lion hearted didn't speak any English. We are talking about the first decade in the 1200s. Robin of Loxley was (according to some) the son of a nobleman and probably spoke French' (*Yahoo answers*).

4 Blumenfeld (2002: 199) establishes five levels: from the very slight to the very heavy accent.

5 By including animation films in the corpus, I deal with different forms of performances where salient features are overemphasized. In a documentary on the work of voice talents, *I Know That Voice* (Shapiro 2013), two professionals explain: 'Voice over is a different kind of acting, it's much bigger, it's much more theatrical' (Diedrich Bader, actor and voice talent); '[Voice talents] have to do all the cryptic expressions that you get on camera on mic ... that's their gift' (Ginny McSwain, voice director). Moreover, there is no doubt that there is a tendency in animation to *overdo it* (i.e. adopt crazy voices and over-the-top accents).

6 The character was voiced by Mel Blanc, a real star in the world of animated films' voices – also known for voicing nearly every major character of the Warner Bros' cartoons (Bugs Bunny, both Tweety and Sylvester, Porky Pig, etc.).
7 In this excerpt (which can easily be viewed online), one notes few linguistic specificities such as the typical French pronunciation of /r/'s as well as the spectacular fragments of French on which I shall expand in the next section.
8 http://www.film.com/movies/janeane-garofalo-talks-ratatouille [accessed 7 December 2014].
9 ITV3 Interview: https://www.youtube.com/watch?v=MZJpGq6W1bw [accessed 7 December 2014]. See also 'How to play Poirot: David Suchet's method acting trick' (*The Telegraph*, 13 November 2013) http://www.telegraph.co.uk/culture/tvandradio/10441147/How-to-play-Poirot-David-Suchets-method-acting-tricks.html [accessed 7 December 2014].
10 Owing much to Bourdieu's (1984b) work on distinction, and in the way Peter Sellers thought first of a physical attitude before he conceived Clouseau's accent, it seems plausible to see a relation between the perceived precision of the French accent and the prissiness of French characters that I described earlier.
11 https://www.youtube.com/watch?v=6rICFoH5P5A [accessed 7 December 2014].
12 The strength of appreciation of accents also depends on the context and types of character as the following anecdote shows. In 2008, when Juliette Binoche played Kathy in a new theatrical adaptation of the British classic *Wuthering Heights*, her performance drew severe criticism from a film reviewer who christened the actress 'Catherine Clouseau' – apparently judging her accent in the light of the *Pink Panther*'s main character (from *The Independent*).
13 The *Trail of the Pink Panther* was released in 1982, after the actor's death, and used unseen footage from his previous films.
14 Is it for its similarity with the typically French onomatopoeia *euh*?
15 In their study, Dewaele and McCloskey (2014) find that, due to high expectations, multilingual participants were significantly more bothered by their own foreign accent than by others'.
16 And it seems that there has been a recent tendency in the world of animation films to use Scottish accents (*Shrek*, 2001; *How to Train Your Dragon*, 2010; etc.).
17 '[L]e terme *kathègoresthai*, d'où sont issues nos catégories, signifie accuser publiquement' (Bourdieu 1984: 268–270).

Chapter 6: The Case of Poirot's Voice

1 This chapter was first published in 2008 under the title '"Who can tell, mon ami?": representations of bilingualism for a majority monolingual audience' in *Sociolinguistic Studies*, in E. Ellis (ed.), special issue on Monolingualism, 2(3): 425–440.

2 Retrieved on 7 August 2008 from http://www.youtube.com/watch?v=KkCdDffb4LE.
3 Monolingual speech in the foreign language is used in brief speech acts by secondary characters too, such as the French *Inspecteur* ('*Envoyez le garçon de cabine*'), a policeman in Nice station ('*Calmez-vous calmez-vous monsieur mes condoléances*') and a nun in the convent where Van Alden's wife is being kept ('*Allez Jeanne, viens, viens*'). These lines are always uttered in the background and as it is not so important that the viewers understand them, they seem to contribute to the local ambiance. They act as a linguistic decor and remind us of the '"language as soundtrack" approach' as described by Kelly-Holmes (2005: 186).
4 For Li (2007: 6), a 'minimal bilingual' is someone 'with only a few words and phrases in a second language'.
5 Intersentential switches occur between different sentences while intrasentential switches are found within the same segment.

Chapter 7: Performances in French on Vancouver's Dining Scene: The Case of French Restaurants' Menus

1 '*Le repas ne serait rien sans le discours avant, pendant et après. Des mots badins ou sentencieux, autour d'intitulés fracassants*' ('Light-hearted or sentential words, surrounding sensational headings') (Abellard 2013).
2 According to Croizé-Pourcelet (2011), the French discursive practices that were traditional of Haute Cuisine restaurants are no longer about long and poetic descriptions of dishes but rather aim at more precise and lighter menus. According to Alain Solivérès, chef of the Parisian restaurant *Taillevent*, which was awarded two stars by the prestigious Michelin guide, menus should be short, go straight to the point and deliver the essential ('*Faire court et juste . . . J'aime aller droit au but, à l'essentiel*'): 'Styles have changed, menus like cooking have been skimmed' ('*les styles ont changé: on a allégé les menus en même temps que la cuisine*' – Solivérès, in Croizé-Pourcelet 2011) – for a detailed history of menus, see Rambourg (2013).
3 In this chapter, I am as faithful as possible to the restaurants' choice of fonts (italics, bold, etc.). If the analyses provided are mainly textual, I acknowledge the fact that menus are polysemiotic and that choices of typefaces, fonts (italics or block letters for example), line spacing, punctuation (quotation marks), or accents (present or absent) play a part in the overall impression that restaurants intend to give of themselves and of the food that they sell.
4 This is a rare case where the word *Escargots* is translated. It is possible that the dish is so emblematic that it is therefore not necessary to provide a translation. Or is it rather that the word *snail* refers to a too concrete reality that would appear to be far

5. Some menus display grammatical mistakes (in genre or spelling). However, it is difficult to tell whether this was due to lack of attention or to a deliberate choice (i.e. in order to obtain the best sounding French) – for example, Zwicky and Zwicky (1980: 90) note that in American menus, *petite* is often chosen as the unmarked form (see an example of such use in note 16).

from appetizing on a restaurant's menu? Zwicky and Zwicky (1980) mention a case in which such dish served in an Italian restaurant in New York is given a translation in French rather than in English (1980: 89).

6. The rare cases that provide articles may first appear incongruous such as in *Pastis'* menu: 'Le tartare et les frites', 'La frisée et les lardons', etc. In these cases, the wording draws on the emblematic use of the French article *le*, which highlights the fact that the dishes are French classics, but also the restaurant's unique rendition of the particular dishes.

7. It is not necessarily the case in other countries where an alternative version of the menu (usually a translation in English) may be handed out to tourists, for example.

8. *The French Table*'s website provides a visual version of their menus in a separate slide show. http://thefrenchtable.ca/lunch-menu-gallery [accessed 13 November 2014].

9. Other meals, such as the controversial horse meat, have not yet attained culinary legitimacy.

10. In the same vein, the coffee company Starbucks described its 'French Roast' blend as inspired by the French intellectuals who were, according to them, at the origin of the French café culture: 'our darkest roast is as sophisticated and intense as the minds that inspired it. We're talking about the French intellectuals who sparked the Parisian coffeehouse culture.'

11. http://www.burnabyheights.com/merchant-directory/merchants/chez-meme-baguette-bistro-2 [accessed 13 November 2014].

12. The restaurant review website *Urbanspoon* adds the term in the keywords that it uses as categories and that they present under each restaurant's name.

13. Whereas in these two films, as well as in popular culture (De Certeau and Giard 2008), the central characters and bearers of the culinary tradition are women, in restaurant culture (and French restaurant culture is not an exception), it is often men who occupy the central stage. Moreover, in the case of *Babette's Feast*, some spectators were shocked by the filmmakers' choice and argued that the *Café Anglais* (a restaurant that had a strong gastronomic reputation in nineteenth-century Paris) never had a female chef. Choosing a female character for the part may have been a good way to present two symbolic values associated with French culture: epicurean pleasures and feminine sensuality.

14. This goes back to the origin of the word restaurant (to restore, i.e. to heal), which originally was a place where medicinal potions were given to cure all sort of illnesses.

15 'French fries back on House menu' http://news.bbc.co.uk/2/hi/americas/5240572.stm [accessed on 13 November 2014].
16 Note the variation in grammatical gender (*fête* is a feminine word), sometimes within the same sentence (*le* is a masculine article whereas *petite* is the feminine flexion of the adjective).
17 The feeling that the French dining experience takes you *there* (i.e. Paris) is commonly expressed in owners', reviewers' and customers' words : 'You feel in Paris without having to fly to Paris' (John Blakeley, *Pastis*' owner); 'It either makes you pine for Paris, or transports you there!' (Mia Stainsby, *The Vancouver Sun*); 'If you can't go to Paris and would like to, eat here. It is a very good copy of the ambiance and character you would find in some Parisian hideaways . . . (Dined on 1/17/2014)' (Opentable.com).
18 Interestingly, the restaurant's lunch menu follows a different format and does not give the names of the dishes in French. This variation from menu to menu says a lot about the formality attached to French language (as dinner is supposedly a more formal meal than lunch).
19 http://blogs.vancouversun.com/2011/08/15/top-20-vancouver-restaurants [accessed 13 November 2014].
20 http://lecrocodilerestaurant.com/awards [accessed 13 November 2014].
21 According to the 2011 census, the percentage of Vancouverites who can speak French (whether as a first or as a second language) approximates 1.2% www12.statcan.gc.ca/census-recensement/2011/as-sa/98-314-x/98-314-x2011003_1-eng.pdf [accessed 13 November 2014].

Conclusion

1 https://www.youtube.com/watch?v=MZJpGq6W1bw [accessed 15 January 2015].
2 The heavy presence of celebrities and politicians on social media like Twitter and Facebook arguably contributes to make these media more conservative/traditional with regard to the audibility given to legitimate voices in comparison with other voices.
3 'What is most important about these mediascapes is that they provide (especially in their television, film and cassette forms) large and complex repertoires of images, narratives and "ethnoscapes" to viewers throughout the world, in which the world of commodities and the world of "news" and politics are profoundly mixed . . . The lines between the "realistic" and the fictional landscapes they see are blurred, so that the further away these audiences are from the direct experiences of metropolitan life, the more likely they are to construct "imagined" worlds' (Appadurai 1996: 35).

4 Apart from Tony Gatlif's films and until the recent TV appearances of Anina Ciuciu ('*Anina Ciuciu incarne la «Rom intégrée». Elle n'est pas la seule, mais c'est la seule qu'on entend*' – 'Anina Ciuciu embodies the "integrated Rom", she is not the only one, but she is the only one that we hear' – *Liberation* 2013), there is a noticeable absence of Rom voices in the French media.

References

Abellard, A. (2013), 'Avant-propos: L'Art du Repas'. *Le Monde, Hors Série, À table: Artisans, virtuoses et producteurs.* July–September: 3.

Agha, A. (2003), 'The social life of cultural value', *Language and Communication*, 23 (3/4): 231–273.

Agha, A. (2005), 'Voice, footing, enregisterment', *Journal of Linguistic Anthropology*, 15 (1): 38–59.

Aitchison, J. and Lewis, D.M. (eds) (2003), *New Media Language*, London: Routledge.

Alvarez-Pereyre, M. (2011), 'Using films as linguistic specimen: theoretical and practical issues', in R. Piazza, M. Bednarek and F. Rossi (eds), *Telecinematic Discourse: Approaches to the Language of Films and Television Series*, Amsterdam: John Benjamins Publishing Company, pp. 47–67.

Anderson, K.T. (2007), 'Constructing "otherness": ideologies and differentiating speech style', *International Journal of Applied Linguistics*, 17 (2): 178–197.

Androutsopoulos, J. (2007), 'Bilingualism in the mass media and on the Internet', in M. Heller (ed.), *Bilingualism: A Social Approach*, New York: Palgrave Macmillan, pp. 207–230.

Androutsopoulos, J. (2010), 'Ideologizing ethnolectal German', in S. Johnson and T.M. Milani (eds), *Language Ideologies and Media Discourse*, London: Continuum, pp. 182–202.

Androutsopoulos, J. (2012a), 'Introduction: language and society in cinematic discourse', *Multilingua*, 31: 139–154.

Androutsopoulos, J. (2012b), 'Repertoires, characters and scenes: sociolinguistic difference in Turkish-German comedy', *Multilingua*, 31: 301–326.

Appadurai, A. (1988), 'Introduction: place and voice in anthropological theory', *Cultural Anthropology*, 3: 16–20.

Appadurai, A. (1996), *Modernity at Large: Cultural Dimensions of Globalization*, Minneapolis: University of Minnesota Press.

Armstrong, N. and Jamin, M. (2002), 'Le français des banlieues: uniformity and discontinuity in the French of the Hexagon', in K. Salhi (ed.), *French in and out of France: Language Policies, Intercultural Antagonisms and Dialogues*, Bern: Peter Lang, pp. 107–136.

Arnold, A. (2015), 'Voix et transidentité: changer de voix pour changer de genre?', *Langage et société*, Éditions de la maison des sciences de l'homme, 151 (1): 87–105.

Arundale, R.B. (2006), 'Face as relational and interactional: a communication framework for research on face, facework, and politeness', *Journal of Politeness Research*, 2 (2): 193–216.

Aubenas, F. (2004), 'La banlieue par la bande', *Libération*, 7 January 2004.
Auer, P. (2007), 'The monolingual bias in bilingualism research, or: Why bilinguals talk is (still) a challenge for linguistics', in M. Heller (ed.), *Bilingualism: A Social Approach*, New York: Palgrave Macmillan, pp. 319–339.
Austin, J.L. (1962), *How to Do Things with Words*, New York: Oxford University Press.
Baker, P., Gabrielatos, C. and McEnery, T. (2013), *Discourse Analysis and Media Attitudes: The Representation of Islam in the British Press*, Cambridge: Cambridge University Press.
Bakhtin, M.M. (1981), 'Discourse in the novel', in M. Holquist (ed.), C. Emerson and M. Holquist (trans.), *The Dialogic Imagination: Four Essays*, Austin, TX: University of Texas Press, pp. 259–422.
Bakhtin, M.M. (1984), *Rabelais and His World*, H. Iswolsky (trans.), Bloomington: Indiana University Press.
Bakhtin, M.M. (1986), 'The problem of speech genres', in C. Emerson and M. Holquist (eds), V.W. McGee (trans.), *Speech Genres and Other Late Essays*, Austin, TX: University of Texas Press, pp. 60–102.
Barthes, R. (1951), *Mythologies*, Paris: Éditions du Seuil.
Barthes, R. (2013 [1961]), 'Toward a psychosociology of contemporary food consumption', in C. Counihan and P. Van Esterik (eds), *Food and Culture: A Reader*, New York: Routledge, pp. 23–30.
Bauman, R. (1975), 'Verbal art as performance', *American Anthropologist*, 77 (2): 290–311.
Bauman, R. (1977), *Verbal Art as Performance*, Prospect Heights, IL: Waveland Press.
Bauman, R. (2001), 'Genre', in A. Duranti (ed.), *Key Terms in Language and Culture*, Malden: Blackwell, pp. 79–82.
Bauman, R. (2011), 'Commentary: foundations in performance', *Journal of Sociolinguistics*, 15 (5): 707–720.
Bauman, R. and Briggs, C.L. (1990), 'Poetics and performance as critical perspectives on language and social life', *Annual Review of Anthropology*, 19: 59–88.
Bayle, A. and Fix, F. (2013), *Rire et émancipation féminine. Identités, Genre, Sexualités*, Paris: L'Harmattan.
Baym, N. (1995), 'The emergence of community in computer-mediated communication', in S.G. Jones (ed.), *Cybersociety: Computer-mediated Communication and Community*, Thousand Oaks, CA: Sage, pp. 138–163.
Baym, N. (1998), 'The emergence of on-line community', in S.G. Jones (ed.), *Cybersociety 2.0: Revisiting Computer-mediated Communication and Community*, Thousand Oaks, CA: Sage, pp. 35–68.
Bazin, A. (1967), *What is Cinema? Vol. 2*, H. Gray (trans.), Berkeley, CA: University of California.
Bednarek, M. (2010), *The Language of Fictional Television: Drama and Identity*, London: Continuum International.
Bednarek, M. (2012), 'Constructing "nerdiness": characterisation in the *Big Bang Theory*', *Multilingua*, 31: 199–229.

Bell, A. (1984), 'Language style as audience design', *Language and Society*, 13: 145–204.
Bell, A. (1991), *The Language of News Media*, Oxford: Blackwell.
Bell, A. (1999), 'Styling the other to define the self: a study in New Zealand identity making', *Journal of Sociolinguistics*, 3 (4): 523–541.
Bell, A. and Garrett, P. (eds) (1998), *Approaches to Media Discourse*, Oxford: Blackwell.
Bell, A. and Gibson, A. (2011), 'Staging language: an introduction to the sociolinguistics of performance', *Journal of Sociolinguistics*, 15 (5): 555–572.
Bentolila, A. (2002), 'Il existe en France une inégalité linguistique', *L'Express*. http://www.lexpress.fr/actualite/societe/education/il-existe-en-franceune-inegalite-linguistique_497804.html [accessed July 2011].
Bentolila, A. (2007), 'Contre les ghettos linguistiques', *Le Monde*, 21 December.
Biber, D. and Conrad, S. (2009), *Register, Genre, and Style*, Cambridge, New York: Cambridge University Press.
Blackledge, A. (2009), 'Lost in translation? Racialization of a debate about language in a BBC news item', in S. Johnson and T.M. Milani (eds), *Language Ideologies and Media Discourse: Texts, Practices, Politics*, London: Continuum International Publishing, pp. 143–161.
Blanchard, A.L. and Markus, L.M. (2004), 'The experienced "sense" of a virtual community: characteristics and processes', *The DATA BASE for Advances in Information Systems*, 35 (1): 65–79.
Bleichenbacher, L. (2008), *Multilingualism in the Movies: Hollywood Characters and Their Linguistic Choices*, Tübingen: Francke Verlag.
Bleichenbacher, L. (2012), 'Linguicism in Hollywood movies? Representations of, and audience reactions to multilingualism in mainstream movie dialogues', *Multilingua*, 31: 155–176.
Bloomfield, L. (1944), 'Secondary and tertiary responses to language', *Language*, 20 (2): 45–55.
Blumenfeld, R. (2002), *Accents: A Manual for Actors*, New York: Limelight Editions.
Bolter, D. and Grusin, R. (1999), *Remediation: Understanding New Media*, Cambridge, MA: MIT Press.
Borba, R. and Ostermann, A.C. (2007), 'Do bodies matter? Travestiste' embodiment of (trans)gender identity through the manipulation of the Portuguese grammatical gender system', *Gender and Language*, 1 (1): 131–147.
Boughton, Z. (2006), 'When perception isn't reality: accent identification and perceptual dialectology in French', *Journal of French Language Studies*, 16: 277–304.
Bouillon, P. (2004), 'Le marivaudage version banlieue fait parler les spectateurs du "9–3"', *La Croix*, 19 January 2004.
Bourdieu, P. (1984a), *La dernière instance*, in *Le siècle de Kafka*, Paris: Centre Georges Pompidou, pp. 268–270, in *Choses dites*, Paris, Les Éditions de Minuit, 1987.
Bourdieu, P. (1984b), *Distinction: A Social Critique of the Judgment of Taste*, R. Nice (trans.), London: Routledge and Kegan Paul.

Bourdieu, P. (1991), *Language and Symbolic Power*, Cambridge, MA: Harvard University Press. [Published in paperback in 1992.]

Bourdieu, P. and Passeron, J.-C. (1990), *Reproduction in Education, Society and Culture*, London: Sage.

Boyer, H. (2001), 'Le français des jeunes vécu/vu par les étudiants: Enquêtes à Montpellier, Paris, Lille', *Langage et société*, 95: 75–87.

Brown, P. and Levinson, S.C. (1987), *Politeness: Some Universals in Language Usage*, Cambridge: Cambridge University Press.

Bucholtz, M. (2011), 'Race and the re-embodied voice in Hollywood film', *Language & Communication*, 31: 255–265.

Bucholtz, M. and Lopez, Q. (2011), 'Performing blackness, forming whiteness: linguistic minstrelsy in Hollywood film', *Journal of Sociolinguistics*, 15 (5): 680–706.

Burger, M. (2006), 'L'analyse du discours appliquée à la communication médiatique: comment la presse romande parle-t-elle de l'Islam?', *Bulletin suisse de linguistique appliquée*, 83 (2): 201–212.

Buscombe, E. (2013), '"They will speak in our language": Indian speech in Western movies', in J. Jaeckle (ed.), *Film Dialogue*, New York: Wallflower Press, pp. 157–171.

Butler, J. (1990), *Gender Trouble*, New York and London: Routledge.

Cameron, D. (1994), 'Verbal hygiene for women: linguistics misapplied?', *Applied Linguistics*, 15: 382–398.

Carrière, C. (2012), 'Omar Sy: "Je ne veux pas être le Noir à la mode"', *L'Express* Cinéma. http://www.lexpress.fr/culture/cinema/intouchables-l-interview-d-omar-sy_1084869.html [accessed 3 November 2014].

Carroll, H.B. (2013), 'Identifying stylizations in ethnically salient talk among disc jockeys', *Language in Society*, 42: 259–286.

de Certeau, M. and Giard, L. (2008), 'The nourishing arts', in C. Counihan and P. Van Esterik (eds), *Food and Culture: A Reader*, 2nd ed., New York: Routledge, pp. 67–77.

Chambers, J.K. (2013), 'Studying language variation: an informal epistemology', in N. Schilling-Estes and J.K. Chambers (eds), *The Handbook of Language Variation and Change*, Hoboken: Wiley-Blackwell, pp. 1–15.

Charron, M. and Desjardins, R. (2011), 'Introduction: food, language, and identity cuisine, langue et identité', *Cuizine: The Journal of Canadian Food Cultures / Cuizine: revue des cultures culinaires au Canada*, 3 (1). http://id.erudit.org/iderudit/1004725ar [accessed 14 November 2014].

Chetcuti, N. and Greco, L. (eds) (2012), *La face cachée du genre: Langage et pouvoir des normes*, Paris: Presses Sorbonne nouvelle.

Child, J., Berthold, L. and Beck S. (1971), *Mastering the Art of French Cooking*, New York: Alfred A. Knopf.

Chion, M. (1999), *The Voice in Cinema*, C. Gorbman (trans.), New York: Columbia University Press.

Christie, A. (2003[1928]), *The Mystery of the Blue Train*, in *Poirot, The French Collection*, London: HarperCollins Publishers, pp. 171–373.

Chun, E.W. (2009), 'Ideologies of legitimate mockery: Margaret Cho's revoicings of mock Asian', in A. Reyes and A. Lo (eds), *Beyond Yellow English: Toward a Linguistic Anthropology of Asian Pacific America*, Oxford: Oxford University Press, pp. 260–287.

Chung, S.H. (2013), 'From "me so horny" to "I'm so ronery": Asian images and yellow voices in American films', in J. Jaeckle (ed.), *Film Dialogue*, New York, Chichester: Wallflower Press, pp. 172–191.

Churchill, W. (1998), *Fantasies of the Master Race: Literature, Cinema and the Colonization of American Indians*, San Francisco: City Lights Books.

Conboy, M. (2010), *Language of Newspapers: Socio-historical Perspectives*, London: Continuum International Publishing.

Cottle, S. (ed.) (2000), *Ethnic Minorities and the Media*, Milton Keynes: Open University Press.

Coulmas, F. (1981), 'Introduction: conversational routine', in F. Coulmas (ed.), *Conversational Routine: Explorations in Standardized Communication Situations and Prepatterned Speech*, The Hague: Mouton, pp. 1–17.

Coupland, N. (2001), 'Dialect stylization in radio talk', *Language in Society*, 30: 345–375.

Coupland, N. (2004), 'Stylised deception', in A. Jaworski, N. Coupland and D. Galasinski (eds), *Metalanguage: Social and Ideological Perspectives*, Berlin: Mouton de Gruyter, pp. 249–274.

Coupland, N. (2007), *Style: Language Variation and Identity*, Cambridge: Cambridge University Press.

Coupland, N. and Jaworski, A. (2004), 'Sociolinguistic perspectives on metalanguage: Reflexivity, evaluation and ideology', in A. Jaworski, N. Coupland and D. Galasinski (eds), *Metalanguage: Social and Ideological Perspectives*, Berlin: Mouton de Gruyter, pp. 15–51.

Croizé-Pourcelet, H. (2011), 'Les cartes des grands restaurants français n'en font plus des tartines', *Slate.fr* http://www.slate.fr/story/45981/langage-carte-grands-restaurants-gastronomie [accessed 10 November 2014].

Crystal, D. (2006), *Language and the Internet*, 2nd ed., Cambridge: Cambridge University Press.

Crystal, D. (2011), *Internet Linguistics: A Student Guide*, New York: Routledge.

Culpeper, J. (1996), 'Towards an anatomy of impoliteness', *Journal of Pragmatics*, 25 (3): 349–367.

Danet, B. (1998), 'Text as mask: gender, play and performance on the internet', in S.G. Jones (ed.), *Cybersociety 2.0: Revisiting Computer-mediated Communication and Community*, Thousand Oaks, CA: Sage, pp. 129–158.

De Bruyn, O. (2008), 'Cinéma français: où sont les Noirs?', *Rue 89 Nouvel Obs*, 25/11/2008 http://rue89.nouvelobs.com/2008/11/25/cinema-francais-ou-sont-les-noirs [accessed 3 November 2014].

De Fina, A. (2013), 'Top-down and bottom-up strategies of identity construction in ethnic media', *Applied Linguistics*, 34 (5): 554–573.

Deleuze, G. (1989), *Cinema 2: The Time-Image*, H. Tomlinson and R. Galeta (trans.), Minneapolis: University of Minnesota Press.

Derrida, J. (1984), 'Voices ii: Jacques Derrida and Verena Andermatt Conley', *Boundary 2*, 12 (2): 68–93.

Derrida, J. (2001), 'Le cinéma et ses fantômes (interview)', *Cahiers du Cinéma*, April 2001: 75–85.

Derrida, J. (2011), *Voice and Phenomenon: Introduction to the Problem of the Sign in Husserl's Phenomenology*, L. Lawlor (trans.), Evanston, IL: Northwestern University Press.

Derville, G. (1997), 'La stigmatisation des "jeunes de banlieue"', *Communication et langages*, 113: 104–117.

Desjardins, R. (2011), 'L' étude du menu comme représentation de l'identité culinaire québécoise: le cas des menus au Château Frontenac', *Cuizine: The Journal of Canadian Food Cultures / Cuizine: revue des cultures culinaires au Canada*, 3 (1). http://id.erudit.org/iderudit/1004729ar [accessed 10 November 2014].

Dewaele, J.-M. and McCloskey J. (2014), 'Attitudes towards foreign accents among adult multilingual language users', *Journal of Multilingual and Multicultural Development*, 36 (3): 221–238.

Dick, H.P. and Wirtz, K. (2011), 'Introduction – racializing discourse', *Journal of Linguistic Anthropology*, 21 (1): 2–10.

Dickerman, S. (2003), 'Eat your words: a guide to menu English', *Slate.com* http://www.slate.com/articles/life/food/2003/04/eat_your_words.single.html [accessed 10 November 2014].

Dubet, F., Cousin, O., Macé, E. and Rui, S. (2013), *Pourquoi moi? L'expérience des discriminations*, Paris: Editions du Seuil.

Dubois, R. (2012), *Les Noirs dans le cinéma français: Images et imaginaires d'hier et d'aujourd'hui*, Paris: The Book Edition.

Duchêne, A. and Heller, M. (eds) (2012), *Language in Late Capitalism: Pride and Profit*, New York: Routledge.

Duchêne, A. and Moïse, C. (eds) (2011), *Langage, genre et sexualité*, Québec: Éditions NotaBene.

Durant, A. and Lambrou, M. (2009), *Language and Media: A Resource Book for Students*, London: Routledge.

Duveen, G. and Lloyd, B. (eds) (1990), *Social Representations and the Development of Knowledge*, Cambridge: Cambridge University Press.

Eagleton, T. (1991), *Ideology: An Introduction*, London and New York: Verso.

Eastman, C.M. and Stein, R.F. (1993), 'Language display: authenticating claims to social identity', *Journal of Multilingual and Multicultural Development*, 14 (3): 187–202.

Eckert, P. and McConnell-Ginet, S. (2003), *Language and Gender*, New York: Cambridge University Press.

Eitzen, D. (1999), 'The Emotional Basis of Film Comedy', in C. Plantinga and G.M. Smith (eds), *Passionate Views: Film, Cognition, and Emotion*, Baltimore: Johns Hopkins University Press, pp. 84–99.

Elliott, C. (2008), 'Consuming the other: packaged representations of foreignness in *President's Choice*', in K. LeBesco and P. Naccarato (eds), *Edible Ideologies: Representing Food and Meaning*, New York: State University of New York Press, pp. 179–198.

Ess, C. and the AoIR ethics working committee (2002), 'Ethical decision-making and internet research: Recommendations from the AoIR ethics working committee'. http:/www.aoir.org/reports/ethics.pdf [accessed 25 April 2009].

Eysenbach, G. and Till, J.E. (2001), 'Ethical issues in qualitative research on internet communities', *British Medical Journal*, 323: 1103–1105.

Fagyal, Z. (2003), 'La prosodie du français populaire des jeunes à Paris: traits héréditaires et novateurs', *Le Français aujourd'hui, Français de l'école et langues des élèves: quel statut, quelles pratiques?*, 143: 47–55.

Fagyal, Z. (2004), 'Action des médias et interactions entre jeunes dans une banlieue ouvrière de Paris: Remarques sur l'innovation lexicale', *Cahier de Sociolinguistique*, 9: 41–60.

Fagyal, Z. (2010), *Accents de banlieue: aspects prosodiques du français populaire en contact avec les langues de l'immigration*, Paris: L'Harmattan.

Fairclough, N. (1989), *Language and Power*, Harlow, London, New York: Longman.

Fairclough, N. (1992), *Discourse and Social Change*, Cambridge: Polity Press.

Fairclough, N. (1995), *Media Discourse*, London and New York: E. Arnold.

Fajardo, I. (2004), 'Entretiens avec Abdellatif Kechiche et Cécile Ladjali', *Télérama*, 2817, 10 January 2004.

Faure, A. (2006), 'Un faubourg, des banlieues ou la déclinaison du rejet', in J.C. Depaule (ed.), *Les mots de la stigmatisation urbaine*, Paris: Éditions Unesco/Maison des sciences de l'homme, pp. 8–39.

Ferber, L. (2008), 'Pardon our French: French stereotypes in American media', *The Osprey Journal of Ideas and Inquiry*, University of North Florida, 7 (7). http://digitalcommons.unf.edu/ojii_volumes/7 [accessed 5 November 2014].

Ferenczi, A. (2011), 'Jamel Debbouze: "Les Français ont peur de leur immigration: c'est normal, c'est TF1 qui a fait les présentations"', *Télérama*, 3184, 22 January 2011. http://www.telerama.fr/scenes/jamel-debbouze-les-francais-ont-peur-de-leur-immigration-c-est-normal-c-est-tf1-qui-a-fait-les-presentations,64722.php [accessed 3 November 2014].

Ferguson, P.P. (2004), *Accounting for Taste: The Triumph of French Cuisine*, Chicago: The University of Chicago Press.

Fiske, J. (1987), *Television Culture*, London: Routledge.

Fiske, S.T. (1998), 'Stereotyping, prejudice, and discrimination', in G. Lindzey, D. Gilbert and S.T. Fiske (eds), *The Handbook of Social Psychology*, Vol. 2, 4th ed., New York: McGraw-Hill, pp. 357–411.

Fowler, R. (1991), *Language in the News: Discourse and Ideology in the Press*, London and New York: Routledge.

Fraser, B. and Nolan, W. (1981), 'The association of deference with linguistic form', *International Journal of the Sociology of Language*, 27: 93–109.

Gabel, J. (1997), *Ideologies and the Corruption of Thought*, New Brunswick, NJ and London: Transaction Publishers.

Gaertner, J. (2005), 'Aspects et représentations du personnage arabe dans le cinéma français: 1995–2005, retour sur une décennie', *Confluences Méditerranée*, 55 (4): 189–201.

Gal, S. (2009), 'Perspective and the politics of representation: a commentary', in A. Reyes and A. Lo (eds), *Beyond Yellow English: Toward a Linguistic Anthropology of Asian Pacific America*, Oxford: Oxford University Press, pp. 325–328.

Gal, S. and Irvine, J. (1995), 'The boundaries of languages and disciplines: how ideologies construct difference', *Social Research*, 62 (4): 967–1001.

Gallazzi, E. and Molinari, C. (eds) (2007), *Les français en émergence*, Bern: Peter Lang.

Garel, R., de la Brétèque, B.A. and Brun, V. (2012), *La voix parlée et la voix chantée*, Montpellier: Sauramps médical.

Garfinkel, H. (1967), 'Passing and the managed achievement of sex status in an intersexed person', in *Studies in Ethnomethodology*, Englewood Cliffs, NJ: Prentice-Hall, pp. 116–185.

Gélas, J. and Blanchard, P. (2012), *Noirs de France* [video], Paris: La Compagnie des Phares et Balises.

Gibson, A. and Bell, A. (2010), 'Performing Pasifika English in New Zealand: the case of bro'Town', *English World-Wide*, 31: 231–251.

Gignoux, S. (2004), 'Tchatchez-moi d'amour dans le «neuf cube»', *La Croix*, 7 January 2004.

Giles, H. and Coupland, N. (1991), *Language: Contexts and Consequences*, Milton Keynes: Open University Press.

Goffman, E. (1959), *Presentation of Self in Every Day Life*, London: Penguin.

Goffman, E. (1963), *Stigma: Notes on the Management of Spoiled Identity*, Englewood Cliffs, NJ: Prentice-Hall.

Goffman, E. (1967), *Interaction Ritual: Essays on Face-to-face Behavior*, Garden City, NY: Anchor Books.

Goffman, E. (1981), *Forms of Talk*, Philadelphia, PA: University of Pennsylvania Press.

Goffman, E. (1983), 'The interaction order', *American Sociological Review*, 48 (1): 1–17.

Greco, L. (2012), 'Production, circulation and deconstruction of gender norms in LGBTQ speech practices', *Discourse Studies*, 14 (5): 567–585.

Gruffydd Jones, E.H. and Uribe-Jongbloed, E. (2013), *Social Media and Minority Languages: Convergence and the Creative Industries*, Clevedon: Multilingual Matters.

Guillot, M. (2010), 'Film subtitles from a cross-cultural pragmatics perspective: issues of linguistic and cultural representations', *The Translator*, 16 (1): 67–92.

Guillot, M. (2012a), 'Film subtitles and the conundrum of linguistic and cultural representation: a methodological blind spot', in S. Hauser and M. Luginbühl (eds), *Contrastive Media Analysis*, Amsterdam, Philadelphia, PA: John Benjamins, pp. 101–122.

Guillot, M. (2012b), 'Stylization and representation in subtitles: can less be more?', *Perspectives*, 20: 479–494.

Gusfield, J.R. (1975), *The Community: A Critical Response*, New York: Harper and Row.

Haarmann, H. (1986), 'Verbal strategies in Japanese fashion magazines – a study in impersonal bilingualism and ethnosymbolism', *International Journal of the Sociology of Language*, 58: 107–121.

Hall, K. and Bucholtz, M. (2013), 'Epilogue: facing identity', *Journal of Politeness Research*, 9 (1): 123–132.

Hall, S. (1990), 'Cultural identity and diaspora', in J. Rutherford (ed.), *Identity: Community, Culture, Difference*, London: Lawrence & Wishart, pp. 222–237.

Hall, S. (1996), 'What is black in black popular culture?', in D. Morley and K.-H. Chen (eds), *Stuart Hall: Critical Dialogues in Cultural Studies*, London, New York: Routledge, pp. 465–475.

Hall, S. (1997), *Race, The Floating Signifier*, Featuring Stuart Hall [video], Northampton, MA: Media Education Foundation, transcript available online: http://www.mediaed.org/assets/products/407/transcript_407.pdf [accessed 15 January 2015].

Hall, S. (2000), 'Encoding decoding', in P. Morris and S. Thornton (eds), *Media Studies: A Reader*, 2nd ed., New York: New York University Press, pp. 51–61.

Hall, S., Critcher, C. and Jefferson, T. [et al.] (1978), 'The social production of news', in *Policing the Crisis: Mugging, the State, and Law and Order*, London and Basingstoke: Macmillan Press, pp. 53–77.

Halliday, M.A.K. (1978), *Language as Social Semiotic: The Social Interpretation of Language and Meaning*, London: Edward Arnold Publishers.

Halliday, M.A.K. (1988), *New Developments in Systemic Linguistics*, London: Pinter.

Haque, E. (2012), *Multiculturalism within a Bilingual Framework: Language, Race, and Belonging in Canada*, Toronto, Buffalo, London: University of Toronto Press.

Haydée, S. (2008), 'Te comprinds ch'picard?', *Libération*, 16 April 2008. http://www.liberation.fr/grand-angle/010178882-te-comprinds-chpicard [accessed July 2011].

Heller, M. (2009), 'Media, the state and linguistic authority', in S. Johnson and T.M. Milani (eds), *Language Ideologies and Media Discourse: Texts, Practices, Politics*, London: Continuum International Publishing, pp. 277–282.

Heller, M. (2010), *Paths to Post-nationalism: A Critical Ethnography of Language and Identity*, Oxford: Oxford University Press.

Herman, L. and Herman, M.S. (1997), *Foreign Dialects: A Manual for Actors, Directors, and Writers*, New York, London: Routledge.

Herring, S.C. (1999), 'Posting in a different voice: gender and ethics in computer-mediated communication', in P.A. Mayer (ed.), *Computer Media and Communication: A Reader*, New York: Oxford University Press, pp. 241–265.

Herring, S.C. (2000), 'Gender differences in CMC: findings and implications', *Computer Professionals for Social Responsibility Newsletter*. http://cpsr.org/issues/womenintech/herring [accessed 25 April 2009].

Herring, S.C. (2001), 'Computer-mediated discourse', in D. Tannen, D. Schiffrin and H. Hamilton (eds), *Handbook of Discourse Analysis*, Oxford: Blackwell, pp. 612–634.

Herring, S.C. (2007), 'A faceted classification scheme for computer-mediated discourse', *Language@Internet*, 4, article 1 http://www.languageatinternet.de/articles/2007/761 [accessed 25 April 2009].

Higbee, W. (2013), *Post-beur Cinema: North African Émigré and Maghrebi-French Filmmaking in France since 2000*, Edinburgh: Edinburgh University Press.

Higgins, C. and Furukawa, G. (2012), 'Styling Hawai'i in Haole wood: white protagonists on a voyage of self discovery', *Multilingua*, 31: 177–198.

Hill, J.H. (1993), 'Hasta la vista, baby: Anglo Spanish in the American Southwest', *Critique of Anthropology*, 13 (2): 145–176.

Hill, J.H. (1995), 'Mock Spanish: a site for the indexical reproduction of racism in American English', *Language & Culture, Symposium 2*.

Hill, J.H. (1998), 'Language, race, and white public space', *American Anthropologist*, New Series, 100 (3): 680–689.

Hill, J.H. (1999), 'Styling locally, styling globally: what does it mean?', *Journal of Sociolinguistics*, 3 (4): 542–556.

Hill, J.H. (2009), 'On using semiotic resources in a racist world: a commentary', in A. Reyes and A. Lo (eds), *Beyond Yellow English: Toward a Linguistic Anthropology of Asian Pacific America*, Oxford: Oxford University Press, pp. 84–89.

Hill, J.H. and Irvine, J. (1993), *Responsibility and Evidence in Oral Discourse*, Cambridge, New York: Cambridge University Press.

Hobson, M. (2001), 'Derrida and representation: mimesis, presentation, and representation', in T. Cohen (ed.), *Jacques Derrida and the Humanities: A Critical Reader*. Cambridge: Cambridge University Press, pp. 132–151.

Hodson, J. (2014), *Dialect in Film and Literature*, Basingstoke: Palgrave Macmillan.

Holmes, J. (1995), *Women, Men and Politeness*, London and New York: Longman.

hooks, b. (1992), *Black Looks: Race and Representation*, Boston, MA: South End Press.

hooks, b. (1997), *bell hooks: Cultural Criticism and Transformation* [video], The Media Education Foundation.

Houdebine-Gravaud, A.-M. (2002), *L'imaginaire linguistique*, Paris: L'Harmattan.

Howarth, C. (2006), 'A social representation is not a quiet thing: exploring the critical potential of social representations theory', *British Journal of Social Psychology*, 45 (1): 65–86.

Hutchby, I. (1991), 'The organization of talk on talk radio', in P. Scannel (ed.), *Broadcast Talk*. Sage Publications, pp. 119–137.

Irvine, J. (1993), 'Insult and responsibility: Verbal abuse in a Wolof village', in J. Irvine and J. Hill (eds), *Responsibility and Evidence in Oral Discourse*, Cambridge: Cambridge University Press, pp. 105–134.

Irvine, J. (2001), 'Style as distinctiveness: the culture and ideology of linguistic differentiation', in P. Eckert and J. Rickford (eds), *Style and Sociolinguistic Variation*, Cambridge: Cambridge University Press, pp. 21–43.

Jaffe, A. (2007), 'Corsican on the airwaves: media discourse in a context of minority language shift', in S. Johnson and A. Ensslin (eds), *Language in the Media: Representations, Identities, Ideologies*, London: Continuum, pp. 149–171.

Jaffe, A. (2009), 'The sociolinguistics of stance', in A. Jaffe (ed.), *Stance: Sociolinguistic Perspectives*, New York: Oxford University Press, pp. 2–28.

Jaffe, A. (2011), 'Sociolinguistic diversity in mainstream media: authenticity, authority and processes of mediation and mediatization', *Journal of Language and Politics*, 10 (4): 562–586.

Jaworska, S. and Larrivée, P. (2011), 'Women, power and the media: assessing the bias', *Journal of Pragmatics*, 43: 2477–2479.

Jaworski, A. and Coupland, N. (2004), 'Sociolinguistic perspective on metalanguage: reflexivity, evaluation and ideology', in A. Jaworski, N. Coupland and D. Galasinski (eds), *Metalanguage: Social and Ideological Perspectives*, Berlin: Mouton de Gruyter, pp. 15–45.

Johnson, S. and Milani, T.M. (eds) (2009), *Language Ideologies and Media Discourse: Texts, Practices, Politics*, London: Continuum International Publishing.

Johnson S., Milani T.M. and Upton, C. (2010), 'Language ideological debates on the BBC "Voices" website: Hypermodality in theory and practice', in S. Johnson and T.M. Milani (eds), *Language Ideologies and Media Discourse: Texts, Practices, Politics*, London: Continuum, pp. 223–251.

Johnston, J. and Baumann, S. (2007), 'Democracy versus distinction: a study of omnivorousness in gourmet food writing', *American Journal of Sociology*, 113 (1): 165–204.

Johnstone, B. (2008), *Discourse Analysis*, Malden, MA: Blackwell.

Kaganski, S. (2004), 'Nique Rohmer!', *Les Inrockuptibles* 423, 7 January 2004.

Kelly-Holmes, H. (2005), *Advertising as Multilingual Communication*, Basingstoke and New York: Palgrave Macmillan.

Kelly-Holmes, H. and Atkinson, D. (2007), '"When Hector met Tom Cruise": attitudes to Irish in a radio satire', in S. Johnson and A. Ensslin (eds), *Language in the Media: Representations, Identities, Ideologies*, London: Continuum, pp. 173–187.

Kozloff, S. (2000), *Overhearing Film Dialogue*, Berkeley, CA: University of California Press.

Kramsch, C. (1998), *Language and Culture*, Oxford: Oxford University Press.

Kress, G. and van Leeuwen, T. (1996), *Reading Images: The Grammar of Visual Design*, London and New York: Routledge.

Kress, G. and van Leeuwen, T. (1998), 'Front pages: (the critical) analysis of newspaper layout', in A. Bell and P. Garrett (eds), *Approaches to Media Discourse*, Oxford: Blackwell, pp. 186–219.

Kress, G. and van Leeuwen, T. (2001), *Multimodal Discourse. The Modes and Media of Contemporary Communication*, London: Arnold.

Labov, W. (1972), *Sociolinguistic Patterns*, Philadelphia, PA: University of Pennsylvania Press.

Labov, W. (1984), 'Field methods of the project in linguistic change and variation', in J. Baugh and J. Sherzer (eds), *Language in Use: Readings in Sociolinguistics*, Englewood Cliffs, NJ: Prentice-Hall, pp. 28–53.

Lalanne, J.-M. (2004), 'M. Hulot dans les 9–3', *Les Inrockuptibles* 423, 7 January 2004.

Lalanne, J.-M. and Fevret, C. (2007), '"La Graine et le Mulet": entretien avec Abdellatif Kechiche', *Les Inrockuptibles*. http://www.lesinrocks.com/2007/12/11/cinema/actualite-cinema/entretien-abdellatif-kechiche-la-graine-et-le-mulet-1207-1158380 [accessed 3 November 2014].

Lazar, M.M. (2009), 'Language ideologies and state imperatives: the strategic use of Singlish in public media discourse', in S. Johnson and T. Milani (eds), *Language Ideologies and Media Discourse: Texts, Practices, Politics*, London: Continuum, pp. 121–140.

Le Breton, D. (2011), *Éclats de voix: Une anthropologie des voix*, Paris: Editions Métailié.

Li, W. (2007), *The Bilingualism Reader* (2nd ed.), London: Routledge.

Lippi-Green, R. (1994), 'Accent, standard language ideology, and discriminatory pretext in the courts', *Language in Society*, 23 (2): 163–198.

Lippi-Green, R. (1997), 'Teaching children how to discriminate: what we learn from the Big Bad Wolf', in *English with an Accent: Language, Ideology and Discrimination in the United States*, London: Routledge, pp. 79–103.

Livia, A. (1997), 'Disloyal to masculinity: linguistic gender and liminal identity in French', in K. Hall and A. Livia (eds), *Queerly Phrased: Language, Gender and Sexuality*, Oxford and New York: Oxford University Press, pp. 350–368.

Locher, M.A. and Bousfield, D. (2008), 'Introduction: impoliteness and power in language', in D. Bousfield and M.A. Locher (eds), *Impoliteness in Language: Studies on its Interplay with Power in Theory and Practice* (Language, Power and Social Process 21), Berlin and New York: Mouton de Gruyter, pp. 1–13.

Locher, M.A. and Watts, R.J. (2005), 'Politeness theory and relational work', *Journal of Politeness Research*, 1 (1): 9–33.

Lodge, A. (1993), *French, from Dialect to Standard*, London; New York: Routledge.

Lorenzo-Dus, N. (2008), *Television Discourse: Analysing Language in the Media*, Basingtoke and New York: Palgrave Macmillan.

Mairesse, M. (2010), 'Sami Bouajila: "J'adore les femmes!"', *Marie-Claire*, http://www.marieclaire.fr/,sami-bouajila,20178,360147.asp [accessed on 3 November 2014].

Marshand, F. (2013), 'Three hot spots for poutine in Vancouver', *Vancouver Sun*, http://www.vancouversun.com/life/Three+spots+poutine+Vancouver/7829663/story.html [accessed on 3 November 2014].

Matheson, D. (2005), *Media Discourses: Analysing Media Texts*, Maidenhead: Open University Press.

McKenna, Y.A.K. and Bargh, J.A. (1998), 'Coming out in the age of the internet: identity "demarginalization" through virtual group participation', *Journal of Personality and Social Psychology*, 75 (3): 681–694.

McMillan, D.W. and Chavis, D.M. (1986), 'Sense of community: a definition and theory', *Journal of Community Psychology*, 14 (1): 6–23.

Meek, B.A. (2006), 'And the Injun goes "How!": representations of American Indian English in white public space', *Language in Society*, 35, 93–128.

Meinhof, U. (1994), 'Double talk in news broadcasts', in D. Graddol and O. Boyd-Barrett (eds), *Media Texts: Authors and Readers*, Clevedon, UK: Multilingual Matters and The Open University, pp. 212–223.

Meinhof, U. (2004), 'Metadiscourses of culture in British TV commercials', in A. Jaworski, N. Coupland and D. Galasinski (eds), *Metalanguage: Social and Ideological Perspectives*, Berlin: Mouton de Gruyter, pp. 275–288.

Melinard, M. (2004), '"Cette jeunesse n'a pas de place dans le paysage audiovisuel". Entretiens avec Abdellatif Kechiche', *L'Humanité*, 7 January 2004.

Mellowes, M. (2005), 'About Julia Child', *PBS American Masters*. http://www.pbs.org/wnet/americanmasters/episodes/julia-child/about-julia-child/555 [accessed 12 November 2014].

Mills, S. (2003), *Gender and Politeness*, Cambridge: Cambridge University Press.

Mills, S. (2005), 'Gender and impoliteness', *Journal of Politeness Research*, 1 (2): 263–280.

Milroy, J. and Milroy L. (1985), *Authority in Language: Investigating Language Prescription and Standardisation*, London: Routledge (2nd rev. ed., 1992).

Modestine, Y. (2008), 'Témoignage. Cinéma: "Le métier du doublage a un problème avec la couleur"', *Rue89, Le nouvel Observateur*, http://rue89.nouvelobs.com/2008/04/05/cinema-le-metier-du-doublage-a-un-probleme-avec-la-couleur [accessed 3 November 2014].

Montanari, M. (2006), *Food is Culture*, New York: Columbia University Press.

Morice, J. (2007), 'Rencontre avec Abdellatif Kechiche, réalisateur de "La Graine et le Mulet"', *Télérama*, 3022, 15 December 2007, http://www.telerama.fr/cinema/23146-rencontre_avec_abdellatif_kechiche_realisateur_de_la_graine_et_le_mulet.php [accessed 3 November 2014].

Morrison, D. (2007), 'The death of French culture', *Time*, 21 November 2007.

Moscovici, S. (1988), 'Notes towards a definition of social representations', *European Journal of Social Psychology*, 18: 211–250.

Moscovici, S. (1998a), 'Social consciousness and its history', *Culture and Psychology*, 4 (3): 411–429.

Moscovici, S. (1998b), 'The history and actuality of social representations', in U. Flick (ed.), *The Psychology of the Social*, Cambridge: Cambridge University Press, pp. 209–247.

Moscovici, S. and I. Marková (1998), 'Presenting social representations: a conversation', *Culture and Psychology*, 4 (3): 371–410.

Moyer, A. (2013), *Foreign Accent: The Phenomenon of Non-Native Speech*, Cambridge: Cambridge University Press.

Myers-Scotton, C. (1988), 'Code-switching as indexical of social negotiations', in M. Heller (ed.), *Code-Switching: Anthropological and Sociolinguistic Perspectives*, Berlin: Mouton de Gruyter, pp. 151–186.

Naficy, H. (2001), *An Accented Cinema: Exilic and Diasporic Filmmaking*, Princeton, NJ: Princeton University Press.

Ndiaye, P. (2008), *La Condition Noire: Essai sur une minorité française*, Paris: Calmann-Lévy.

Neumark, N., Gibson, R. and Van Leeuwen, T. (2010), *Voice: Vocal Aesthetics in Digital Arts and Media*, Cambridge, MA: The MIT Press.

Odicino, G. (2011), 'Omar Sy: "La banlieue, je la porte en moi"', *Télérama*, 3225, 2 November 2011, http://www.telerama.fr/cinema/omar-sy-la-banlieue-je-la-porte-en-moi,74663.php [accessed 3 November 2014].

de Oliveira, S.M. (2007), 'Breaking conversational norms on a Portuguese users' network: men as adjudicators of politeness?', in B. Danet and S. Herring (eds), *The Multilingual Internet*, Oxford and New York: Oxford University Press, pp. 256–277.

Panayametheekul, S. and Herring, S. (2007), 'Gender and turn allocation in a Thai chat room', in B. Danet and S. Herring (eds), *The Multilingual Internet*, Oxford and New York: Oxford University Press, pp. 233–255.

Pasquier, M. (2008), 'Rabah Ameur-Zaïmèche (2). Pour la sortie de son film "Dernier Maquis"', *Critikat*, 21 October 2008, http://www.critikat.com/actualite-cine/entretien/rabah-ameur-zaimeche-2.html [accessed 3 November 2014].

Permis de vivre la ville (collectif) (2007), *Lexik des cités: dictionnaire illustré*, Alain Rey (*Préface*), Dizis la Peste (*Préface*), Paris: Fleuve noir.

Petrucci, P. (2008), 'Portraying language diversity through a monolingual lens: on the unbalanced representation of Spanish and English in a corpus of American films', *Sociolinguistic Studies*, 2 (3): 405–423.

Petrucci, P. (2012), 'The translation of cinematic discourse and the question of character equivalence in *Talk to me*', *Multilingua*, 31 (2/3): 231–251.

Piazza, R., Bednarek, M. and Rossi, F. (eds) (2011), *Telecinematic Discourse: Approaches to the Language of Films and Television Series*, Amsterdam and Philadelphia, PA: John Benjamins.

Piazzo, P. (2004), '*L'Esquive*, jeu de l'amour et du cinéma', *Le Monde/Aden*, 7 January 2004.

Pitte, J.-R. (2002), *French Gastronomy: The History and Geography of a Passion*, New York: Columbia University Press.

Planchenault, G. (2008a), '"Who can tell, mon ami?": representations of bilingualism for a majority monolingual audience', *Sociolinguistic Studies*, 2 (3): 425–440.

Planchenault, G. (2008b), '"C'est ta live!": Doublage en français du film américain *Rize* ou l'amalgame du langage urbain des jeunes de deux cultures', in M. Abecassis (ed.), *Glottopol, Revue de Sociolinguistique en Ligne*: Pratiques langagières dans le cinéma francophone, 12: 182–199.

Planchenault, G. (2010), 'Displacement and plurilingualism in *Inch'Allah dimanche*: appropriating the Other's language in order to find one's place', in V. Berger and M. Komori (eds), *Polyglot Cinema: Migration and Transcultural Narration in France, Italy, Portugal and Spain*, Berlin: Lit Verlag, pp. 99–111.

Planchenault, G. (2011), 'Les standards du français parlé dans le cinéma *francophone* et la langue de l'autre: réception du cinéma québécois en France', in M. Abecassis (ed.), *La francophonie ou l'éloge de la diversité*, Cambridge: Scholars Publishing, pp. 43–55.

Planchenault, G. (2012), 'Accented French in films: performing and evaluating in-group stylisations', *Multilingua*, 31 (2/3): 253–275.

Pochon, C. (2011), 'Cinéastes noirs en France – Cannes 2011: Jean-Claude Barny et Fabrice Pierre', *Clap Noir Cinémas et Audiovisuels Africains*, 28 May, http://www.clapnoir.org/spip.php?article737 [accessed 3 November 2014].

Pooley, T. (1996), *Chtimi: The Urban Vernaculars of Northern France*, Clevedon: Multilingual Matters.

Pooley, T. (2008), 'Analyzing urban youth vernaculars in French cities', in D. Ayoun (ed.), *Studies in French Applied Linguistics*, Amsterdam and Philadelphia, PA: John Benjamins, pp. 317–344.

Porton, R. (2005), 'Marivaux in the "Hood": an interview with Abdellatif Kechiche', *Cineaste*, winter 2005: 46–49.

Potet, F. (2005), 'Vivre avec 400 mots', *Le Monde*, 18 March 2005.

Preston, D.R. (2004), 'Folk metalanguage', in A. Jaworski, N. Coupland and D. Galasinski (eds), *Metalanguage: Social and Ideological Perspectives*, Berlin: Mouton de Gruyter, pp. 75–101.

Rambourg, P. (2013), *A table . . . le menu!*, Paris: Honoré Champion.

Ramdani, N. (2009), 'Language still a barrier in the banlieue', *theguardian.com*, Wednesday 16 December 2009, http://www.theguardian.com/commentisfree/belief/2009/dec/16/language-banlieue-islamophobia-france-sarkozy [accessed 31 December 2014].

Rampton, B. (1995), 'Language crossing and the problematisation of ethnicity and socialisation', *Pragmatics*, 5 (4): 485–513.

Rampton, B. (1998), 'Language crossing and the redefinition of reality', in P. Auer (ed.), *Code-Switching in Conversation: Language, Interaction and Identity*, London: Routledge, pp. 290–317.

Rampton, B. (1999), 'Styling the other: introduction', *Journal of Sociolinguistics*, 3 (4): 421–427.

Rasin, J. (2010), *Beautiful Darling* [video], Flowerside Creations, JJay Productions.

Reah, D. (1998), *The Language of Newspapers*, London: Routledge.

Révis, J. (2013), *La voix et soi. Ce que notre voix dit de nous*, Bruxelles: De Boeck Solal.

Reyes, A. (2009), 'Asian American stereotypes as circulating resources', in A. Reyes and A. Lo (eds), *Beyond Yellow English: Toward a Linguistic Anthropology of Asian Pacific America*, Oxford: Oxford University Press, pp. 260–287.

Richardson, J. (2007), *Analyzing Newspapers: An Approach from Critical Discourse Analysis*, Basingstoke: Palgrave Macmillan.

Richardson, K. (2010), *Television Dramatic Dialogue: A Sociolinguistic Study*, New York: Oxford University Press.

Rossi, F. (2011), 'Discourse analysis of film dialogues: Italian comedy between linguistic realism and pragmatic non-realism', in R. Piazza, M. Bednarek and F. Rossi (eds), *Telecinematic Discourse: Approaches to the Language of Films and Television Series*, Amsterdam: John Benjamins Publishing Company.

Roux, B. (2008), 'Tu n'as rien vu à Bergues', *Positif*, 568: 59.

Rumsey, A. (1990), 'Wording, meaning, and linguistic ideology', *American Anthropologist*, 92 (2): 346–361.

Saeed, T. (2008), 'Doing Nakl: a mimicry of resistance by British-born South Asian adolescents in east London', *Working Papers in Urban Language & Literacies*, http://www.kcl.ac.uk/sspp/departments/education/research/ldc/publications/workingpapers/54.pdf [accessed 15 January 2015].

Said, E.W. (1978), *Orientalism*, New York: Pantheon Books.

Salhi, K. (ed.) (2002), *French In and Out of France: Language Policies, Intercultural Antagonisms and Dialogues*, Bern: Peter Lang.

Sammut, G. and Howarth, C. (2014), 'Social representations', in T. Teo (ed.), *Encyclopedia of Critical Psychology*, New York: Springer, pp. 1799–1802.

Scannell, P. (1991), *Broadcast Talk*, London: Sage Publications.

Schilling, N. (2013), 'Investigating stylistic variation', in N. Schilling-Estes and J.K. Chambers (eds), *The Handbook of Language Variation and Change*, Malden, MA, Oxford and Chichester: Wiley-Blackwell Publishing, pp. 327–349.

Seaberg, A.G. (1991), *Menu Design: Merchandising and Marketing*, New York: Van Nostrand Reinhold.

Seargeant, P. and Tagg, C. (eds) (2013), *The Language of Social Media: Identity and Community on the Internet*, London: Palgrave Macmillan.

Silverman, M. (1999), *Facing Postmodernity: Contemporary French Thought on Culture and Society*, London, New York: Routledge.

Silverstein, M. (1979), 'Language structure and linguistic ideology', in P. Clyne, W. Hanks, and C. Hofbauer (eds), *The Elements*, Chicago: Chicago Linguistic Society, pp. 193–248.

Silverstein, M. (2003), 'Indexical order and the dialectics of sociolinguistic life', *Language & Communication*, 23: 193–229.

Silverstein, M. and Urban, G. (eds) (1996), *Natural Histories of Discourse*, Chicago: UCP.

Soltane, A. (2012), 'Le film Intouchables écarte l'Algérien Abdel', *L'Expression*, 9 January 2012. http://www.lexpressiondz.com/culture/lecran_libre/145962-le-film-intouchables-ecarte-l-algerien-abdel.html [accessed 3 November 2014].

Starr, M. (1991), *Peter Sellers: A Film History*, Jefferson, NC: McFarland & Co.

Strand, D. (2009), '*Être et parler*: being and speaking French in Abdellatif Kechiche's *L'Esquive* (2004) and Laurent Cantet's *Entre les murs* (2008)', *Studies in French Cinema*, 9 (3): 259–272.

Swamy, V. (2007), 'Marivaux in the suburbs: reframing language in Kechiche's *L'Esquive* (2003)', *Studies in French Cinema*, 7 (1): 57–68.

Taguieff, P.A. (1988), *La Force du préjugé. Essai sur le racisme et ses doubles*, Paris, La Découverte, « Armillaire », reedited in 1988 by Gallimard, Paris.

Tajfel, H. and Turner, J.C. (1979), 'An integrative theory of intergroup conflict', in W.G. Austin and S. Worchel (eds), *The Social Psychology of Intergroup Relations*, Monterey, CA: Brooks-Cole.

Tannen, D. and Trester, A.M. (2013), *Discourse 2.0: Language and New Media*, Washington, DC: Georgetown University Press.

Tarr, C. (2005), *Reframing Difference: Beur and Banlieue Filmmaking in France*, Manchester: Manchester University Press.

Teo, P. (2000), 'Racism in the news: a critical discourse analysis of news reporting in two Australian newspapers', *Discourse Society*, 11 (1): 7–49.

Tessé, J.-P. (2004), 'Cité dans le texte', *Les Cahiers du Cinéma*, 586: 52–53.

Thompson, J.B. (1991), 'Editor's introduction', in P. Bourdieu, *Language and Symbolic Power*, Cambridge, MA: Harvard University Press, pp. 1–31.

Toscer, O. (2008), 'Discrimination dans le cinéma français: Le dossier "noir" du doublage', *Le Nouvel Observateur*, 15 February 2008: 84.

Trim, R. (2002), 'The lexicon in European languages today: unification or diversification', in P. Gubbins and M. Holt (eds), *Beyond Boundaries: Language and Identity in Contemporary Europe*, Clevedon: Multilingual Matters, pp. 35–45.

Trimaille, C. and Billiez, J. (2007), 'Pratiques langagières de jeunes urbains: peut-on parler de "parler"?', in E. Gallazzi and C. Molinari (eds), *Les français en émergence*, Bern: Peter Lang, pp. 95–109.

Trubek, A.B. (2000), *Haute Cuisine: How the French Invented the Culinary Profession*, Philadelphia, PA: University of Pennsylvania Press.

Truong, F. (2010), 'Le "jeune de banlieue" n'existe pas', *Libération*, 4 November 2010, http://www.liberation.fr/societe/2010/11/04/le-jeune-de-banlieue-n-existe-pas_691211 [accessed 15 January 2015].

van Dijk, T.A. (1988), *News as Discourse*, Hillsdale, NJ: L. Erlbaum Associates.

van Dijk, T.A. (2000), 'New(s) racism. A discourse analytical approach', in S. Cottle (ed.), *Ethnic Minorities and the Media*, Milton Keynes, UK: Open University Press, pp. 33–49.

Walker, A. (1982), *Peter Sellers: The Authorized Biography*, London: Hodder and Stoughton.

Watts, R.J. (2003), *Politeness*, Cambridge: Cambridge University Press.

Weck, F. (2008), *Putain d'accent! Comment les Méridionaux vivent leur langue*, Paris: L'Harmattan.

Weissberg, J. (2011), 'Film Review: "Untouchable"', *Variety*, 29 September 2011, http://variety.com/2011/film/reviews/untouchable-1117946269/# [accessed 3 November 2014].

West, C. and Zimmerman, D.H. (1987), 'Doing gender', *Gender and Society*, 1 (2): 125–151.

Wodak, R. and Busch, B. (2004), 'Approaches to media texts', in J. Downing, D. McQuail, P. Schlesinger and E. Wartella (eds), *Handbook of Media Studies*, Thousand Oaks, London, New Delhi: Sage, pp. 105–123.

Woolard, K.A. (2008), '"Why dat now?": linguistic-anthropological contributions to the explanation of sociolinguistic icons and change', *Journal of Sociolinguistics*, 12 (4): 432–452.

Yaguello, M. ([1988] 2008), *Catalogue des idées reçues sur la langue*, Paris: Points.

Yuen, N.W. (2004), 'Performing race, negotiating identity: Asian American professional actors in Hollywood', in J. Lee and M. Zhou (eds), *Asian American Youth: Culture, Identity, and Ethnicity*, New York: Routledge, pp. 251–267.

Zwicky A.D. and Zwicky, A. (1980), 'America's national dish: the style of restaurant menus', *American Speech*, 55: 87–92.

Filmography

Part 1

Chapter 2. Performances of non-standard voices in French films

Bienvenue chez les Ch'tis [*Welcome to the Sticks*] (2008), dir. Dany Boon, screenplay by Dany Boon, Alexandre Charlot, Franck Magnier (Pathé Renn Productions; Hirsch; TF1 Films Productions; Les Productions du Chicon)

L'Esquive [*Games of Love and Chance*] (2003), dir. Abdellatif Kechiche, screenplay by Ghalia Lacroix (Lola Films; CinéCinémas)

Chapter 4. Performances of ethnic voices in French films

Aide-toi, le ciel t'aidera (2008), dir. and screenplay by François Dupeyron (ARP Sélection, Canal +, CinéCinémas)

Cheba Louisa (2013), dir. Françoise Charpiat, screenplay by Françoise Charpiat and Mariem Hamidat (Wild Bunch, Direct Cinéma, Legato Films)

Chocolat (1988), dir. Claire Denis, screenplay by Claire Denis and Jean-Pol Fargeau (Cerito Films, La Sept Cinéma, MK2 Productions, TF1 Films Production, Wim Wenders Productions)

Dernier Maquis (2008), dir. Rabah Ameur-Zaïmeche, screenplay by Rabah Ameur-Zaïmeche and Louise Thermes (Sarrazink Productions, Les films du Losange)

Huit Femmes [*Eight women*] (2001), dir. François Ozon, screenplay by François Ozon and Marina De Van. (France 2 Cinéma, Mars Distribution)

Inch'Allah Dimanche (2001), dir. and screenplay by Yamina Benguigui (ARP Sélection, Bandits longs)

Intouchables [*The Untouchables*] (2011), dir. and screenplay by Olivier Nakache and Eric Toledano (Quad Télévision, TF1 Films Production, Chaocorp, Gaumont, Ten Films)

La graine et le mulet [*The secret of the grain*] (2007), dir. and screenplay by Abdellatif Kechiche (Pathé Renn Productions; Hirsch; France 2 Cinéma)

Né quelque part (2013), dir. Mohamed Hamidi, screenplay by Alain-Michel Blanc and Mohamed Hamidi (Quad Films, France 3, Canal +, Ciné +)

Romuald et Juliette [*Mama, There is a Man in your Bed*] (1988), dir. and screenplay by Coline Serreau (Cinéa, Cofimage, France 3 Cinéma, France 3)

Rue Case-Nègre [*Sugar Cane Alley*] (1983), dir. and screenplay by Euzhan Palcy, based on Joseph Zobel's novel (Orca Productions)

S'en fout la mort [*No fear, no die*] (1990), dir. Claire Denis, screenplay by Claire Denis and Jean-Pol Fargeau (Cinéa)

Part 2

Chapter 5. Performances of French-accented English in Hollywood films

Algiers (1938), dir. John Cromwell, screenplay by John Howard Lawson and James M. Cain (Walter Wanger Productions)

Beverly Hills Cop (1984), dir. Martin Brest, screenplay by Daniel Petrie Jr (Paramount Pictures, Eddie Murphy Productions)

Chocolat (2000), dir. Lasse Hallström, screenplay by Robert Nelson Jacobs, based on Joanne Harris' novel) (Miramax Films, David Brown Productions, Fat Free)

French Kiss (1995), dir. Lawrence Kasdan, screenplay by Adam Brooks (Polygram Filmed Entertainment, Prufrock Pictures, Twentieth Century Fox Film Corporation, Working Title Films)

Green Card (1990), dir. and screenplay by Peter Weir (Touchstone Pictures, with the participation of Australian Film Finance Corporation–AFFC)

Groundhog Day (1993), dir. Harold Ramis, screenplay by Dany Rubin and Harold Ramis (Columbia Pictures Corporation)

Madagascar 3 (2012), dir. Eric Darnell, Tom McGrath, Conrad Vernon, screenplay by Eric Darnell and Noah Baumbach (DreamWorks Animation, Pacific Data Images)

Matrix Reloaded (2003), dir. and screenplay by Andy Wachowski and Lana Wachowski (Warner Bros, Village Roadshow Pictures, Silver Pictures, NPV Entertainment, Heineken Branded Entertainment)

Ocean's Thirteen (2007), dir. Steven Soderbergh, screenplay by Brian Koppelman and David Levien (Warner Bros, Village Roadshow Pictures, Jerry Weintraub Productions, Section Eight)

Shrek (2001), dir. Andrew Adamson and Vicky Jenson, screenplay by William Steig and Ted Elliott, Terry Rossio, Joe Stillman and Roger S.H. Schulman (DreamWorks Animation, DreamWorks SKG, Pacific Data Images)

Star Trek: The Next Generation (1987), dir. Screenplay by (Paramount Television)

The Cat's Bah (1954), dir. Chuck Jones, screenplay by Michael Maltese (Warner Bros)

The Da Vinci Code (2006), dir. Ron Howard, screenplay by Akiva Goldsman, based on Dan Brown's novel (Columbia Pictures, Imagine Entertainment, Skylark Productions)

The Lion King (1994), dir. Roger Allers and Rob Minkoff, screenplay by Irene Mecchi, Jonathan Roberts and Linda Woolverton (Walt Disney Pictures)

The Pink Panther (1976) [*The Pink Panther strikes again*], dir. Blake Edwards, screenplay by Frank Waldman and Blake Edwards (Amjo Productions)

The Pink Panther (1978) [*The Revenge of the Pink Panther*], dir. Blake Edwards, screenplay by Frank Waldman, Ron Clark and Blake Edwards (Jewel Productions, Seller-Edward Productions, Pimlico Films)

The Pink Panther (1982) [*Trail of the Pink Panther*], dir. Blake Edwards, screenplay by Frank Waldman, Tom Waldman and Blake Edwards United Artist, Titan Productions, Lakeline Productions Ltd, Amjo Productions)

The Pink Panther (2006), dir. Shawn Levy, screenplay by Len Blum, Steve Martin (Metro-(Goldwyn-Mayer, Columbia Pictures, Robert Simonds Productions)

The Pink Panther (2009) [*The Pink Panther 2*], dir. Harald Zwart, screenplay by Scott Neustadter, Michael H. Weber, Steve Martin and Blake Edwards (Goldwyn-Mayer, Columbia Pictures, Robert Simonds Productions)

The Wolf of Wall Street (2013), dir. Martin Scorsese, screenplay by Terence Winter, based on Jordan Belfort's book (Paramount Pictures, Red Granite Pictures, Appian Way, Sikelia Productions, EMJAG Productions)

Chapter 7. Performances in French on Vancouver's dining scene

Babette's Feast (1987), dir. Gabriel Axel, screenplay by Gabriel Axel, based on Karen Blixen's novel (Panorama Film A/S, Det Danske Filminstitut, Nordisk Film, Rungstedlundfonden)

Chocolat (2000), dir. Lasse Hallström, screenplay by Robert Nelson Jacobs, based on Joanne Harris' novel (Miramax Films, David Brown Productions, Fat Free)

The French Chef (2005), dir. Russel Morash (WGBH Boston Video)

Index

accented cinema 54
accents
   ch'timi language 54–7, 61
   in French media 41–6
   performed accents 21–2
   social categorization 42, 49
   standard language ideology 48–50
   see also French-accented English
actors 93, 94–5, 110, 113, 122–3
advertisements 102–3
agency 161–2
'Allo 'Allo! (television series) 128
American cinema, French-accented English 107–23
   see also United States
Ameur-Zaïmeche, Rabah 96
Androutsopoulos, J. 49
Appadurai, A. 159
appropriateness
   gender identities 71
   politeness and 69–71
Arab characters 95
Arabic language 11, 62, 63
Asian-American actors 122–3
audience 18, 38–40, 61–5

Babette's Feast (Axel) 146–8
Bakhtin, Michael 7, 158–9, 161–2
Bankolé, Isaac de 93
banlieue cinema 53
banlieue French 5–6, 8, 10–11, 43, 49, 51
Barny, Jean-Claude 94, 98
Barthes, Roland 156
Barton, Joey 2
Bauman, R. 4, 24, 30–1
Bazin, André 59
Bell, A. 28
beur 11
Beur cinema 53–4, 95–9
biases in media 19
   see also discrimination

Bienvenue chez les Ch'tis (Boon)
   ch'timi accent 61
   excerpts 55–6
   linguistic ideology 54–7
   non-standard voices 47–8, 49, 58
   realism 59
   stylization 60
Binoche, Juliette 113
bistros 152–3, 155–6
black actors 93, 94–5
Boon, Dany 54–7, 59, 60, 61
Bourdieu, Pierre 8–13, 39, 53
broadcast media 15, 19–20
Butler, J. 69

Canada, culinary identities 154–5
Caribbean identities 98
carnival/carnivalesque 45
Carroll, H.B. 9
CDA *see* critical discourse analysis
Child, Julia 145, 146, 148
Chion, M. 33, 158
Chocolat (Hallström) 148
Christie, Agatha 125
ch'timi language 54–7, 61
Chung, S.H. 122
Cicero 42
cinema
   Cinéma de banlieue 53
   comic genres 43–4, 47
   ethnic voices 89–100
   films de banlieue 11
   foreign accents 101
   non-standard voices in French films 47–66
   post-beur cinema 89
   racial discrimination 90–2
   realism 59–61, 63
   sociolinguistic study of 21–2
   Turkish German cinema 44
   voice-body separation 158
   Walt Disney films 21, 104, 107–8, 119

Clouseau, Inspecteur 118–22
cod-French accent 2, 128
code-switching 134–5, 151–2
'colonial experience' 90–1
comic genres 43–4, 45, 47
commercials 102–3
commodification 37–8, 46, 92–5, 121
community membership 73–4, 78–81
computer-mediated communication
    linguistic study of 22–3
    performance 68–73
    politeness and gender 72–3
condescension strategy 8–9
connoisseurship 148
contrasting voices 23, 159
Corsican radio 20
Coupland, N. 28, 29, 128
critical discourse analysis (CDA) 17, 18
Le Crocodile (restaurant) 140, 143, 150, 152
culinary experience, French language and 153–6
culinary identities 154–5
cultural appropriation 105
cultural capital 39
cultural flows 159
cultural identities 100
cultural maps 17

Darah, Maik 90, 92
Darling, Candy 85
'The death of French Culture' 103
Deleuze, Gilles 59
Denis, Claire 93
Depardieu, Gérard 112, 117
Derrida, Jacques 1, 6, 45–6
Dexter's Laboratory (Cartoon Network) 103
dialects 24
dialogism 161
dining experience, French language and 153–6
discourses 53
discrimination, in French film industry/media 41–6, 90–2
discursive markers 132, 133
diversity 159
'domesticated words' 102
drag-queens 86
Dubet, F. 91
Dubois, R. 99

English actors 110
'enregisterment' 26
entextualization 36–7
'envoice' 1, 111
L'Esquive (Kechiche)
    Arabic words 62, 63
    audience perceptions 61–5
    excerpts 57–8
    linguistic features 62–3
    linguistic ideology 50–4
    non-standard voices 47–8, 49
    realism 59, 63
    review of 3–4
    standard French in 63
    stylization 56, 60
    verbal aggressiveness 62
    verlan usage 63
ethnic voices
    commodification 92–5
    in French cinema 89–100
    stereotypes 90–4

face 68, 70
fake accents 2, 121, 128
Faure, Alain 6
feminine identity
    internet 67–87
    markers of 76–7
    stereotypes 71–2
feminine politeness 83
Ferber, L. 104
Ferguson, P.P. 139, 145
fiction, sociolinguistic study of 21–2
films de banlieue 11
    see also cinema
Flamand Barny, Jean-Claude 94, 98
folk linguistics 126–7
food culture, United States 144–8
    see also menus
foreign accents 101
frames/framing 35, 130
French cinema/films see cinema
French culture/values 103, 104–5
    see also 'The death of –'
'French lover' trope 107
French restaurant menus see menus
French stereotypes 104
French-accented English 26, 101–56
    American cinema 107–23
    film character types 109–10

French characters' features 110–13
Inspecteur Clouseau 118–22
lexical features 116
linguistic practices/features 108–18
names of characters 112
phonological features 114–15, 117
pragmatic features 116
spectacular fragments 118
syntactic/morphological features 115–16
French-Canadian culinary identities 154–5
Frenchman as philanderer trope 111

Gaertner, J. 95
Garofalo, Janeane 113
gender
dysphoria 85
identities 84–7
performance as 69, 84–7
and politeness 71–2
stereotypes 83
genres 24–30, 43–4, 45, 47
Goffman, Erving 42–3, 68
Google searches 103
Green Card (Weir) 112, 117

Halberstadt, Michèle 94–5
Hall, Stuart
Caribbean identity 98
'colonial experience' 90–1
cultural identity 100
'maps of meaning' 39
'newsworthy' concept 17
popular culture 92
hegemonic ideologies 161–2
Herman, L. and Herman, M.S. 114, 117, 119
Herring, S.C. 72
heteroglossia 128, 158, 159
Hollywood films, French-accented English 107–23
hooks, bell 93
humor, stigmatization 43–4

identities
Caribbean 98
culinary 154–5
cultural 100
feminine 67–87
gender 84–7
'ideologizing' 49

'imaginaire linguistique' concept 127
Inch'Allah Dimanche (Benguigui) 95, 97
indexicality, orders of 50, 149
individual agency 161–2
Les Inrockuptibles 39
Inspecteur Clouseau 118–22
insult poetry 45
'internationalisms' 133
internet
linguistic study of 22–3
transvestites' website 67–87
The Intouchables 44, 92, 94
Irish language 20
Irvine, J. 45
Islam, media biases 19

Le jeu de l'amour et du hasard (Marivaux) 51, 52

Kaganski, Serge 3–4, 8, 9
Kechiche, Abdellatif 50–4, 58, 64, 91–2, 96, 97
Kelly-Holmes, H. 102, 133–4
Krimo (*L'Esquive*) 52, 53

lexical borrowings 133
linguistic exchanges 9–13
'linguistic ghettos' 8
linguistic ideologies
Bienvenue chez les Ch'tis 54–7
definition 3
L'Esquive 50–4
registers 6–7
as social representations 5–6
linguistic market 10
The Lion King (Allers & Minkoff) 107
lip-synching industry, racial discrimination 90–2
Lippi-Green, R. 108, 111
literary studies 158–9
Lodge, A. 56

macro-genres 25, 26
Maghrebi youth 6
'maps of meaning' 39
Marivaux, Pierre Carlet de Chamblain de 51, 52
marked/unmarked voices 160
Martin, Steve 1–2, 120, 121
masculinity 112

Mastering the Art of French Cooking (Child) 145
media texts, linguistic study of 16–24
mediated language 35–6
mediated performances 31
menus 139–56
    bilingual menus 142, 152–3
    code-switching 151–2
    in French without English translation 153
    French words on 148–50
    as genre 141–4
    spectacular fragments 151
    structure and function 141–4
micro-genres 25
minority languages 20, 23
mock accents 2, 121, 128
mock languages 29–30
Modestine, Yasmine 90, 91
Morin, Edgar 59
Moscovici, S. 5
movies *see* cinema
Moyer, A. 101
'multiple voicing' (heteroglossia) 128, 158, 159
Muslims, media biases 19
The Mystery of the Blue Train (*Poirot* episode) 129–37

natural language 36
Né quelque part (Hamidi) 97–8
new media 22–4
news 18
'newsworthy' concept 17
nique ta mère expression 4, 6–7, 36
North African actors/directors 95–9
North America, French-dining experience 147
novels (Bakhtin) 158–9
    see also heteroglossia

online communication
    linguistic study of 22–3
    transvestites' website 67–87
orders of indexicality 50, 149

Pepe Le Pew (Looney Tunes character) 111
performance
    computer-mediated communication 68–73

definitions 30–1
feminine identity 76–7
gender 84–7
sociolinguistic study of 15–40
performance of voice 1–4, 7–9
    audience 38–40
    characteristics 34–8
    research questions 12
    subversive potential 45
performers 32–4
philanderer trope 111
Picard French 56
Pink Panther films 1–2, 118–22
platform events 32
plurality 158–9
Poirot, Hercule 113, 125–38
    code-switching 134–5
    formal register 136
    French lexicon 131–4
    French stylization 129–37
    speech analysis 126
    syntactic forms 136–7
politeness
    and appropriateness 69–71
    feminine politeness 83
    formulaic politeness 81–2, 83
    gender and 71–2
    markers 132
politic behaviour 70
popular culture 92
pragmatic markers 132, 133
prejudice, in French film industry/media 41–6, 90–2
Preston, D.R. 126, 127
print media 18–19
puns 118–19

Quebecois culture 155

racial discrimination, in French film industry 90–2
racist jokes 44
Ratatouille (Bird) 119
realism, cinematic 59–61, 63
recorded voices 1
'referee design' 127
registers 6–7, 24–5
restaurant reviews 153–4
    see also menus
Richard, Firmine 93–4

Rohmer, Eric 4
romance 107
Romuald and Juliette (Serreau) 93
rudeness 82–3, 112

Scannell, P. 15
schools 52
Seaberg, A.G. 140, 141–2, 148
seduction 111–12
self-presentation 68, 76–7
Sellers, Peter 119–20
sexist jokes 44
Shrek (Adamson & Jenson) 116
signalization 122
silent voices 160
Silverstein, M. 50, 149
Singapore 20
slang 63
social representations 5–6
solidarity 74, 78–81
spectacular fragments 118, 151
speech genres 25
staged language 31–2, 34–5
stance-taking 32
standard language ideology 48–50
Star Trek films 118
stereotypes
    ethnicity 90–4, 122
    feminine identity 71–2
    French stereotypes 104
    gender 83
    media reliance on 44
stigma 41–6
'strategy of condescension' 8–9
style
    definitions 27
    politics of 29–30
    style shifting 27
styling 27–8, 128
stylization 28–9, 56–7, 60
    ethnic voices 89
    French speakers of English as a foreign language 127–9
    politics of 29–30
    'styling' contrast 128
stylized French English 127–9
sub-genres 25, 26
suburban accents/vernaculars (*banlieue* French) 5–6, 8, 10–11, 43, 49, 51

Suchet, David 113, 128–9
swearwords 7, 57–8, 64, 118
Sy, Omar 92, 94, 99

taboo words 7, 57–8, 64, 118
Tarr, Carrie 53
television
    cod-French accent 128
    sociolinguistic study of 21–2
textual cross-dressing 73
Time magazine 103
transvestites
    gendered identity 86–7
    stylized performance 160–1
transvestites' website 67–87
    data analysis 76–83
    data presentation 75–6
    formulaic politeness 81–2, 83
    French group 78–9, 80
    'girlfriends' corner' 75
    Quebecois group 79, 80–1
    rudeness, avoiding 82–3
    sense of community 73–4, 78–81
    solidarity 74, 78–81
'tribal stigmas' 43
Turkish German cinema 44

United States (US)
    food culture 141, 144–8
    and French culture 103
    menus 141
    see also American cinema
unmarked voices 160
urban space 5

Vancouver, French restaurants 150–6
verbal art 2–3
verlan ('back slang') 63
virtual communities, transvestites 67–87
voice
    appropriation of 105
    contrasting voices 23, 159
    definition 34
    disembodied voices 45, 158
    marked/unmarked voices 160
    paradoxes 34
    silent voices 160
    sociolinguistic study of 15–40

voice-body separation 45, 158
 see also 'envoice'

Walt Disney cartoons/films 21, 104, 107–8, 119
websites *see* transvestites' website
Welshness 20
wine-tasting 149

womanhood, performance of 85–7
 see also feminine ...
Wurst, Conchita 84, 86, 87, 161

'yellow voices' 122

Zwicky, A.D. and Zwicky, A. 142–4, 148, 149